MANAGING THE INDUSTRY/UNIVERSITY COOPERATIVE RESEARCH CENTER

A Guide for Directors
and Other Stakeholders

EDITORS

DENIS O. GRAY, Ph.D.
Department of Psychology, North Carolina State University, NC

S. GEORGE WALTERS, M.S., M.B.A., Ph.D.
Management Studies, Rutgers University, NJ

CONTRIBUTORS

MITCHELL FLEISCHER, Industrial Technology Institute, Ann Arbor, MI
ELIEZER GEISLER, University of Wisconsin, Whitewater, WI
HOWARD LEVINE, California College of Arts and Crafts, San Francisco, CA
KAY LOVELACE, University of North Carolina, Greensboro, NC
VIRGINIA SHAW-TAYLOR, Evaluator Emeritus, Consultant, Golden, CO
LOUIS TORNATZKY, Southern Technology Council, Research Triangle, NC

 BATTELLE PRESS
Columbus • Richland

Library of Congress Cataloging-in-Publication Data

Managing the industry/university cooperative research center : a guide
   for directors and other stakeholders / edited by Denis O. Gray,
   S. George Walters
      p.   cm.
   Includes bibliographical references and index.
   ISBN 1-57477-053-5 (pbk. : alk. paper)
   1. Research institutes—Management—Handbooks, manuals, etc.
2. University and colleges—Research—Management—Handbooks,
manuals, etc.   3. Research, Industrial—Management—Handbooks,
manuals, etc.   I. Gray, Denis O.   II. Walters, S. George.
Q180.57.M36   1998
001.4´068—dc21

                                                    98-23189
                                                    CIP

Printed in the United States of America

Battelle Press
505 King Avenue
Columbus, Ohio 43201-2693, USA
614-424-6393 or 1-800-451-3543
Fax: 614-424-3819
E-mail: press@battelle.org
Website: www. battelle.org/bookstore

CONTENTS

FIGURES

ACKNOWLEDGMENTS

Many colleagues in industry, government and academia were very enthusiastic in providing suggestions that were helpful in formulating the objectives and content of this book. All these individuals, including National Science Foundation (NSF) Industry/University Cooperative Research Center (I/UCRC) program managers, 50 center directors, and 35 evaluators, have our appreciation and thanks. A list of the NSF I/UCRCs can be found in Appendix 2-8.

Special acknowledgment must be made of the support given by the National Science Foundation under award EEC-9222356 and by Dr. Alex Schwarzkopf, Program Coordinator of the NSF-I/UCRC program for the development of an earlier version of this book.

Contributions were also made by an Editorial Review Board which reviewed individual chapters. The Board included Dr. Schwarzkopf and seven I/UCRC directors: Dr. Alden Bean, Lehigh University, Center for Innovation Management Studies; Dr. Jerome Congleton, Texas A&M, Center in Ergonomics; Dr. Arlene Garrison, University of Tennessee, Center for Measurement and Control Engineering; Professor Edward Haug, University of Iowa, Center for Virtual Proving Ground Simulation: Mechanical and Electro-Mechanical Systems; Dr. Dale Niesz, Rutgers University, Center for Ceramic Research; Dr. Ira Pense, Director Emeritus, Georgia Institute of Technology, Center for Material Handling/

Logistics; Dr. Daniel Watts, New Jersey Institute of Technology, Center for Emission Reduction Research.

Other editorial assistance was provided by Courtland Lewis, Melbourne, Florida; Arlene Horowitz, Editor Emeritus, New Jersey Institute of Technology/HSMRC Newsletter; Professor Jim Swindall, Director, Questor Centre for Environmental Research, Queens University, Belfast, Northern Ireland; and Cheryl Cathey, NSF I/UCRC Program.

Research assistance was provided by graduate students Mark Linblad and Stephanie Tarant, at North Carolina State University, Raleigh, and Robert Mastice at the New Jersey Institute of Technology.

Additionally, we express our grateful appreciation to Dr. Saul K. Fenster, President, New Jersey Institute of Technology (NJIT) and Dr. Gary Thomas, Provost, NJIT for delivery of the copyright to the editors, and to Dr. Richard Magee, Executive Director of the I/UCRC for Hazardous and Toxic Substances at New Jersey Institute of Technology. He provided insights on growing and managing centers. He also made available research space and resources for this project, as well as the expertise of center Assistant Director Maggie Griscavage, who managed the coordination, assembly and preparation of our original manuscript.

PREFACE

DENIS O. GRAY, *North Carolina State University, Raleigh*

S. GEORGE WALTERS, *Professor Emeritus, Rutgers University, NJ*

In the early 1980s we became involved in the evaluation of a small initiative supported by the National Science Foundation (NSF), the Industry/University Cooperative Research Centers (I/UCRC) Program. A primary objective of the program was to see if NSF could replicate the successful industry-university partnership it had produced in the pioneering Massachusetts Institute of Technology (MIT) Polymer Processing Center. Several years ago, we looked back on this humble beginning and marveled at what this modestly funded program had accomplished.

More than 80 cooperative research centers involving over 100 universities had been created and 55 of those centers were still in operation! With $4 million in NSF funding annually, these centers supported 600 faculty and 1,000 students, attracted 600 industrial members, and generated an annual budget of $60 million per year. Remarkably, feedback indicated both industry and university participants felt they benefitted from these partnerships. We also found that individual industry members can leverage their own typical $30,000 membership fee at least ten, or even 30 times or more in funded center research.

More importantly, I/UCRC surveys revealed that the research knowledge generated by these centers triggers an additional $100 million in new industry research activities. This represents a 1.66 precompetitive research dollar multiplier and shows IUCRC research results are good enough to invest in.

The I/UCRC program has also helped pave the way for several larger center-based programs, including Engineering Research Centers, Science and Technology Centers, and state I/UCRCs. As we were quoted in *Chemical Engineering News* (January 1994) the NSF I/UCRC program is one of "the most significant pieces of social technology for managing cooperative research to emerge from the National Science Foundation."

Consistent with this view, Richard Cyert (1993), President Emeritus of Carnegie Mellon University, has said these centers have had a major impact on the "relevance to competitiveness" of academic research in the U.S. and "are models that could be used in the management area to a great advantage."

As we shared our observations on the I/UCRC model with our colleagues, we realized there was great interest both inside and outside the I/UCRC program in understanding what factors accounted for the I/UCRC model's effectiveness and, more importantly, how to emulate that success. Center Directors appeared to have an insatiable interest in learning how to improve their performance to the level achieved by "the best in class" centers. At the same time, other stakeholders including university, industry and government representatives from across the U.S. and abroad continually approached I/UCRC participants with questions about how to start their own centers. Persuaded that there would be an interest in learning how to build and manage lasting "win-win" partnerships between industry and university, we set out to write this book.

In preparing this volume we have gone to great lengths to incorporate input from a variety of relevant sources and perspectives. Detailed chapter outlines were reviewed by 30 I/UCRC evaluators and 50 Center Directors. Seven evaluators with six to 15 years of program experience co-authored the chapters. These contributors had complete access to some 14 years of NSF industrial and faculty center participants surveys and historical profiles. They also held discussions with company members, directors, faculty and student researchers. After several iterations, individual chapters were reviewed by an Editorial Review Board of seven successful Center Directors. The NSF-I/UCRC Senior Program Director reviewed all chapters. Additional reviews were provided by Battelle Press.

While our strategy emphasized experience-based knowledge and principles accumulated over 20 years of NSF I/UCRC experimentation, each of our eleven chapters begins with an introduction which provides a literature-based conceptual framework for the

principles and practices which follow. The chapters include:
(1) The Background and Evolution of the I/UCRC model,
(2) Planning and Establishing an I/UCRC, (3) The Structure and
Protocols of an I/UCRC, (4) Recruiting and Maintaining
Membership in an I/UCRC, (5) Planning Center Research, (6) Implementing the Cooperative Research Program, (7) Knowledge
and Technology Transfer, (8) Control, Budgeting, and Evaluation,
(9) Communication, (10) Leadership, and (11) Growth and
Diversification. All of the chapters have been written to meet the
needs of university, industry and government stakeholders.

It is our belief that a university science or engineering professor
with entrepreneurial skill and committed faculty and industry colleagues can achieve successful, lasting and mutually-beneficial
partnerships by building and sustaining I/UCRC-type centers. We
hope that this book will facilitate and support such efforts.

REFERENCES

Cyert, R.M. *Universities, competitiveness, and TQM: A plan of action for the year 2000*. Public Administration Quarterly, Spring, 1993.

CHAPTER 1

CREATING WIN-WIN PARTNERSHIPS:

Background and Evolution of Industry/University Cooperative Research Centers Model

DENIS O. GRAY, *North Carolina State University, Raleigh*

INTRODUCTION

Research cooperation between industry and university has increased dramatically over the past few decades. Fueled by a number of social forces, including shrinking federal support for research, pressures from global competitiveness, and the increasing importance of science-based knowledge to the innovation process (Feller, 1997), industry's share of academic research has more than doubled over the past two decades, from 3.1 percent in 1975 to 6.9 percent in 1995 (NSB, 1996).

Interestingly, this growth has been accomplished without a commensurate closing of the "cultural gap" which separates institutions from these two sectors. Contemporary universities and industry continue to follow very different paths in terms of structure (problem-driven vs. disciplinary), time horizons (short vs. long), and goals/values (profit vs. education and knowledge dissemination) (Fairweather, 1988). How have industry and universities increased cooperation in spite of persistent cultural differences? The answer to this apparent paradox lies in the development, deployment, and widespread adoption of a diverse collection of specialized organizational "bridges," what we will refer to as *industry-university (I/U) linkage mechanisms*. These structures including centers, labs, and institutes, have allowed universities and industry to meet each other half-way, at their organizational periphery,

1

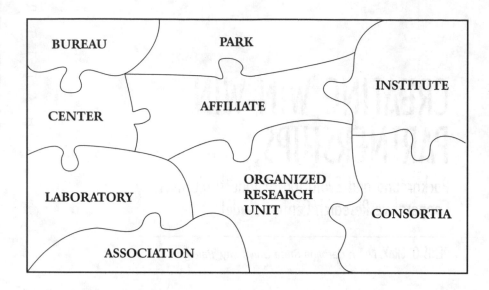

in spite of persistent core cultural differences. These structures have been so successful that most of today's industry-sponsored academic research is performed through various I/U linkage mechanisms.

Unfortunately, while I/U linkage mechanisms have increased the amount of interaction between these two sectors, they haven't always changed the *way participants interact*. In truth, much of the work performed through these mechanisms looks a lot like traditional academic or industrial research. In some cases, faculty do their own thing, but with support from industry. In other cases, industry gets specific problems solved, but the work is done by faculty instead of employees or contractors. Such arrangements have fueled a variety of criticisms ranging from, they offer nothing new to one side or the other is being exploited (e.g., Brooks, 1993). These one-sided exchanges stand in stark contrast to the long-term, truly collaborative and mutually beneficial partnerships forged by the National Science Foundation's (NSF) Industry/University Cooperative Research Centers (I/UCRC) Program.

In I/UCRCs, instead of working on small-scale, narrowly defined disciplinary problems, faculty work on large problems which are *both* scientifically important and relevant to industry. Instead of developing projects based on their personal predilections, faculty develop projects based on a meaningful dialogue with industry. Instead of working solo, projects are carried out in multidisciplinary and often cross-sector teams. While open publication remains their primary objective, faculty recognize the economic and social value of their research and take responsibility for protecting and proactively transferring knowledge and technology to the private and governmental sectors. In these partnerships, the stereotype of the "ivory tower" professor is a distant memory.

The changes in industry involvement are equally dramatic. Instead of using the university as a convenient and cheap subcontractor for solving short-term problems, firms make long-term commitments to universities to support fundamental research and also to team with other firms, often competitors, in these activities. While knowledge, technology transfer and commercialization are the primary industry objectives, student educational needs and publishing findings in a timely fashion are high priorities too.

In short, I/UCRC collaborations, and others which successfully imitate this model, are "win-win" partnerships that have strengthened the ability of our universities to conduct high-quality and relevant research and the ability of industry to compete globally.

Since industry's support for basic and applied research and federal government support for civilian research are expected to decline over the next decade (Council on Competitiveness, 1996), the need for research cooperation is expected to grow. As a consequence, we believe there will be an even greater need for I/U partnerships in the future, particularly the "win-win" variety. Unfortunately, precious little attention has been devoted to understanding and explaining how to start, manage and sustain these new and complex industry/university organizational forms. The purpose of this book is to begin to fill this void.

In this chapter we describe the circumstances that have supported the growth of IU linkage mechanisms. We then describe the development, impact and principles behind a model, pioneered by the National Science Foundation's Industry-University Cooperative Research Center (I/UCRC) program, for creating win-win partnerships.

Cooperative Research: An Historical Perspective

Until relatively recently, relations between industry and university traditionally have been very strong in the US. A variety of factors including support of higher education by a pragmatically oriented state government (as opposed to federal), enlightened public policy like the Morril Act of 1862 and the Hatch Act of 1887 (which created the land grant university system and the agricultural extension system, respectively), and integration of engineering training into mainstream universities all contributed to close, if informal and short-term, ties between universities and local industry up till the 1940s (Gray et al., 1996). This changed in the 1950s and 1960s. Expanded federal support for university research after World War II, which emphasized training the next generation of professors, and disillusionment with industry and the military-industrial complex greatly weakened relations between industry and universities.

During the 1970s most of the forces that contributed to the decline in cooperation either abated or reversed themselves: federal support for research leveled off and then declined, the demand for graduate-trained scholars lessened, and bitterness toward the military-industrial complex began to fade. Thus, it was only natural that the level of cooperation and interaction would begin to rebound in the universities and departments (e.g., the land grants, engineering) that historically had strong ties to industry (Nelkin & Nelson, 1987).

However, the expansion in industry-university interaction witnessed over the past two decades is both quantitatively and qualitatively different from what preceded it. We would attribute this growth to two factors: competitiveness pressures which caused U.S. companies to pursue an innovation-based strategy for competing in the new global economy; and an emergent public policy that has attempted to aide and abet this strategy, in part, by trying to encourage and support research cooperation with universities. While discussing both of these developments in depth is beyond the scope of this chapter, a brief overview of government efforts is warranted.

Government Efforts

Government policy toward industry-university cooperation has had two foci. The first has been a series of legislative reforms, including the Bayh-Dole Act, Stevenson-Wydler Act, and the National Cooperative Research Act, designed to remove a variety of institutional disincentives (e.g., patent rights and anti-trust penalties) to public-private partnerships in general and to industry-university partnerships in particular (Gray et al., 1996). The second, more interventionist thrust, promoted by both federal and state policy, encouraged more intense and meaningful cooperation by promoting the adoption and implementation of a variety of I/U linkage mechanisms (Coburn, 1995) such as the NSF I/UCRC program.

These efforts have proven very useful. The number of universities reporting they receive 10 percent or more of their funding from industry has doubled. In fact, increased support from industry accounts for most of the growth in academic research during this period (National Science Board, 1993). These efforts have also resulted in a fundamental change in the way industry supports universities. Increasingly, firms are bypassing traditional mechanisms (e.g., contracts, gifts) and providing support through I/U linkage mechanisms.

Industry-University Linkage Mechanisms

"Among the most interesting changes in American colleges and universities over the past quarter of a century is the rather prolific growth of institutes, centers, laboratories, bureaus, and other research and service units that parallel the conventional departmental structure. No easy description of these additions to the academic landscape is possible. They carry out a bewildering variety of purposes, use many different organizational models, are supported at widely disparate levels of investment, are sometimes housed in the obscure corners of the campus, and are found at all levels of the organizational hierarchy."—Ikenberry, 1973

What is an I/U linkage mechanism? An I/U linkage mechanism is an organizational structure (e.g., department, unit) designed to house and support transactions between industry and university. In the organizational literature, this relatively specialized organizational form is referred to as a boundary-spanning structure (Aldrich, 1977). Boundary-spanning structures can be as simple as a role (e.g., liaison to an outside organization) or as complex as an organization with its own structure, goals, and strategy.

I/U linkage mechanisms are relatively complex boundary-spanning structures because they must link dissimilar institutions and buffer conflict or friction. They achieve this, in part, by adopting features which represent a compromise between corporate and academic norms. For instance, staffing is usually multidisciplinary but not industry matrix-level. These compromises allow I/U linkage mechanisms to handle large-scale, multidisciplinary, applied, task-related projects which could never be handled through an academic department (Freidman and Freidman, 1986). At the same time, I/U linkage mechanisms can be a catalyst for incremental change in core structures like departments.

Universities have been interacting with outside institutions, including the government, via linkage mechanisms like research institutes since before W.W.II (Kidd, 1959). According to Baba (1988), at least 28 different industry-university linkage mechanisms have evolved since the early 1900s. Some of the most prominent research linkage mechanisms are described in Figure 1-1.

However, the popularity of these structures in recent years has been nothing short of phenomenal. According to Cohen, Florida &

Figure 1-1   Research linkage mechanisms.

Linkage Mechanism	Innovation Stage	Participants*	Scope	Impact
Industrial Affiliates	Research and Development	I: Large firms U: Research universities F: Regular faculty G: Minor to no role	Suffering from major decline; replaced by I/UCRCs	Minor
Applied Research Institutes	Development to Applied Engineering	I: Large Firms U: Research Universities F: Full-time staff and faculty G: Joint sponsor of some institutions	Widely used; small to very large budget	Conduct a significant amount of applied research
Firm-sponsored laboratory	Research	I: Large R&D intensive; biotechnology U: Private universities F: Regular faculty G: No involvement	Very limited; large budgets; received great deal of publicity	Not clear
IU Cooperative Research Centers	Research to Development	I: Large R&D intensive firms U: Research universities F: Regular faculty G: Major federal role; state participation	Widely used mechanism; budgets average about $1 M per site	Data on I/UCRC demonstrate effectiveness in transferring knowledge and technology; education benefits

continued

Figure 1-1	Research linkage mechanisms (continued).			
Linkage Mechanism	**Innovation Stage**	**Participants***	**Scope**	**Impact**
I-U Projects	Development to Applied Engineering	I: Large and small firms U: Diverse group F: Regular faculty G: Primarily state	Widely used; small budgets	Focuses collaboration on downstream knowledge and technology transfer
Small Business Technology Transfer	Research to Development	I: Small firms; U: Open to all but research universities dominate F: Regular faculty G: State and federal support	Widely used by states; small budgets	Focuses collaboration on downstream knowledge and technology transfer
Industrial Associations and Consortia	Research to Development	I: Diverse; Agriculture U: Diverse F: Regular G: Little or none	Widely used; unknown	Unknown; expect similar to CRC
Research Parks	Commercialization	I: Diverse; U: Research universities F: Regular G: State	Widely used, >100	Positive interactions; economic development unknown

*I = Industry; U = University; F = Faculty; G = Government

Goe (1994), there were over 1,000 I/U research linkage mechanisms in the US in 1990 with total expenditures of $4.12 billion, approximately $2.53 billion of it for R&D[1]. This represents almost 15 percent of university research expenditures. Industry's share of these costs ($779 million) represents an astounding 69 percent of all industrial support for academic research and development! In other words, I/U linkage mechanisms have become the primary vehicle for industrial support of academic research. However, in spite of their popularity, it would be a mistake to believe that this diverse collection of I/U linkage mechanisms is the cure for all that ails I/U relations.

Effects of Linkage Mechanisms

Cohen, Florida and Goe (1994) found huge differences within the sample of linkage mechanisms they studied on a variety of performance measures. Some did very well on publications or technology transfer or down-stream commercialization while others fared poorly. While they didn't have much luck identifying the source of these variations, we believe these differences are due to two factors they didn't examine: organizational form and management.

Since each type of I/U linkage mechanism is a slightly different organizational form, some types will be better suited than others for performing certain kinds of research and achieving certain goals. Consistent with this premise, our own research has demonstrated that I/U projects, typified by a bench-level collaboration between an industrial and university investigator on a specific project, are much more likely to result in research targeted at patent and product development than I/U centers (Gray, et al., 1986). Similarly, there is a broad consensus that the industrial affiliates model, providing early access to faculty findings for an annual fee, usually results in very traditional academic research, and the research institutes model, typified by individually funded projects performed by a team of investigators, usually results in relatively applied and short-term projects.

At the same time, how a linkage mechanism is managed will also affect performance. Consistent with this view, one industrial

---

[1]Cohen and Florida use the term center in this report. However, they define a university-industry center as including university-affiliated research centers, institutes, laboratories, facilities, stations or other organizations. In order to avoid confusion with the centers discussed in this report, we will use the term "linkage mechanisms" to describe the general class.

observer estimates that only four percent of university-based centers actually exceeded corporate expectations (Hesselberth, 1991).

Not surprisingly, these principles reflect the standard organizational axiom: "do the right thing" and then "do things right." In other words, decisions about which specific I/U linkage mechanism one chooses (e.g., affiliate, institute, center) and how well one manages that form will influence the kinds of outcomes one will attain.

But what constitutes the "right thing," if you're interested in creating win-win research partnerships between industry and university? We answer that question in the next section by describing the development and outcomes of the NSF I/UCRC program. We turn our attention to "doing things right" in the remainder of this volume.

I/UCRC PROGRAM AND MODEL:
A BRIEF HISTORY OF THE I/UCRC PROGRAM

The Industry-University Cooperative Research Centers Program began as part of the Experimental R&D Incentives Program (ERDIP) initiated by the National Science Foundation during the early 1970s. The ERDIP was a time-limited, experimental program to test the viability of different R&D initiatives. It included four public sector-oriented components: the Cooperative Research and Development Experiment (which evolved into the Industry-University Cooperative Research Centers Program), the Laboratory Validation Assistance Experiment, the Innovation Centers Experiment, and the Medical Instrumentation Experiment (Colton, 1982). These four programs were supposed to increase non-federal investment in R&D, and increase the rate of adoption of the results of science and technology in the private sector.

During the one-year planning phase of the Cooperative Research and Development Experiment 14 grant recipients defined and proposed different cooperative models and sought industrial support. During the four-year second phase, three models of cooperative research were implemented and evaluated: an R&D extension model which emphasized low technology operational problems (Furniture Applications Institute at North Carolina State University); a model using a third-party broker between industries and universities (the New England Energy Development Systems, run by Mitre Corporation); and a university-based research consortium (MIT Industry Polymer Processing Center). An independent evaluation concluded that while each model showed technical achievement, only the MIT Industry Polymer Processing Center demonstrated an ability to attract sustained industrial support and proved to be a profitable approach, both scientifically and administratively (Burger, 1982).

In spite of these findings, not everyone was convinced of the value of the so-called "MIT model." Mirroring these sentiments Baer (1980) concluded, "A principal question is estimating how many successful university-based centers can be created on the MIT model. Professor Suh's success at MIT may be so unique that few individuals and institutions can emulate it without descending into research mediocrity and administrative nightmares" (pp. 19-20). In essence, Baer was questioning the generalizability of what has become known as the "I/UCRC model." Was the Polymer Processing Center's success the product of good timing and effective local leadership or had NSF identified a model, a social technology if you will, that was broadly replicable?

Contemporary Development

The I/UCRC Program began in earnest around 1980. Since then it has become one of the country's largest cooperative research programs cited as an administrative, scientific, and technological success (Hesselberth, 1991; Illman, 1994).

By 1997, the I/UCRC program included 55 cooperative research centers encompassing over 80 universities; 700 member firms; over 800 faculty; almost 800 graduate and over 250 undergraduate students; and a budget of over $75 million. Center technologies run the gamut from advanced telecommunications to steel processing. Approximately 70 percent of the centers are still operating after 17 years.

More importantly, the I/UCRC program has resulted in a win-win partnership for university and industry. One indication of this is the fact that 90 percent of industrial representatives and faculty report they are satisfied with their involvement. I/UCRC evaluations over the past dozen years, provides additional support for these assertions (see Figure 1-2). In brief, they demonstrate that faculty receive substantial research support and conduct industrially relevant fundamental research, report higher levels of interaction with other faculty, and continue to publish at a high rate. Students rate their educational experience higher, continue to enjoy academic freedom, and receive more job offers than their departmental peers. Industry reports leveraging their research investment 30-to-1 in a given center, recruiting talented students,

Figure 1-2   Indicators of success for the I/UCRC program (as of FY 1997).

Administrative and Financial

- 55 I/UCRCs in operation at end of FY1996; 60 percent of these five years or older

- Approximately 75 percent of I/UCRCs funded over the past 17 years are still in operation

- Total effective I/UCRC Program budget is $75 million

- I/UCR centers average $1.1 million in direct funding per year

- NSF provides less than 7 percent ($4.1 million) of the funding received by I/UCRCs

Generalizability of the Model

- Diverse technological areas

- Implemented by small and medium-sized universities and a variety of academic departments

- I/UCRC models are operating successfully in Europe

Impact of Model

- Over 80 universities involved in I/UCRCs

- Over 800 faculty and 800 graduate students and 250 undergraduate students are actively involved in conducting research within I/UCRCs

- Over 700 industrial memberships held in I/UCRCs

Scientific

- On average, faculty member publishes three papers and two journal articles per year based on I/UCRC research

- On average, faculty member supervises one dissertation to completion per year

- Faculty awards from academic and professional associations

Student

- I/UCRC students rate their educational experience more highly than departmental peers (Scott and Schaad, 1991)

- I/UCRC students perceive as much academic freedom as their departmental peers (Gidley, 1989)

- I/UCRC students report more job offers than their departmental peers (Scott and Schaad, 1991)

Technological

- Average center produces at least one disclosure and patent per year

- Annual follow-on research averages $170,000 per firm, $2 million per center, and $100 million for the program

- Over 70 percent of members report a knowledge or technology transfer success; 79 percent of these report transfer resulted in technical advances or development (Scott and Schaad, 1994)

- I/UCRC research has resulted in the development of number of significant commercial products and processes developed

Note: Unless noted otherwise the source for these findings include: Gray, D.O. and Lindblad, M. (1997). *NSF Industry-University Cooperative Research Centers: Structural Information 1995-96.* Raleigh, N.C.: North Carolina State University; Gray, D.O. and Lindblad, M. (1997). *NSF Industry-University Cooperative Research Centers: Process-Outcome Results 1996.* Raleigh, N.C.: North Carolina State University. Gray, D.O. and Lindblad, M. (1997). *NSF Industry-University Cooperative Research Centers: Memberships and Milestones 1995-96.* North Carolina State University; Gray, D.O. and Lindblad, M. (1997).

making new internal research investments of over $170,000 per firm per year, and achieving high levels of technology transfer.

Examples of I/UCRC faculty achievements and awards and some of the commercially successful developments which have come from their research are described in Figure 1-3 and Figure 1-4, respectively. Not surprisingly, given these findings, the I/UCRC program has provided the basis for designing a number of other programs including NSF's Engineering Research Centers and State-I/UCRC programs and a variety of state university-based centers of excellence.

Remarkably, this growth and success has required only a modest amount of federal funding. While the NSF I/UCRC Program budget has increased from $1 million to $4 million since 1980, funding per center has actually declined from approximately $250,000 per year to $50,000 per year. NSF provides only seven percent of the program's budget, with industry (45 percent), state (13 percent), other federal sources (28 percent) and the balance university (8 percent).

I/UCRC FORMULA FOR SUCCESS

What accounts for the high and widespread success achieved by the NSF I/UCRC Program? In our view, its success can be attributed to three program components: the "I/UCRC model," the organizational form which has been refined and elaborated to the point it represents a reliable "social technology"; the screening and selection process used by NSF; and financial and technical support provided through a multi-year grant.

I/UCRC Model

The I/UCRC model is a complex hybrid organizational form which incorporates features found in three other I/U linkage mechanisms: organized research units, industrial affiliates, and R&D consortia (see Figure 1-5).

At a fundamental level, an I/UCRC is an **organized research unit**. That is a semi-autonomous research unit which exists within the university independent from academic departments (Friedman & Friedman, 1986). As such it is better equipped than an academic department to draw faculty from across departmental boundaries, provide norms and incentives which encourage multidisciplinary and problem-driven research and manage large multi-task projects for its sponsors.

Figure 1-3 I/UCRC faculty and student awards and achievements.

National Medal for Technology

IEEE Prize, Best Paper (twice)

Recipient, NSF Career Development Award (twice)

Basic Energy Sciences Award, Sandia National Laboratory

American Chemical Society's Ralph K. Iler Award (twice)

Lockheed Martin Nova Corporate Award for Technical Excellence

Student Awards, Mentor Graphics/Sun VLSI Design Contest

Student Award, SPE Polymer Modifiers and Additives Division Scholarship

Finalist, American Chemical Society Sherwin Williams Award

Bounder Faculty Award for Excellence in Research and Faculty

Silver Medal, Technology Transfer Society

IEEE Circuits and Systems Society, Darlinton Award

IEEE Presidential Faculty Fellow

American Control Conference, Best Paper

Figure 1-4 I/UCRC commercial success stories.

Plastics Recycling

A plastics recycling research center developed a large-scale (5 million pounds per year) pilot plant for recycling plastic bottles for 21 licensees. One licensee invested $10 million in a 60,000 square foot recycling plant that processes 40 million pounds per year of reclaimed plastics from the northeastern US.

Better Fit for US-Made Autos

An I/UCRC developed a dimensional measurement methodology that allowed Chrysler Corporation's Jeep Grand Cherokee plant to reduce the dimensional tolerance in the assembly of automobile body panels from 5mm to 2mm. This standard tolerance improvement makes Chrysler a world-class competitor against foreign automobile manufacturers.

Improved Handling of Materials

A manufacturer decentralized sourcing for components across a number of plants in a large metropolitan area. The result was a high rate of between-plant transport, large inventories, and an uncertain supply of parts. Using technology developed at an I/UCRC devoted to material handling research, the company modified its material configuration. It reported that the changes reduced the work-in process inventory by $100 million, reduced personnel costs associated with materials handling by $3 million, and saved an additional $10 million per year in carrying costs.

Note: These cases are included in the 1993 NSF I/UCRC Program brochure.

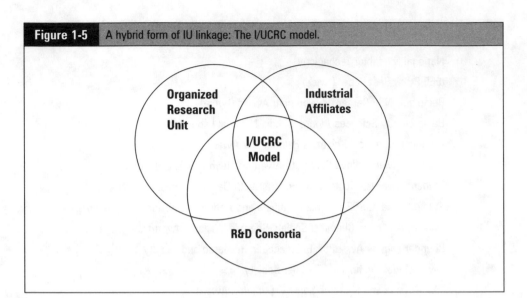

Figure 1-5   A hybrid form of IU linkage: The I/UCRC model.

Because it involves collective support by a number of firms, as opposed to one-on-one support, an I/UCRC incorporates features found in the **industrial affiliates** model. Consistent with the affiliates approach, the collective format ensures that the center will focus on research that is of interest to multiple firms or a whole industry and thus be generic and precompetitive in nature. However, in contrast to the affiliates approach, the I/UCRC model provides a strong and prominent role for industry in all aspects of center management and thus draws heavily on an industrial linkage form, the **R&D consortia** (Davis, 1985). Since government often supports Centers, the prominent role given to industry ensures that the center will run based on "technology pull" (industry's needs) rather than "technology push" (government's perception of industry's needs) principles.

The I/UCRC Model as Social Technology

While it's clear that the I/UCRC model is a complex hybrid organizational form, we think it's more than that. We believe it represents an effective social technology.

Although it might come as a surprise to most engineers and scientists, innovation scholars have long accepted the existence of "social," "organizational," "administrative," or "programmatic" technologies (Rogers, 1983). In order for something to be considered a social technology it should meet three criteria: a replicable set of structures, procedures, roles, behavior patterns; knowledge-based; and demonstrable and replicable effects (Tornatzky and Fleischer, 1990).

The I/UCRC model meets these standards. The model is supported by a body of theory and research (e.g., Aldrich, 1977; Cummings, 1984). It has a replicable set of structures, procedures, roles, and practices for linking industry and university research needs and activities. More important, the effect of these procedures (e.g., focus on industrially-relevant fundamental research, education and technology transfer benefits) has been demonstrated over and over again in a wide variety of settings and circumstances. As a consequence, we would argue that the I/UCRC model can and should be viewed as more than a promising idea, it should be considered a proven, reliable social technology for creating win-win partnerships.

While a detailed description of the practices which constitute this social technology is beyond the scope of this chapter, some of the "core" features include (1) an organizational structure; (2) a membership agreement or bylaws; (3) a set of standard procedures related to periodic meetings, project selection, and other issues.

Building a Foundation: NSF's Role

While this volume will focus on describing the generic I/UCRC model and how to make it work with or without the assistance of a government sponsor like NSF, it's important to recognize the valuable role NSF has played in the centers it has sponsored. As any student of the innovation literature will tell you: "Build a better mouse trap and sometimes people will beat a path to your door." The fact of the matter is many superior technologies, social and otherwise, fail to achieve their intended effect. Remember beta format VCRs? Failure is usually related to two factors: how the technology is disseminated to potential users and the manner in which it is implemented (Tornatsky and Fleischer, 1990). In the NSF I/UCRC program, the model's dissemination is enhanced by a screening and selection process and its implementation is supported by a financial and technical support system. These factors have also contributed to the program's success.

Screening and Review: Providing the Right Ingredients

NSF plays an important role in the creation and success of I/UCRCs by screening and reviewing center proposals. Five year center operating grants are awarded based on a peer review process which focuses on knowledge of the I/UCRC model, scientific merit emphasizing multidisciplinary, leadership, industrial support, institutional support, marketing strategy and research strategy.

The Operating Grant Award: Empowering Success

The NSF I/UCRC operating grant also contributes to the success of the I/UCRC centers. While the direct financial support provided through this award is minimal, it provides prestige associated with NSF and technical assistance in establishing and operating centers.

Financial support. It's difficult to argue that this modest amount of funding contributes substantially to the program's success. However, two incidental benefits may accrue from this situation. The program appears to attract only applicants who are highly motivated and entrepreneurial in orientation. It also reinforces a "customer orientation" (e.g., industry) among centers. Nonetheless, funding to plan a center and some cost- sharing undoubtedly reduces some of the risk involved in starting a new center.

Prestige. The NSF is the primary source of funding for academic science and engineering research within the US. It has a well respected system of peer review. It is held in high regard by both academic and industrial scientists. As a consequence, considerable prestige is associated with receiving support from NSF so its centers win approval and respect within their institutions. NSF opens doors to potential I/UCRC industrial sponsors. The growing reputation of the I/UCRC program has also helped in this arena.

Technical assistance. The I/UCRC model has evolved with help from NSF staff who took an active role in helping Center Directors figure out how to manage the uncertainties and problems inherent in running a center. As centers had their successes and failures, NSF staff communicated and reinforced the principles and practices imbedded in these experiences with new Center Directors. This process was enhanced and amplified by the "feedback-based continuous improvement" approach to evaluation used throughout the program (See Chapter 8). This continues to this day and has certainly contributed to the program's enviable success rate.

SUMMARY

Over the last 40 years, I/U linkage mechanisms have evolved from a novel organizational strategy to bridge the gap between industrial and university participants to the dominant mechanism for industrial support of university research. Their proliferation, in fact routinization, on our college campuses may represent the most significant change to the way research universities operate over the past half century.

Cuts in federal R&D, industry's need for fundamental research no longer done in-house, and the university's need for financial support will almost certainly dictate expanded use of these intermediary organizations. However, neither industry nor university nor government can afford to invest time and energy in partnerships which don't deliver or are consistently one-sided. The I/UCRC model, social technology developed and championed over the past 20 years, offers hope in this regard.

While there are certainly a number of profitable mechanisms for industry and university to work together, the I/UCRC Program has established an enviable and long-standing track record of producing win-win partnerships. The results speak for themselves: a manageable model which generalizes across a wide spectrum of industries, universities, and academic departments; a powerful leveraging vehicle for federal and industrial sponsors; financial, scientific, technical and social benefits for universities, their faculty and students, and industry.

A number of programmatic ingredients have contributed to these results, including: a screening and selection process which insures that the proper factors for a successful center are present; an operating grant which helps reduce some of the financial risk involved in starting a center and provides prestige; and most importantly, a highly evolved "I/UCRC model" that has proven to be an effective and robust social technology—"the right thing" if you will.

Up until now, a system of informal and intermittent technical assistance offered by NSF, its network of directors and evaluators has helped participants "do things right." Unfortunately, because I/UCRCs are complex boundary-spanning structures, this ad hoc approach hasn't always been adequate to meet the needs of current and would-be I/UCRC directors, industry sponsors, and the federal and state program managers who would like to help universities and firms emulate the I/UCRC program's success. To meet their needs, we will attempt to document some of the research and experience-based know-how represented in the "I/UCRC model" in this book. This will involve coverage of a variety of topics including: planning and initiating a new center (Chapter 2), organizational structure (Chapter 3), membership (Chapter 4), planning the cooperative research program (Chapter 5), implementing the cooperative research program (Chapter 6), communications (Chapter 7), control, budgeting and evaluation (Chapter 8), knowledge and technology transfer (Chapter 9), leadership (Chapter 10), growth and diversification (Chapter 11).

In closing, it's important to point out that *there is no perfect way to implement the I/UCRC model*. An effective social technology is usually comprised of a small number of essential or "core" principles and a variety of features which can and probably should be handled differently based on local circumstances. As a consequence, each chapter included in this volume includes an overview of the topic under discussion which emphasizes general concepts, principles and contingencies for action, followed by specific strategies, practices, sample forms etc. Our assumption is a reader who knows why a strategy works can improvise when his or her circumstances are atypical. We hope the combination of both perspectives will meet the needs of directors looking for "best practices," while encouraging the kind of experience-based experimentation which has contributed to the development and refinement of the I/UCRC model.

REFERENCES

Aldrich, H. Boundary spanning roles and organizational structure. *Academy of Management Review*, 217-230, 1977.

Baba, M. L. Innovation in university-industry linkages: university organization and environmental change. *Human Organization, 47(3)*, 260-269, 1988.

Baer, W.S. *Strengthening University-Industry Interactions*, Rand Corp., Santa Monica, CA: 1980.

Brooks, H. Research universities and the social contract for science. In Branscomb, L.M. (Ed.) *Empowering technology*. MIT Press, Cambridge, MA, 1993.

Burger, R.M., Cole, S.H., & Burnette, Jr., C.H., Analysis of the NSF's University-Industry Cooperative Research Centers Experiment: An effort to stimulate university-industry cooperative research in solving R&D problems in American industry. In Colton, R.M.(Ed.) *Analyses of five NSF experiments to stimulate increased technological innovation in the private sector.* National Science Foundation, Washington, DC, 1982.

Coburn, C. *Partnerships: A Compendium of State and Federal Cooperative Technology Programs.* Battelle, Columbus, OH, 1995.

Cohen, W., Florida, R., & Goe, W. R. *University-Industry Research Centers in the United States.* Carnegie Mellon University, Pittsburgh, PA, 1994.

Colton, R.M. (Ed.) *Analyses of five NSF experiments to stimulate increase technological innovation in the private sector.* National Science Foundation, Washington, DC, 1982.

Council on Competitiveness. *Endless Frontier, Limited Resources.* Council on Competitiveness, Washington, D.C. , 1996.

Cummings, T. G. . Transorganizational development. In B. M. Staw & L. L. Cummings (Eds.), *Research in Organizational Behavior.* JAI Press, Greenwich, CN, 367-422, 1984.

Davis, D.B., R&D Consortia, *High Technology,* 5 48-52, 1985.

Fairweather, J. S. *Entrepreneurship and higher education: lessons for colleges, universities, and industry* (ASHE-ERIC Higher Education Report 6): Association for the Study of Higher Education, 1988.

Feller, I. Technology Transfer from Universities. *Higher Education: Handbook of Theory and Research,* XII, Agathon Press, NY, 1997.

Friedman, R. S., & Friedman, R. C. *Sponsorship, organization and program change at 100 universities.* No. (NSF Grant SRS-840288). Institute for Policy Research and Evaluation, Pennsylvania State University, University Park, PA, 1986.

Gidely, T.R. *Industry funded research and graduate education: A national study of chemical and electrical engineering students.* Unpublished doctoral dissertation, North Carolina State University, Raleigh, N.C., 1989.

Gray, D. O., Johnson, E. C., & Gidley, T. R. Industry-university projects and centers: An empirical comparison of two federally funded models of cooperative science. *Evaluation Review,* 10, 776-793, 1986.

Gray, D.O., Behrens, T.R., & Oldsman, E. Industry-university linkage mechanisms in the United States. In Brimble, P. (Ed.) *Proceedings of an international workshop: Modalities of university-industry cooperation in the APEC region.* Ministry of University Affairs, Bangkok, Thailand, 1996.

Hesselberth, J. F.Consortia: Making them work. *ChemTech,* p. 271-273, 1991.

Illman, D. L.NSF Celebrates 20 years of industry-university cooperative research. *Chemistry and Engineering News,* 25-30, 1994.

Ikenberry, S. O., & Friedman, R. C. *Beyond academic departments: The story of institutes and centers.* Jossey-Bass, San Francisco, CA, 1972.

Kidd, C.V. *American universities and federal research.* Harvard University Press, Boston, MA, 1959.

National Science Board. *Science and Engineering Indicators 1993.* U.S. Government Printing Office, Washington D.C.,1993.

National Science Board. *Science and Engineering Indicators 1996*. U.S. Government Printing Office, Washington D.C., 1996

Rogers, E.M. *Diffusion of innovations*. Free Press, NY, NY, 1983.

Rosenberg, N., & Nelson, R. R. American universities and technical advance in industry. *Research Policy, 23*, 323-348, 1994.

Scott, C., & Schaad, D. *Understanding Technology Transfer in NSF Industry/ University Cooperative Research Centers.* University of Washington, Seattle, WA, 1994.

Scott, C. S., Schaad, D. C., & Brock, D. M. *A Nationwide Follow-up Study of Graduates of NSF Industry/University Cooperative Research Centers.* National Science Foundation, Washington, D.C., 1991.

Tornatzky, L. G., & Fleischer, M. *The processes of technological innovation*. Lexington, MA: Lexington Books, 1990.

GETTING STARTED:

Planning and Initiating a New Center

CHAPTER 2

S. GEORGE WALTERS, *Professor Emeritus, Rutgers University, NJ*
DENIS O. GRAY, *North Carolina State University, Raleigh*

INTRODUCTION

"The growth of university-industry and university-industry-government collaborative R&D programs is the single most important development in the character of university technology transfer endeavors since the early 1980s. University-industry research centers (UIRCs) are the primary vehicle through which industry supports academic R&D." (Feller, p. 31, 1997)

Since there is growing uncertainty surrounding future federal and industrial support for R&D, we may need to rely even more heavily on the highly leveraged, yet mutually beneficial, partnerships described by Feller.

Centers are created in a variety of different ways: as a response to a government-sponsored centers initiative, based on the instigation of a number of firms or a whole industry, as a survival strategy when a large federal grant expires, or as a gradual evolution of an informal small partnership. In spite of this diversity, evidence suggests a number of common features associated with the "birthing" of new cooperative research center involving industry and university.

First, while industry can and has been the driving force behind the creation of cooperative research centers, an entrepreneurial faculty member or team of faculty is typically the catalyst for creating a new center. This should come as no surprise. Faculty need to support their research programs, and centers have become a viable way of expanding the market for faculty and graduate student research.

Second, while the title of this volume stresses the partnership between industry and university, the overwhelming majority of cooperative research centers receive funding from federal or state government sources (Coburn, 1995). As a consequence, the growth and success of cooperative research centers in the U.S. is really a product of industry-university-government partnerships. Thus, most individuals interested in creating a new center will typically find themselves involved in meeting the requirements of a federal or state sponsor.

Finally, creating a center tends to be action-oriented. It involves much more than writing a successful grant proposal (although this is usually involved). As we will point out, the process is closer to planning and implementing a new business start-up. As a consequence, creating a new center is best understood as a **process** which is articulated over time, involves a series of steps, feedback loops, and periodic follow through.

Given these common features, the material presented in this chapter will emphasize the central role of the faculty entrepreneur and attempts to secure sponsorship and funding from a government agency (illustrated by the NSF IUCRC program). However, in doing so we will emphasize a generic action-oriented process which can and has been used profitably by faculty and non-faculty with a variety of federal or state agencies, and by individuals trying to start a center without government support.

The Center Development Process

New centers usually evolve during a three-stage process.

Exploratory Stage

Individuals collect preliminary information about the feasibility of establishing a center and begin to formulate their center vision. This stage involves a great deal of self-assessment and reality testing, which culminates in the development and submission of a concept paper to an agency for internal review. Proposed centers which meet program criteria and are considered potentially viable are encouraged to submit a formal proposal.

Pre-Planning Stage

Collaborators develop a full-blown plan for evaluating the feasibility of establishing a center and developing the industry and university interaction necessary to support an operational center. This may involve the development and submission of a planning grant proposal to a government agency.

Planning Stage

Collaborators test the feasibility of establishing a center, gain industrial commitments, and refine the center operating plan. A proposal to establish a new center is submitted to industrial sponsors and eventually to a government agency.

Government Funding

As we described above, the vast majority of cooperative research centers involve sponsorship and/or co-funding by a government agency. The NSF I/UCRC program has figured prominently in the growth of cooperative research centers in the U.S. It was the first major government initiative to attempt to systematically create cooperative research centers, it served as a model for other programs, and it remains one of the largest (at least in terms of number of participants). As a consequence, we will use the NSF I/UCRC and its application process to illustrate how the center development process can dovetail with government granting procedures.

However, it's important to remember that the NSF I/UCRC program's fifty plus centers account for less than five percent of the centers identified by Cohen, Florida and Goe (1994). Therefore, individuals interested in starting new centers should consider a broad spectrum of federal and state funding options.

THE NSF I/UCRC PROGRAM AND MODEL

Currently over 50 I/UCRCs exist at universities around the nation (see Appendix 2-8). According to NSF, I/UCRCs pursue three objectives:

- To pursue fundamental engineering and scientific research having industrial relevance.

- To produce graduates who have a broad, industrially oriented perspective in their research and practice.

- To accelerate and promote the transfer of knowledge and technology between university and industry.

Since NSF does not provide financial support for an indefinite period of time, centers must pursue a fourth objective: *"to achieve self-sufficiency from NSF support within ten years."* I/UCRCs may also re-invent themselves with innovative research themes and compete for funding beyond ten years (see Chapter 11).

In order to achieve these objectives, the I/UCRC program framework has the following characteristics:

- develops a partnership among academe, industry and other organizations participating in the center;

- consults with center members to set a research agenda focused on shared research interests and opportunities;

- shares the intellectual property developed by the center equally among center members;

- has center members monitor and advise on the progress of the research, which speeds two-way transfer of knowledge between universities and industry;

- has industrial and other partners that are the primary financial resource for the center;

- has a formal structure and policies for center members outlined in an I/UCRC membership agreement;

- relies primarily on graduate student involvement in the research projects, thus developing students who are knowledgeable in industrially relevant research;

- has a center director, based at a university or college, who is responsible for all center activities, and

- has formal evaluation of the partnership conducted by an independent evaluator.

Universities and colleges with sufficient research and graduate education capabilities are eligible as lead institutions for I/UCRC program support. Since organizations of this type are difficult to create, the NSF I/UCRC program provides two kinds of assistance: a screening process designed to provide feedback on the viability of proposed centers, and modest financial support for the planning and operation of centers.

Criteria for supporting a new I/UCRC are very straightforward (see Figure 2-1). Proposed centers must demonstrate $300,000 of industrial support from at least six firms in order to be eligible for up to $100,000 a year in NSF support. Additional details on NSF

Figure 2-1	I/UCRC program funding criteria.

New Centers

- Minimum of $300,000 annually from at least six firms.

- In first five years, are eligible for up to $100,000 per year from NSF, renewable annually.

Multi-University Centers

- Partner universities must have a minimum of $150,000 per year industry support from at least three firms, and are eligible for up to $50,000 funding per year from NSF, renewable annually.

- Affiliate universities must have a minimum of $75,000 industrial support annually, and are eligible for up to $25,000 per year from NSF.

funding guidelines and options are described in the "NSF I/UCRC Program Announcement" and at the NSF website: *http://www. eng.nsf.gov/eec/i-ucrc.htm*

A Program Metaphor—Developing a Small Business

Establishing an I/UCRC is like starting a small business (Lauer, 1994). The prospective Center Director must be an entrepreneur with vision and ambition to realize a thriving academic team of investigators who produce high-quality research ideas, new knowledge, and graduates. Research results are disseminated to a diverse market of industry, federal, and state government agencies.

Consistent with this metaphor, the process involved in developing a new I/UCRC is similar to developing and refining a business plan, and submitting a concept paper and planning and operations proposals to a government agency are similar to seeking seed and venture capital for a new start-up.

In the case of the NSF I/UCRC program, the business venture represented by an I/UCRC is like a unique franchise. The NSF application process is designed to screen potential franchisees for qualifications and strengths critical for long-term technical and educational success. Successful applicants receive start-up funding; a proven model for center development, structure, operation, management, and evaluation; and a valuable NSF seal of approval in the form of a peer-reviewed NSF award.

The I/UCRC application process screens potential cooperative research franchisees for a variety of qualities (see Figure 2-2).

Local Capabilities

Successful centers require junior and senior faculty researchers who **understand the I/UCRC model** and demonstrate capabilities which coincide with industrial needs. Since industry values **multidisciplinary work**, faculty should represent a variety of relevant disciplines.

Center **leadership** should reflect entrepreneurship, technical vision, commitment to boundary spanning, commitment to team work, administrative capability, and self-knowledge (see Chapter 10).

Successful centers are usually built on a pre-existing **network of industrial contacts**. This is essential for recruiting industrial members and for targeting research in an area of strong industrial needs. Healthy revenue from consulting and industrial collaborative research in a sponsoring department demonstrates the university's and the department's ability to address industry research needs.

Favorable Environment

Centers must address a research **need** of industry. An industry-relevant research program is a prerequisite because industry's financial support is mandatory. Though most firms involved in

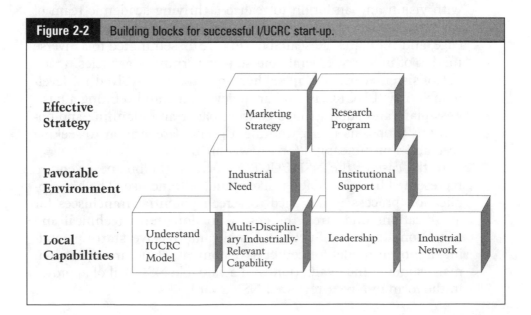

Figure 2-2   Building blocks for successful I/UCRC start-up.

I/UCRCs perform and support a great deal of R&D, firms which are not R&D intensive may also be candidates for recruitment. The important point is that centers must be able to identify industry members who will recognize the value of their proposed research agenda and who can apply the center's research outputs.

Strong **institutional support** from academic administrators, the university president, deans, and department chairs is vital in attracting cross-disciplinary research teams of quality faculty members and students. Issues of tenure, funding allocation, overhead reimbursement or waiver, space assignment, access to equipment, and course development and credit may hamper an I/UCRC if key administrators are not supportive.

Effective Strategy

While a pre-existing industrial network is essential when a center is getting started, few if any centers have sustained themselves on one. Center leadership must reach outside and develop an I/UCRC **marketing plan** that continues throughout the life of the center. Strategic alliances between industry and university are not permanent and need constant renewal and upgrading. Marketing is a center way of life. While the Center Director shoulders most of these responsibilities, faculty and industrial members should also be involved in recruiting new members.

An I/UCRC proposal must match a university's research strengths to an industry's research needs and funding capability. Sharpening this focus is a major activity throughout the NSF three-phased process. This process does not end when a new center is established. Ongoing development of a **relevant research agenda** is critical to a center's continued success and is discussed in detail in Chapter 5.

Venture capitalists look for certain qualities before investing in a new enterprise. The I/UCRC screening process does the same thing. All of these qualities are not expected to be in place at once, but are developed throughout the evolution of the center from idea to operation. This chapter provides guidance on this developmental process and describes early warning signs of problems, or dimensions one must strengthen (e.g., research agenda).

EXPLORATORY STAGE: DO YOU HAVE WHAT IT TAKES?

Creation of a cooperative center does not begin with writing a proposal. In fact it begins by deciding *whether* a proposal should be written at all! Often the enthusiasm among faculty for creating a center may be out of touch with the actual probability of success. As a consequence, we recommend that the process of developing a center begin with an exploratory stage. A thorough self-assessment and informal external assessment may be reflected in a concept paper.

Beginning Self Assessment

Do Your Homework

First, carefully review the relevant funding announcements. At this stage, it is also recommended to identify by name a number of potential member firms in a given industry and their characteristics. The next step is to review Chapters 1 through 5 in this handbook.

Do a Feasibility Scan

It is more effective to involve at least one or two other faculty and close industrial supporters in this task. Conduct a day-long mini-retreat to brief the group on the I/UCRC model and requirements. Every participant is asked to answer the following questions prior to the retreat:

- Do available faculty have the multidisciplinary technical capability that is relevant to industrial need in the prospective research area, research themes and specific projects?

- Is the center leadership strong (especially the director) in terms of technical, administrative, and entrepreneurial skills and commitment?

- Does the leadership have much experience and a network of contacts in the relevant industry?

- Will the research focus be in an area in which there is a critical mass of firms which need it?

- Will university administrators support a cross-disciplinary research center?

- Is the necessary supporting university infrastructure of labs, equipment, instrumentation, students in place?

Through candid discussion and straw votes during the retreat participants examine several key questions:

- *Scientific and organizational **strengths** of the university and the likely team members?* For example, what is their experience with companies? In what research areas does the institution have national acclaim? Does the administration have a mission to promote university-industry relations?

- *Scientific and organizational **weaknesses** of the university and the likely team members?* For example, are there administrative practices that inhibit faculty from participating in cooperative research with industry? Are there research competencies missing at the institution? Are there personality conflicts?

- ***Opportunities** in the external environment relevant to the proposed center?* For example, what are the acute technology needs of key industries that fit the scientific capacities of the university? Has a foundation recently established an endowed chair in the research area? Have new government regulations imposed on the target industries accelerated the need for research?

- *The **threats** in the external environment relevant to the proposed center?* For example, is there a competing center established at another university? Has the state legislature recently passed a faculty conflict-of-interest law which makes it difficult to work with industry?

Results of these discussions will decide: (1) do not go any further; (2) wait until certain internal weaknesses or external threats are resolved; or (3) yes, full speed ahead. A memorandum or similar document detailing the decision is useful. The same problems tend to turn up later.

Concept Paper

Preparation

When the decision is to go forward, the next step is a concept paper which should be submitted to the NSF-I/UCRC program office (see Figure 2-3) or other government agency. Since NSF's suggested outline for this is described in considerable detail in the NSF I/UCRC Program Announcement, we emphasize the process of developing a successful proposal rather than the content.

Most of the information collected during the self-assessment process will be useful for the concept paper, but there is need for

Figure 2-3	Concept paper outline.

Proposed Center: Description of the research focus;

Industrial Need: Description of the industry and its research needs;

University Capabilities: Summary of the university's capability to address those research needs, including center leadership and university commitment;

Financial Potential: Brief analysis of anticipated industry, university, state, or other funding commitments;

Proposed Model: Summary of center structure, policies, management research focus, and planned budget;

Endorsements: At least five potential industry supporters.

more formal data collection. For instance, an objective catalogue of university research resources, faculty, students, and facilities matched to industrial needs would be extremely helpful. It is necessary to contact key researchers to ascertain their interest. This includes faculty researchers as well as industry colleagues who may become corporate members. It is important to list the grants, contracts and consulting experience of the center research team. This indicates the potential for the center to become self-sustaining.

University administration support, especially from relevant department chairs and deans, is essential. Similar cross-disciplinary, industry-oriented research support is the most concrete indication. Consultation with these individuals is advisable. In particular, the office of the president of the university should be consulted. It is this office that reviews patent policy, center structure, and overheads, and gives permission to plan new centers.

Feedback

It is important to remember that a concept paper is *not* a formal proposal. It is an *informal* way to gauge potential for the center before you make a huge investment in planning, recruiting, and proposal writing. Concept papers should be limited to 4 to 8 pages, no more. NSF staff will review and comment on the concept paper within two months.

After the concept paper has been endorsed and the potential center can respond favorably to comments, the decision to proceed can be made by the proposer.

PRE-PLANNING STAGE:
DEVELOPING A PRELIMINARY BUSINESS PLAN

Consistent with our franchise metaphor, to make a proposed center a reality it is necessary to develop a business plan, operating proposal, or a prospectus, including a marketing plan for prospective members. Since this process can be time consuming and costly, NSF provides seed funding in a (up to $10,000) pre-planning grant/meeting award.

Pre-planning proposals address in greater detail the same concept paper issues: local capabilities, model understanding, multi-disciplinary industry-relevant capabilities, leadership, local network, environment, industrial need, and institutional support. In addition, a coherent research agenda and proposed marketing strategy should be articulated.

Who's Involved in Developing a Pre-Planning Grant/Meeting Proposal

As in the concept paper, it is advisable for the potential Center Director to draw together a small team of faculty who share the vision of the center. Collaboration is one of the hallmarks of a co-operative research center and this team will put the pre-planning proposal together and later, if approved, implement it. The team may include a representative from the university research office or an associate dean for research. Then add three or four industrial allies with whom the core group have had long professional relationships and who are supportive of the effort.

University support is needed in regard to patent policy, delays in publication, center structure, membership fees, and cost sharing. These must be documented in the pre-planning proposal. Someone should be added to the team to address these issues with appropriate university officials. Industrial allies serve as team members and a sounding board during these critical pre-planning and implementation phases.

Center Directors should be able to remind influencers and collaborators of the significance of basic, pre-competitive research merit and the ability of I/UCRCs to deliver such research. Close to half of all the productivity gains may be the result of innovation —the application by managers/innovators of knowledge generated by talented scientists and engineers. This leads to higher standards of living and global pre-eminence. I/UCRC leveraging is 10 to 15 times and R&D dollar multipliers of 1.5 to 7 are the profile of the I/UCRC centers. (Barker, 1991; Clinton and Gore, 1994; Crawford, 1994; Illman, 1994; Walters, 1987.) This documentation helps position basic research and its linkage to productivity alongside of such other issues as monetary and fiscal policy, inflation, employment, and balancing the budget. I/UCRCs are part of the solution to maintaining and enhancing U.S. vitality.

Chapter 6 details a number of strategies for soliciting team input. The Center Director may flesh out a draft of the proposal and ask team members to critique it; team members can be convened as a group to brainstorm; individuals can be given responsibility for authoring specific sections which are then passed around for comment, revision and integration; or some combination of these approaches. (See Appendix 2-9.) Obviously, the more interaction and participation one solicits, the better.

Preparing the Pre-Planning Proposal

Figure 2-4 summarizes the format for preparing a proposal. A formal analysis of industrial needs and capabilities should be provided, including national, regional, or local statistics on the size and importance of the target industry, literature or expert opinion on needs or gaps in that industry's research, or on emerging scientific or technological trends, etc. A general description of the center's proposed research program research areas, thrusts, topics, and projects should also be provided.

Proposals also address how the I/UCRC organizational model may need to be customized to meet particular university circumstances. For centers which involve a number of departments and other colleges or even other universities, it may be desirable to consider the addition of a new layer of management to supervise activities in their respective discipline or respective school.

In addition to NSF funding and the industrial membership fees, state sources, federal agencies, and special program grants which might be included in center funding should be identified. Centers which show funding leverage along with world-class research have a greater probability of attracting industrial firms and obtaining NSF and other government approval.

The plan for developing an industrial-relevant research program and marketing the center to industrial sponsors should be spelled out in a time line or other scheduling device. These are the objec-

Figure 2-4	Preparing the pre-planning proposal.

Introduction

- Analysis of the industry on which the proposed center plans to focus, its importance to the nation's economic health and its research interests and needs, especially in those areas of research that could be considered appropriate for a university.

- Description of the center research focus.

- University capabilities to address the industrial research interests and needs noted above, including faculty and infrastructure.

Model of the Envisioned Center

- Proposed center structure, organization, policies, and operational procedures.

- Management and staffing plan.

- One- or two-page description of each anticipated research project including a discussion of its industrial relevance and appropriateness for the center.

- Budget and sources of funding, noting potential for obtaining a minimum of $300,000 from industry in each year of operation.

- Evaluation plan.

Project Description

- Detail how the pre-planning research objectives will be achieved.

- Outline for a meeting which will determine the research agenda and its viability with possible industrial sponsors.

- Roles the proposed Center Director and other researchers will have in performing this pre-planning study.

- Managerial experience of the proposed Center Director.

Budget

- Complete Form 1030 found in NSF Publication 95-27 for travel, an industry pre-planning meeting, publications and faculty time.

- Note any other sources of funds to be used in this study.

Industry Endorsements

- Letters from at least 5 potential participant companies noting the center's concept and proposed research agenda and that the firm would consider joining if the center were formed.

tives of the pre-planning grant/meeting, and the most important elements of the proposal.

The budget should be specified for travel, expenses of pre-planning meetings, faculty time evaluation, and reference other sources of funds which might be used in the pre-planning study; not infrequently, some industrial funding may be available along with funding and support from the university itself[2].

Letters of interest from potential industrial participants should be included. They should endorse the proposed center's concept, policies and the proposed research agenda and indicate that the center's research has the potential to have a positive impact on the industry. They should state that the company is interested in becoming a center member. These letters should be signed by someone within the company who has the responsibility and authority to authorize later the flow of funds to the center.

Review Criteria

While the venture capitalist evaluates proposals based on their probability of producing a financial return, NSF and other government agencies will invest in those proposals which appear to have the highest probability of becoming technically and educationally successful and financially stable (see Figure 2-5).

Figure 2-5	NSF I/UCRC pre-planning grant/meeting criteria.

- Center is consistent with characteristics and operations of an I/UCRC.
- There is enough potential university support, faculty and facilities involved to build a viable center.
- Research interests focus on an industry that is in a position to support the center.
- Center has potential for sufficient industrial and other financial commitments.
- The center proposes to develop a research program that does not duplicate that of an existing I/UCRC.

---

[2]NSF budget forms are posted on the NSF website at www.nsf.gov/bfa/cpo/forms.

PLANNING STAGE: REFINING AND IMPLEMENTING THE BUSINESS AND MARKETING PLAN

The final stage focuses on the refinement and implementation of the pre-planning proposal. In the NSF program, the goal is to attract members totaling $300,000 or more in annual support. This process usually reaches closure during a two-day recruiting meeting attended by potential industrial sponsors.

Getting Ready: Developing Materials

It is advisable to prepare a brochure/prospectus describing the proposed center venture, policies, research, projects, proposed budgets, and faculty. Most of this information is obtained in the pre-planning proposal.

Preliminary Marketing

It is at this stage that the Center Director tries to identify potential members from the wider industrial environment in the chosen area of research (see Figure 2-6). It is wise to use the center's industry members to initiate such contacts. The entire industrial network of the prospective director and other core faculty should be contacted. The Center Director and core faculty must be prepared to make cold calls, individually or in groups. Contacts may

Figure 2-6	Targeting industry prospects.

Allies: Identify and get feedback from a small group of firms or individuals that you consider your allies. This group is contacted for advice early and often. They must commit to the creation of the center and become its advocates.

Top Prospects: Identify twenty highest-quality firms that you think should join the center, based on strong technical or industrial convergence with center, proximity, or personal network. Have extensive one-on-one phone calls or visits with this group during the pre-planning stage about the research program. Identify likely allies or decision-makers to optimize outcome.

Relevant Prospects: Identify firms that might join based on technical overlap. Communicate with this group via letters or announcements, providing them opportunity to become top prospects.

involve visits to the university or company to detail the research mission, the operations, and the potential benefits of participation. Center Directors must devote considerable effort to preparing solid, professional presentations for they are a continuous aspect of center life.

Presentations should inform the prospective member about the proposed center, solicit input on the proposed research program, convince the prospect to attend an already-scheduled pre-planning conference, and ultimately get a commitment to join the center.

The Pre-planning and Recruiting Meetings

An organizational pre-planning conference or series of such meetings should be the capstone of the pre-planning process and a bridge to the operations proposal. Shumacher (1992) has provided a checklist for organizing such a meeting (see Appendix 2-1). These conferences provide an opportunity to draw together faculty, students, and potential industrial members in one room to focus on the establishment of a center, agreement on research thrusts and specific research proposals, obtain letters of commitment from each industrial company; and so on.

Figure 2-7 shows a typical agenda for such a meeting. Pre-planning meetings may be opened by the president of the university who welcomes the industrial participants. A representative of the NSF, or other government agency describes the program and what can be expected in the way of support. The meeting is chaired by the potential Center Director. One purpose of the meeting is to convey a vision of the center, its organizational structure, its policies, and its proposed research agenda. Another purpose is to confirm that there is a need for the specific research projects being proposed by faculty members. Every effort should be made to be sensitive and responsive to industry suggestions for changes in research mission, thrusts, and individual projects.

Every effort must be made during and following this meeting to obtain formal letters of intent committing the industrial participants to recommending to appropriate authorities in their company the budgeting of the membership fee and the conditions upon which those funds would be released for center use. These letters accompany the center operations proposal or requests for funding from any other funding agency.

The entire meeting should be structured to elicit fullest participation of industry, and include opportunities for informal social interactions between faculty and industrial members. Feedback

Figure 2-7	Typical agenda for a pre-planning conference.

Center for _____

Sunday–Month, Day

6:00–7:30 p.m.	Meeting Registration
7:30–9:30 p.m.	Informal Cocktail Reception and Discussion

Monday–Month, Day

7:00–8:30 a.m.	Breakfast
8:45–9:00 a.m.	Welcome—President of the University
	Introduction to the University
9:00–9:10 a.m.	Introduction of Participants
9:10–9:30 a.m.	Introduction to Department(s) in which center will be based.
9:30–10:10 a.m.	Center Structure: presentation by Center Director assisted by a key industrial supporter outlining the need for the proposed research of the new I/UCRC, and describing the organization including major policies and procedures, cost and funding options.
10:10–10:50 a.m.	Research Program: presentation by director or faculty–perhaps double teamed, a high-level overview of the proposed research of the center.
10:50–11:20 a.m.	Coffee Break
11:20–11:40 a.m.	Introduction to NSF I/UCRC Program
11:40–11:55 a.m.	Presentation by the evaluator regarding evaluation procedures and feedback during the meeting, what is envisioned for semi annual meetings, and the administration of the NSF research instruments to gauge measures of intervening center success.
11:55–12:00 a.m.	Outline of the afternoon session.

A break for lunch with devices available for industry members to make contact with their business location.

1:00–1:45 p.m.	Research Area 1: Overview of research followed by 15 minute project presentations; use proposal and LIFE forms (Appendices 2-2, 2-4).
1:45–2:30 p.m.	Research Area 2: (repeat as above)
2:30–3:15 p.m.	Research Area 3: (repeat as above)
3:15–3:45 p.m.	Coffee Break
3:45–4:15 p.m.	Breakout Sessions by Research Area (optional).
	Guided discussion and feedback on the proposed projects—use Discussion Guide (Appendix 2-5).
4:15–5:00 p.m.	Repeat Breakout Session
5:00–5:30 p.m.	Discussion of the organization of the evening and morning session. Use Organization Feedback Form (Appendix 2-7).
6:00–8:00 p.m.	Cocktail Hour and Dinner
8:00 p.m	Industry-only Workshop on the Day's Topics (optional).

Tuesday—Month, Day

7:00–8:30 a.m.	Breakfast
8:30–10:00 a.m.	Discussion of Project Feedback (Director)
	Review and discussion of feedback obtained via LIFE forms and during breakout sessions. Focus on kinds of changes and refinements for which there is a consensus.
10:00–10:30 a.m.	Break
10:30–11:15 a.m.	Discussion of Organizational and Policy Feedback (Director). Define Organization Feedback Forms.
11:15–12:00	Closing Remarks, Action Items.

obtained during the meeting will help in planning the research agenda and formulating specific research projects which meet industry's needs for the first year of the center's operation.

Developing the Research Plan

During the meeting, the research areas and projects are presented by individual faculty members. Copies of research proposals and other materials should be distributed to potential members before the meeting. Survey instruments such as the Level of Interest and Feedback Evaluation (LIFE) form are distributed which provide industrial participants with an opportunity to indicate their level of interest and to make comments regarding suggested changes (see Chapter 5 and Appendix 2-4).

Early on in this process, proposers should begin to use several I/UCRC devices, the project proposal form and the LIFE form. The project form provides a uniform basis for proposing research projects, and the LIFE form provides a uniform basis for capturing industrial feedback. (See Appendices 2-2 to 2-5 and Chapters 5, 6, and 7 for operating details.) Every effort should be made to encourage industrial participants to suggest research ideas that, if appropriate, are then transformed into research proposals either to be included in the start-up stage or added as the center evolves.

The purpose of the meeting and these procedures is: (1) to present the research proposals and have open discussion and an exchange of ideas, (2) to formalize the opinions of the potential industrial members on feedback forms, (3) to quickly tabulate and place those opinions in the hands of the Center Director and core faculty, (4) to brainstorm and have feedback sessions, (5) while the meeting is still in progress change research areas and specifics of a research proposal as needed, and (6) to obtain industrial approval.

Although the greatest interest usually is shown in the research themes and the individual projects, discussion will also touch upon policies on patents, royalties, publication of the research, and levels of funding that would be necessary to initiate a research program of the type that is being proposed and to sustain it over a number of years. Appendix 2-6 illustrates an organizational feedback form that could be used to solicit this input.

A typical pre-planning conference provides a great deal of feedback, which must be digested. Sometimes this feedback may necessitate a rethinking of the center's research program. Appendix 2-7 includes a set of questions proposers may want to address before submitting their operations proposal.

The Operations Proposal

The operations proposal is an expanded version of the pre-planning proposal (see Figures 2-8 and 2-9) that demonstrates that the objectives of the pre-planning study have been achieved and that the center is ready to function. It documents the appropriateness of the research agenda and the willingness of industry to fund it through letters of commitment or cash in hand. Since the proposal

---

Figure 2-8   Center proposal format.

Introduction

Describe need for the center and its technical focus. Describe the research, the industry, and the center expertise and resources to address this need.

Center Structure and Operations

Discuss evidence of university involvement and participation, and available facilities and infrastructure. Describe director management capability and research experience. Explain intellectual property policies (permit non-exclusive, royalty-free licenses for industrial center members and the possibility of exclusive, royalty-bearing license), publication delay policies; public law 98-620 "march in rights;" membership fee structure of the center, role of members; specific benefits of membership categories; and list the proposed evaluator and members of the university policy committee.

Research Plan

For each research project proposed for the center, describe (in no more than three pages per project): the goals, experimental plan, industrial relevance and time scale of the project, the names and capabilities of faculty involved, the involvement of students and industrial advisory personnel in planning and executing the project, if applicable, and the project budget.

Financial Management of the Center

The proposal should include financial operating plans for five succeeding years, and projected allocation of funds by source and function. A separate budget detailing all costs for the initial year should be included. Provide details on the support to the center from the participating universities. Include a proposed budget for NSF funds for each of the first five years of center operation and a five year summary budget as well. Use NSF Form 1030 from the Proposal Forms Kit, Grant Proposal Guide (NSF 95-27/28).

Appendices

Copy of the industrial agreement document, letters of financial commitment from participating companies; a full list of each individual who participates in any center activity. The list should identify institutional and departmental affiliation or discipline and should include biographical information (NSF Form 1362) on the director, faculty members, or other individuals from participating institutions who will be directly involved in the development, operation, and evaluation of the center. The publications list for these individuals is limited to the ten most relevant. Current and Pending Support (NSF Form 1239) for key academic personnel who are requesting salary support from NSF.

| Figure 2-9 | Evaluation criteria for operations proposal. |

A proposal is evaluated according to the technical and management quality of the proposed center, the qualifications of the personnel, the level of industrial involvement and the likelihood of achieving the goals of the I/UCRC program, as follows:

- Aggregate industrial membership fee support of at least $300,000 per year from a minimum of six firms and potential for more memberships;

- High-quality, industry-relevant research;

- Student involvement with industry and the research;

- Clear technical focus, research need, and defined research agenda;

- Strong industry and university collaboration;

- Adherence to the center structure and policies recommended by the I/UCRC Program;

- Center Director and research team capable of developing and operating a center;

- University administration's commitment.

is subjected to an external peer-review, it must also include summaries of the center's proposed research. The proposal should reaffirm the university administration's support. In the case of the NSF I/UCRC program, the proposal will have to address these issues.

Funding

Strong leveraging of NSF funds is a very positive point in evaluation. I/UCRC operational support from NSF is renewable each year and phased out completely at the end of five years. Renewal for a second five-year period (up to $50,000 per year) is possible. A strategic plan for increasing membership over the term of the award is required. Anticipated funding from the state and other federal agencies should also be identified, as appropriate. The proposal must also budget salary, travel, equipment, and support for the evaluation function.

Center Evaluation

NSF requires each center be observed independently and evaluated during its planning and operational phases. The evaluation normally is conducted by an evaluation expert, usually from within the university but not from the department receiving center funding. Funds are provided by NSF to help cover operational support of evaluation.

The evaluator collects data that provides feedback to the center and NSF on the center's performance. The information gathered also provides a basis for NSF presentations to congressional committees and other policy makers such as officials in the Office of the President's Science Advisor. This function is described in detail in Chapter 3 and 8.

SUMMARY

The development process used by NSF's I/UCRC program offers a proven model for setting up and operating a successful industry and university collaborative research center. Organizational structure, policies, management and evaluation protocols, as well as techniques for recruiting members, planning a research program, and transferring technology to industry are all well-established and available to new centers. Thus, much of the entrepreneurial burden and risk of starting an academic research center are minimized. The challenge to a prospective Center Director instead is focused on winning initial NSF approval of his or her concept and successfully advancing all the way through the three-stage approval process.

Although the center model and its many established elements provide substantial assistance, the effort involved in establishing a new center is considerable and the commitment required is great. This does not entail mere grantsmanship. It may be useful to reiterate the steps for proposers to follow.

Exploratory Stage

Self-Assessment and Concept Paper, 2 months and 2 months for NSF review.

- Determine whether there is a critical mass of potential dues-paying members in an R&D-intensive industry in the prospective focus area.

- Look inward to determine objectively whether there is strong leadership (especially the director) in terms of technical, administrative, and boundary-spanning and commitment.

- Ask whether the leadership is experienced, has a network of contacts in the relevant industry, is respected and trusted by colleagues.

- Find faculty and industry colleagues who are willing to help.
- Determine faculty multidisciplinary technical capability relevant to industrial needs in the prospective research area.
- Match university infrastructure, labs, equipment, staff, commitment to industry needs.
- Be sure that all university and industry participants understand the I/UCRC model.
- Obtain university administration support. (Make the Office of the President of the university aware of the undertaking.)
- Proceed with concept paper and developing a center only if self-assessment is positive.
- Submit concept paper to the NSF-I/UCRC program office or other government agency for comment.

Pre-planning Stage

Concept Paper to Planning Grant, 6-12 months and 3 months for NSF review.

- Upon approval of the concept paper, proceed with pre-planning proposal if commitment from university, industry, and researchers is still strong.
- Convene a group of two to three faculty plus the prospective Center Director to prepare and implement the pre-planning proposal.
- Form a larger group to plan the center and advise the proposal-writing team. This group should include representatives from the university research office, the department or college administration, and several industry members.
- Circulate draft copies of the pre-planning proposal to university administrators.
- Obtain university documentation relating to patent policy, delays in publication, center structure, membership fees, and cost sharing.
- Conduct a formal analysis of industry capabilities and needs in the proposed area.
- Meet with potential industry members individually and collectively regarding their research needs. Look for opportuni-

ties to match and build upon these with faculty research expertise.

- Consider alternatives to the generic I/UCRC organizational structure.

- Identify other funding including state, federal, private, and other sources.

- Formulate a marketing plan to recruit industrial members.

- Prepare budget for NSF or other government agency pre-planning grant/meeting award.

- Formulate tentative research areas and specific projects.

- Obtain letters of interest from potential industrial participants.

- Rewrite the pre-planning proposal.

Planning Stage

Planning Grant/Meeting to Operations Proposal, 3-6 months and 3 months for NSF review.

- Upon notification of a planning grant/meeting award, implement the marketing plan.

- Contact the industrial network of the prospective Center Director and other core faculty.

- Ask industry network to contact colleagues in other companies.

- Conduct university or industry site visits to present the research mission, operating protocols, and potential benefits of a company's participation.

- Publish a prospectus describing the proposed center, company members, center policies, research areas specific projects, budgets, and include faculty and prospective Center Director CVs.

- Convene one or more organizational planning conferences for industry to recruit members and flesh out the strategic research plan.

- Recruit nine-to-ten members at $300,000 or more in annual fees.

- At this meeting obtain formal letters of intent from the industrial participants.
- Finalize the proposed research plan.
- Identify a center evaluator within the university.
- Submit an operations proposal to NSF or other government agency.

NEXT STEPS

By the time an operations proposal is submitted, there should be enough momentum built during preparations and development to sustain energy for the center during the proposal review period. A positive prudence in scheduling meetings and making center commitments in advance of an award is advised.

Following notification of a center operating grant award, final preparations for the center should be made. The Industrial Advisory Board (IAB) should convene at an initial meeting to get the research program underway. The Center Director should finalize administrative arrangements, contracts, official bylaws, membership agreements, etc., with the university and the member companies. An evaluator should begin to carry out his/her duties.

The Center Director and colleagues must now lead and manage an I/UCRC successfully. The remainder of this book covers this and more.

REFERENCES

Barker, R. and Brady, J. *Partners in Innovation, Business and Academia,* a Presentation to H.R.H. Prince Charles, Highgrove, McKinsey & Co., Inc., UK, July, 1991.

Block, E. *Human Talent for Competition.* National Science Foundation, Washington, D.C., 1987.

Bush, G.W. *Leadership,* Post-Presidential Speech, Leadership Conference, Drew University, Madison, NJ, video, University Relations Office, 1995.

Clinton, W., and Gore, A. *Science in the National Interest,* Executive Office of the President of the United States, Office of Science and Technology Policy, Washington, D.C., August, 1994.

Coburn, C. *Partnerships: A Compendium of State and Federal Cooperative Technology Programs.* Battelle, Columbus, OH, 1995.

Cohen, W., Florida, R., and Goe, W.R. *University-Industry Research Centers in the United States*. Carnegie-Mellon University, Pittsburgh, PA, 1994.

Crawford, M. *NSF Industry R&D Cooperative Centers Aim to Raise Profile*, New Technology Week, Washington, D.C., January 18, 1994 (reports interview with Schwarzkopf).

Feller, I. Technology Transfer from Universities. *Higher Education: Handbook of Theory and Research*, XII, Agathon Press, NY, 1997.

Gingrich, N. *To Renew America*, Harper Collins, NY, 1995.

Houlder, V. *How to Handle R&D*, Financial Times, London, Aug. 25, 1997, pg. 8.

Illman, D.L. *NSF Celebrates 20 Years of Industry University Cooperative Research*, Chem. Eng. News, NY, Jan. 24, 1994 (reports interviews with Schwarzkopf, Walters and White).

"Industry/University Cooperative Research Centers Program, Program Announcement," National Science Foundation, Arlington, VA, 1997.

Lauer, R.D. *An Analogy of NSF I/UCRCs to a Franchise Operation*. Presentation at NSF- I/UCRC Evaluators Conference, Washington, D.C., Jun. 9-10, 1994.

Schumacher, D. *Get Funded! A Practical Guide for Scholars Seeking Research Support From Business*, Newbury Park, CA: Sage, 1992.

Walters, S.G. *Improving U.S. World Competitiveness Through Industry-University Cooperative Centers*, Food Technology Management, Chicago, IL, Dec. 1987.

Walters, S.G. *Proceedings on Research Progress, Measurement of Management Decision- Making in the Programs of the U.S. Agency for International Development*, U.S. Government Research Programs (VA1-10) NSF. National Research Council, the National Academy of Sciences, Washington, D.C., Dec., 1991.

APPENDIX 2-1

Checklist for Organizing an On-Campus
Symposium for Industry (from Shumacher, 1992, pp. 192)

- Decide who is going to be responsible for organizing and hosting the symposium
- Decide on program objectives; rough out program
- Select convenient (for both academics and corporate people) date that is far enough in advance (preferably at least 6 months)
- Obtain commitments from presenters and introducers
- Reserve meeting rooms and audiovisual equipment
- Write program brochure and registration form; order printing
- Identify corporate representatives to be invited
- Send preliminary, individual letter of invitation (including program date) to corporate invitees
- Send preliminary notice to invited faculty
- Identify academic administrators to be invited; get dates on their calendars; send them confirming memos
- Send program brochure and registration form to corporate representatives
- Arrange meals, reception
- Order name tags, handouts, folders and such
- Follow up with corporate invitees by means of phone calls
- Conduct dress rehearsal

APPENDIX 2-2

Project Proposal or Progress Report Form

Program Name: New:_____

Program Manager: Continuation:_____

Description:	
Experimental Plan:	
Related Work Elsewhere:	How Ours Is Different:
Related Work In:	Milestones:
Deliverables:	Budget:
Potential Member Company Benefits:	
Economics:	
Progress to Date:	
Knowledge Transfer Target Date:	

APPENDIX 2-3

Directions and Sample LIFE Form

Level of Interest Feedback Evaluation (LIFE)

An important objective of an NSF/I/UCRC semi-annual Industrial Advisory Board meeting is to facilitate scientific discussion about center research projects among faculty, students and industrial members.

LIFE forms hold the potential for stimulating project relevant discussion.

- One of these forms is filled out by each IAB voting member during the five to ten minute period set aside for this purpose following each project progress report or new project proposal.

- The form, which includes instructions, can be produced by any commercial printer. It is usually printed on no carbon required (NCR) paper. The white sheet is for the Director, the yellow sheet is for the researcher, and the pink for the IAB member to retain. (See Appendix 2-4.)

- The Evaluator and the NSF Program Officer collect the forms and make the yellow copy available immediately to the faculty in time for them to discuss comments with members during coffee breaks, lunch, and poster sessions.

- Following the poster sessions and any discussions with the researchers, IAB members may modify their forms and give the revised copy to the Evaluator.

- Based on the final comments, faculty prepare a single flip chart size page or view graph with brief, highlighted statements of the comments they wish to respond to and the responses.

- These sheets or a view graph showing the Level of Interest and Comments for each project are then used as a basis for discussion during the Executive Session of the Industrial Advisory Board.

- They also provide a basis for further IAB faculty discussions during the IAB/Faculty debriefing session. This procedure can help foster scientific discussion and exchange of expertise among Center participants.

With some analysis by the Evaluator, LIFE forms also hold the potential of contributing to the Director's project management system and of alerting the Director to those members whose rankings of Level of Interest and Comments signal possible dissatisfaction with Center activities.

When presenting the results for discussion, list project titles and researcher names along the X axis and VHI, I, IWC, NI and ABS Levels of Interest along the Y axis. Post the LIFE Level of Interest data from each LIFE form. Projects and researchers with a third or more votes in the combined IWC, NI, ABS score should be looked at very carefully. They could be entering the "endangered species" area. Director and researchers need to be informed so that discussions can take place and, if appropriate, corrective action taken.

Some Centers also prepare a second matrix listing the company member names along the X axis and the Levels of Interest along the Y axis. This information is prepared for the Director especially. Once again the rule of thumb, to be adjusted by your Center experience, is that a company with a third or more of its votes as IWC, NI, and ABS could become a candidate for withdrawal from the Center and thus should receive special attention.

The use of the LIFE form and process enables the IAB and the Director to gain a sense of the priorities of the research which is being proposed and thus assists the Center in making final selections of research for funding. This process has a great deal of power. Use it carefully.

Oral and/or Written Instructions for use of the LIFE form:

To facilitate scientific and technical interaction between center faculty and Industrial Member Representatives, each company represented is requested to rank each presentation on the LIFE form as follows: Very Interested, Interested, Interested with Changes, No Interest and Abstain (i.e., not qualified to comment). The level of interest checked should reflect the opinion of the company and not a personal interest).

Comments should include: suggested changes, quality of research, scientific merit, innovative nature of the research, industrial relevance, level of effort, (progress since last report for previously funded projects), offers of help, (relevance to Center long range plans, technology road maps, Center research thrusts/objectives, etc.) and other suggestions that might relate in a timely way.

Your completed LIFE forms will be picked up immediately after each research presentation. Please keep the pink sheets for your records.

APPENDIX 2-4

Level of Interest Feedback Evaluation Form (LIFE Form)
(Courtesy Emission Reduction Research Center, NJIT)

Project Title:

Research Leader:

To facilitate scientific and technical interaction between Center Faculty and Industrial Member Representatives, each company represented is requested to rank their company's level of interest and the research relevancy of each presentation. Please mark an X below to reflect the opinion of your company.

Level of Interest: **Relevance to Company:**

____ Very Interested |_____|_____|_____|
____ Interested   High   Moderate Some   None
____ Interested with Change
____ Not Interested
____ Abstain

Comments: (include precompetitive suggestions/ applications/Industry benefits, suggested changes, quality of research, scientific merit, innovations of research, industrial relevance, level of effort, progress since last report, offers of help, etc.)

_____

_____

_____

_____

_____

Your completed LIFE forms will be picked up immediately after each research presentation. Please keep the pink sheets for your records.

Name: _____   Company: _____
    (Please print)   (Please print)

Date: _____

APPENDIX 2-5

Guide for Research Discussion Sessions

Instructions to Discussion Leader:

These questions may help stimulate and structure the discussion in your workshop. Please add or subtract to this list as you see fit. Someone in your area should be responsible for taking notes.

SUGGESTED QUESTIONS:

1. Are there any general observations about the nature and direction of the research proposed in presentations in this area?

2. Does anyone have any suggestions for ways in which the projects might be improved, accelerated or made more relevant to industrial needs?

3. Does anyone see any major obstacles or barriers to conducting these studies that we may not have anticipated?

4. Are there information, people or new technology relevant to these projects that you think we should tap?

5. Are there important problems, questions, or issues for your firm or for the industry in this area that we should be tackling but aren't? What are they? How many other participants are interested in these issues?

APPENDIX 2-6

I/UCRC Organization Feedback Form

NAME: _____

COMPANY_____

In order to finalize the structure, policies and scientific program for X university's I/UCRC, we need your input. In the space provided below, please indicate any questions or concerns you have about the following issues.

A. The organizational structure, general policies and bylaws, patent policies, publication policies, membership fee and scientific program.

B. Any other information that will be needed by your firm before it can arrive at a decision on membership.

C. It would be helpful to know your personal evaluation of the proposed center. What recommendation will you make to your firm about joining center? (Please check one.)

_____ JOIN CENTER

_____ MEMBERSHIP DECISION NEEDS FURTHER INVESTIGATION

_____ DON'T JOIN CENTER

APPENDIX 2-7

Debriefing an I/UCRC Research Planning Meeting for a New Center

1. Are all of the projects presented consistent with the center's stated technical mission and boundaries?
2. *If not,* which ones are not consistent?
   a. Can the mission statement be broadened to accommodate these projects?
   b. *If yes,* is the mission statement still coherent?
   c. What are the pros and cons of making this change? (e.g., what industries/ firms would be interested in this broadened mission?)
3. Are there any obvious holes or redundancies in the technical "menu" reflected by the proposed projects when compared to the center's mission?
   a. *If yes,* what are they?
   b. Can investigators and projects be found to fill these holes?
   c. Can and should some projects be merged to avoid redundancies?
   d. Where and how? (both b and c.)
4. Can the center's research menu be logically grouped into major research areas or thrusts?
   a. *If yes,* what are they? (name and provide statements of goals and objectives.)
   b. Are all of the areas well represented?
   c. Do these areas/thrusts seem for form a coherent whole and are they complementary (show how areas might provide synergy or intersect)?
   d. *If not,* what areas should or could be dropped?
5. Is the center's mission and research program too broad given the available resources?
   a. *If yes,* can it be narrowed to provide a tighter and more focused program?
   b. *If no,* can resources (people) be added to provide better coverage?
6. Were project presentations (and hard copy) consistent with the format and detail needed for a formal presentation to industry representatives?
   a. *If not,* how and when will this be accomplished?
7. Can presentations and mission statements be translated into statements of industrially-relevant needs, problems and concerns?

APPENDIX 2-8

List of I/UCRCs 1996-1997

Status	Year Funded	Center	Academic Affiliation
6 Years or Older	1981	Center for Applied Polymer Research	Case Western Reserve University
	1982	Center for Advanced Computing and Communication	North Carolina State Univ./Duke Univ.
		Center for Ceramic Research	Rutgers University
		Center for Materials Handling/Logistics	Georgia Institute of Technology/ Univ. of Arkansas
		Center for Dielectric Studies	The Pennsylvania State University
		Center for Advanced Steel Processing and Products Research	Colorado School of Mines
	1984	Center for Process Analytical Chemistry	University of Washington
		Hazardous Substance Management Research Center	NJ Inst. of Technology/Princeton U./ Rutgers U./Stevens Inst. Of Tech./ Tufts U./ Univ. Of Medicine and Dentistry of NJ
		Center for Optoelectronic Devices, Interconnects, and Packaging	University of Arizona/University of Maryland
		Surface Engineering and Tribology	Northwestern Univ./Georgia Inst. of Technology
		Center for Microcontamination Control	University of Arizona
		Center for Electromagnetics Research	Northeastern University
		Center for Chemical Process Modeling and Control	Lehigh University
	1985	Center for Iron and Steelmaking Research	Carnegie Mellon University
		Center for Innovation Management Studies	Lehigh University
		Center for Advanced Electronic Materials, Devices and Systems	University of Texas at Arlington/ Texas A&M
		Center for Measurement and Control Engineering	University of Tennessee
		Center for Nondestructive Evaluation	Iowa State University
	1986	Center for Web Handling	Oklahoma State University
		Center for Glass Research	Alfred University/University of Missouri Rolla
		Center for Energetic Materials	New Mexico Institute of Mining and Technology
		Center for Software Engineering	Univ. of Florida/Purdue Univ./Univ. of Oregon
		Center for Sensors and Actuators	University of California, Berkeley

Status	Year Funded	Center	Academic Affiliation
6 Years or Older (cont.)	1987	Center for Virtual Simulation Proving Ground: Mechanical and Electromechanical Systems	University of Iowa/Univ. of Texas at Austin
		Center for Aseptic Processing and Packing Studies	North Carolina State U./Univ. of California at Davis
	1988	Center for Biological Surface Science	SUNY at Buffalo/Univ. of Memphis/NY State College of Ceramics
	1989	Center for Micro-Engineered Materials	University of New Mexico
		Center for Ultra-High Speed Integrated Circuits and Systems	Univ. of California at San Diego
		Center for Analog/Digital Integrated Circuits	Washington State U./Univ. of Washington/Oregon State Univ./SUNY at Stony Brook
	1990	Center for Advanced Air Conditioning and Refrigeration	University of Illinois, Urbana
		Center for Grinding Research	University of Connecticut
		Center for Dimensional Measurement and Control in Manufacturing	University of Michigan, Ann Arbor
3 to 6 Year-Olds	1991	Center for Coatings Research	Eastern Michigan/North Dakota State Univ.
		Center for Nanostructural Materials Research	University of North Texas
	1992	Center for Separations Using Thin Films	University of Colorado at Boulder
		Center for Polymer Interfaces	Lehigh University
		Center for Integrated Pest Management	North Carolina State University
		Center for Wireless Information Networks	Rutgers University
		Center for Advanced Communications	Villanova University
		Center for Building Performance and Diagnostics	Carnegie-Mellon University
		Center for Health Management	Arizona State University
	1993	Center for Corrosion in Multiphase Systems	The Ohio State University
	1994	Center for Machine-Tool Systems	University of Illinois
		Center for Polymer Biodegradation	University of Massachusetts
		Center for Emission Reduction Research	NJ Institute of Technology/Penn State Univ./Massachusetts Inst. Of Technology/ Ohio State Univ.
		Center for Ocean Technology	University of Rhode Island
		Center for Composite Design	Stanford University
		Center for Advanced Control of Energy and Power Systems	Arizona State Univ./Colorado School of Mines/Purdue Univ.

Status	Year Funded	Center	Academic Affiliation
2 Years or Less	1995	Center for Advanced Manufacturing and Packaging of Microwave, Optical and Digital Electronics	Univ. of Colorado
		Center in Ergonomics	Texas A&M
		Center for Pharmaceutical Processing Research	Purdue University
		Center for Particulate Matters	The Pennsylvania State University
	1996	Center for Power System Engineering	Cornell University/Univ. of California at Berkeley/Univ. of Illinois/Univ. of Wisconsin at Madison
		Center for Management of Information	University of Arizona
New	1997	Center for Quality and Reliability Engineering	Rutgers University/Arizona State University
		Center for Advanced Polymer and Composite Engineering	Ohio State
		Center for the Built Environment	University of California, Berkeley
		Center for Wireless Electromagnetic Compact Compatibility	University of Oklahoma
		Center for Management of Information	University of Arizona

APPENDIX 2-9

Information Flow for New Research Missions, Themes, Projects

(Courtesy Center for Wireless Information Networks, Rutgers University)

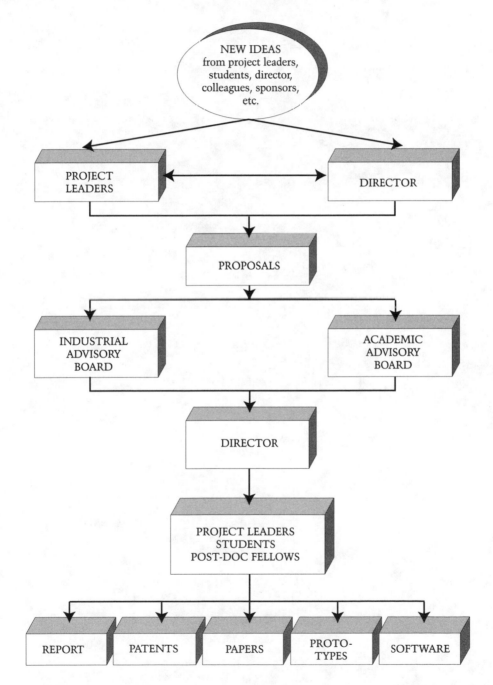

DESIGNING CENTERS:
Principles for Effective Organizational Structure

DENIS O. GRAY, *North Carolina State University, Raleigh*

S. GEORGE WALTERS, *Professor Emeritus, Rutgers University, NJ*

INTRODUCTION

"Just as a keystone supports an arch, so too some organizational mechanism is required to support long-term connections between the business and academic communities."—(Matthews and Norgaaard, 1984, p. 176)

For several decades, American research universities have been confronted with a difficult dilemma: industry has begun to demand research assistance which is long-term, mission-driven, multidisciplinary, and team-based; university values, norms and administrative practices are ill-equipped to handle and often antagonistic towards many of these needs. As we pointed out earlier, most universities have tried to resolve this incompatibility by creating and deploying boundary-spanning structures, specifically centers, which are more consistent with industry's needs and yet well integrated into the university proper. In principle, this so-called centers strategy allows the university to meet a pressing need in its environment without changing its core structure.

It is important to remember that boundary-spanning units are more than organizational bandaids. They should be conceived as an actual organization with their own structure, management, leadership, and strategy. To succeed, these center features must be tailored to meet the needs of its external stakeholders. In this chapter we focus our attention on the most visible and stable organizational feature of a center, its structure.

What Is Structure?

Hall (1977) has drawn an analogy between organizations and buildings. For instance, all buildings have relatively static and stable structural features, including beams, interior walls, passageways, roofs, that dictate the movements and activities of people within the building and within specific rooms. In similar fashion, all organizations have structural features that dictate activities and interactions of organizational participants.

In the context of a center, structure asks: Where would this unit report within the university? Who would report to whom? How would center reporting relationships affect traditional reporting relationships? How would various tasks be defined and allocated? How would priorities be set and decisions made? How would activities and interactions within this unit and between this unit and the university, industry and sponsor groups be coordinated? Structure is important because it encompasses many aspects of a center we can deliberately create; it shapes activities and processes and thereby influences the achievement of organizational goals.

While organizational theorists tend to differ somewhat on specific dimensions of structure, for our purposes, we will use Robbins (1990), who summarizes structure into complexity, centrality, and formality.

Complexity

The extent of differentiation within an organization: horizontal, or the division of labor, degree of horizontal separation between units; vertical, the depth of the organizational hierarchy; and spatial differentiation, the geographic location of offices and personnel.

Centralization

The "degree to which the formal authority to make discretionary choices is concentrated in an individual, unit, or level (usually high in the organization)." (Robbins, 1990, p. 106.) Centralization can vary within a given unit or organization based on the kind of decision involved (e.g., some decisions may be centralized, others decentralized). Decision-making is also a multi-step process. Discretion early-on in decision-making contributes to decentralization.

Formality

The degree to which an organization relies on rules and procedures to direct and standardize the behavior of its members. Formality can vary across jobs and functions and is manifested in job descriptions, rules, policies and procedures. Formalization can also be accomplished by *unwritten* and implicit norms and expectations or can be "internalized" within members by virtue of professionalization.

Design Principle for I/UCRC Structure

Designing an organization involves choices. There is no single ideal organization. Thus, most organizational theorists adopt a contingency approach to design issues, arguing that organizational features including structure, strategy, and goals depend on a number of factors.

For instance, complex organizations are better equipped to handle large, diverse and far flung tasks, but may strain a manager's span of control and require greater coordination and communication. Centralization increases control and in some instances efficiency, but usually has a negative effect on speed of decisions, collaboration, and motivation. Formal structures tend to be more predictable and easy to manage but also tend to be less flexible and innovative.

Fortunately, center designers face a relatively common context of small size, demand for innovative scientific work, a complex and fast-changing environment, and a goal of conducting and transferring high-quality industry-relevant research in a highly professional and individualistic culture. This has allowed centers to use similar structures.

Complexity

Because most centers are relatively small, the structure for an I/UCRC is simple. Figure 3-1 shows vertical differentiation is limited to an administrative function, management by the Center Director, and research.

Horizontal differentiation is also limited. Although the center's research is typically grouped by problem areas, the research function (staffed by a faculty member and graduate students) also exhibits little differentiation.[3] Most centers have faculty from a single university, so spatial differentiation has tended to be quite limited.

---

[3]Even when these factors are taken into account, most theorists argue principle of "equifinality," more than one structure achieves the same result.

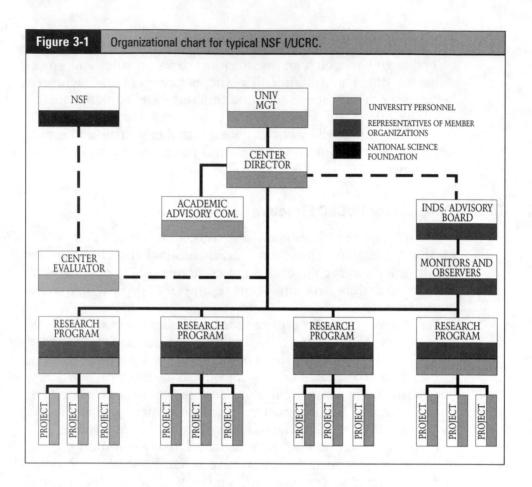

Figure 3-1 Organizational chart for typical NSF I/UCRC.

Probably the most noteworthy element of the organizational chart is the presence of a number of external linkages: an Industrial Advisory Board (IAB) comprised of one representative from each member company, an Academic Advisory Committee (AAC) which represents center academic and administration interests.

Not every center fits these recommendations. In fact, an increasing number of I/UCRCs have grown quite large or have added geographically remote research sites. Structural modifications necessitated by these situations are not great and are described in Chapter 11.

Centralization

Centralization of decision making within a center depends on the kind of decision. According to our research, I/UCRCs follow a fairly consistent and relatively effective pattern of decision making (Gray & Gidley, 1987). First, many administrative matters can and probably should be routinized and centralized with the Center Director having considerable discretion. Strategic matters including planning of the research program and project selection should be carried out in a participatory manner but with industrial sponsors making the final recommendation. This approach also helps prevent the Center Director from conflict of interest among his/her colleagues. In similar fashion, operational research decisions should involve considerable discussion and participation but ultimately should be made at the lowest level possible (e.g., project level).

Obviously, there are occasions when centers will want to deviate from some or all of these guidelines. Some Center Directors prefer to make administrative decisions with considerable colleague collaboration (see Chapter 10). Under certain circumstances such as loss of an IAB member or faculty, the Center Directors should reorder research priorities.

Formality

Formalization can make a center predictable and reliable; it can also make it rigid, inflexible, and bureaucratic. I/UCRCs have addressed this paradox by varying the amount of formalization by function and job. Formalization is high for I/UCRCs when the university center and the sponsor interact, moderate within the administrative function and low within the research and external linkage functions.

An overview of the organizational design of a typical I/UCRC shows a simple structure centralized on strategic issues but very decentralized on research operations, formal at the top and at its industrial network, but low in formalization of the research function. Most of these features can be observed in the organizational chart for a typical I/UCRC (Figure 3-1). Interestingly, the recommended structure for a center bears a strong resemblance to the organic structure observed in many innovative organizations (Tornatzky and Fleischer, 1990).

While these principles provide a rough outline for designing a center (see Figure 3-2), "the devil is in the details." In the next section we describe specific structural features that help define the I/UCRC model.

Figure 3-2	Design principles for an I/URC.

Structural Dimension/Feature	Structural Implications
Complexity	
Small Size (Employees, Sites)	Low General Complexity
Multiple Stakeholders	Higher Complexity (Linkage Function)
Centralization	
Bureaucratic Host	Centralized (Administrative)
Multiple Customers	Centralized (Strategic)
Knowledge Creation	Decentralized (Research)
Consortial Arrangement	Decentralized (Strategic)
Formality	
Research and Development	Low Formality (Research)
Competitive; Fast Changing	Low Formality (Research)
Bureaucratic Host	High Formality (Administrative)
Intellectual Property	High Formality (Sponsor Interface)
Level of Professionalism	Low Formality (Research)
Government-sponsorship	High Formality (Administrative)

CENTER FUNCTIONS, ROLES AND RESPONSIBILITIES

University Administration

An I/UCRC must report somewhere within the university's hierarchy. Over 85 percent of I/UCRCs operating during 1996, reported to a dean's level or higher. And for good reason. Centers are by definition multidisciplinary, boundary-spanning units which may create turf problems among academic units or require dispensation from standard university operating procedure. As a consequence, it is important for a center to report as high within the university hierarchy as possible (dean's level when faculty come from different departments or provost when faculty span across colleges). Reporting at a high level has a number of benefits. Specifically, it increases the chances that a center and its faculty won't get caught up in parochial department turf battles; the responsible university official will have authority, and, it is hoped, the inclination to give the center a certain degree of autonomy; the center will be in line with other units when discretionary resources are being handed out.

It's worth noting that while a center may find itself above departmental politics, most researchers don't. As faculty members, most directors and center researchers are members of academic departments. They report to department heads, are reviewed by senior faculty for promotion and tenure and must publish in journals recognized by their discipline. While serious problems appear to be rare, directors who control more resources than their department head, and young untenured faculty who are expected to publish in disciplinary journals, are well advised to be sensitive to conflicts.

Responsible University Official

The center reports to an official within the university hierarchy who has authority over policies and procedures, decisions about the research programs, and allocation of resources. While the role played by this administrator varies from university to university, few become involved in the direct management of the center or second-guess the research priorities of the IAB. In fact, most limit themselves to monitoring, oversight, including ensuring that the center maintains high standards with respect to education and research, ensuring that the center follows established university procedures, and coordinates with departments and other centers. These responsibilities usually are accomplished by reviewing center reports and planning documents, reviewing and responding to the feedback and recommendations from the IAB, and conducting periodic reviews.

Some administrators go beyond this relatively benign role and become strong advocates for centers and see them as *opportunities* for significantly increasing extramural research and enhancing the university's reputation. Such individuals may dispense with various rules by waiving or reducing overhead rates or using non-traditional criteria such as intellectual property to evaluate center faculty. They assist in recruiting industry members, and try to enhance a center's capabilities when they allocate faculty positions to departments. Research indicates that the presence of such an individual contributes to a center's success (Gray, Stewart, et al., 1991).

Academic Advisory Committee (AAC)

If it ain't broke, don't fix it. If you don't have a problem, don't convene your AAC. — Anonymous Center Director

The Academic Advisory Committee serves as a linkage mechanism for advice and feedback about operations, policy, and research issues between the university's academic core and the Center Director and the responsible university official. It typically includes academic department heads or deans involved in the center and relevant university administrators. AACs are essential when formulating center policies and procedures, when major policy changes occur and when a major problem occurs. As a center matures and policies and procedures become routinized, the AAC's role diminishes. Many successful I/UCRCs have never convened the AAC once they were established.

Center Administration

Depending upon their size, centers can function successfully with only a Center Director and an administrative assistant. However, the scope and complexity of their required tasks are enormous.

Center Director

The key role to center success. S/he is responsible for the management and administration of internal operations, the research program and recruitment of industrial sponsors. A sample job description is provided in Figure 3-3. We recommend that the directorship be a full-time position. Unfortunately, because of budgetary constraints, this has become a luxury only a few NSF funded I/UCRCs can afford. While centers have functioned with part-time directors, the center may lose its technical direction or membership base. Shouldering what is a full-time Center Director's job on a part-time basis can result in burnout and a perception among one's colleagues that you are not sharing equally in departmental duties (Gray, et al., 1991). This probably contributes to the high turnover rate among Directors within the NSF I/UCRC Program.

If budgetary restrictions rule out a full-time director, one is left with two options: either hire a professional-level administrative assistant, or share or delegate some of the responsibilities with other faculty. The latter option is discussed in Chapter 10.

Administrative Assistant

Most centers have an administrative assistant who reports to the Center Director. How this position is defined and filled has tremendous impact on the Center Director's workload and the

Figure 3-3	Sample job description—Center Director.

- Reports to the responsible university representative.
- Responds to recommendations from the Industrial Advisory Board.
- Responsible for the management and administration of internal operations of the center including:
  - Budget control,
  - Maintenance of the center databases, records, and publications,
  - Organization of the semi-annual meetings,
  - Preparation of the center annual report, completion of surveys and reports required by a NSF and university administrations.
- Responsible for the management and administration of research operations of the center including:
  - Preparation and implementation of the center's long-range plan and research plan,
  - Monitoring and oversight of research projects.
- Responsible for the management and administration of external operations of the center including:
  - Coordination of industry recruiting efforts,
  - Facilitation of technology transfer to member firms,
  - Preparation of public relations materials.
- Responsible for communication and coordination among all center operations.

center's success. Administrative assistant responsibilities vary from basic secretarial and clerical duties to primary responsibility for budgets and much of the center's internal management and operations. In some centers, administrative assistants have even assumed some recruitment responsibility and become associate directors. Obviously, duties depend upon the qualifications of the incumbent, grade-level, and salary of the position. Some centers may find it necessary to "create" or improvise a brand new university job description in order to hire a professional level administrative assistant.

Evaluator

NSF I/UCRC program administration requires all centers to include an evaluator who collects information by observation and surveys of IAB members and faculty. Evaluators provide objective feedback on center processes and outcomes to assist in refining operations and to anticipate problems. Because of the experience they have acquired over the years, some evaluators are used by their directors as management and organizational development consultants. The evaluator typically is a faculty member from another department on campus and is supported by NSF. The role and responsibilities of the evaluator are described in Chapter 8.

Research

The research project is the fundamental work unit of any center. However, in order for a center to succeed, it must offer industry more than tangentially related research projects often found within academic departments or university institutes and laboratories. Centers must offer sponsors a coherent collection of industry-relevant, multidisciplinary research projects which exhibit cross-fertilization and demonstrate synergy. In order to accomplish this goal, I/UCRC's core research (which is selected by a consensus of all members and supported by membership fees) is typically organized within program areas and by research project. When properly managed, a center research project should operate like a virtual-team, comprised of university and industrial contributors.

Program Areas

Program areas are research projects which have been grouped around a coherent theme, led by an area coordinator. As Figure 3-4 shows, a program area may be organized around either purely scientific or industrial themes. It is critical that program areas reflect the interests and capabilities of available faculty and have relevance to the center's industrial members. Further, since most centers do not have the resources to cover all of the topics which might interest their sponsors, it is important that its research areas be complementary and provide an opportunity for synergy. Program areas usually emerge over time.

Center program area teams are *ad hoc* and loose rather than the highly structured teams observed in industrial research organizations. This flexible approach produces cross-fertilization across related projects and seems better suited to a university-based consortia for a number of reasons: it allows greater flexibility in addressing emerging needs or opportunities, it allows greater flexibility in capitalizing on the interests and talents of current and new faculty, and is consistent with an organizational culture where faculty can be encouraged but not ordered to work on a given project or topic.

Figure 3-4	Typical I/UCRC research areas.

Center for Non-destructive Evaluation

- Ultrasonics
- Electromagnetic measurement
- Image enhancement techniques
- Microfocus radiography

Center for Grinding Research and Development

- Grinding machine and grinding process dynamics
- Truing and dressing of grinding wheels
- Thermal aspects of the grinding process
- Grinding fluid studies

Berkeley Sensor and Actuator Center

- Scientific fundamentals
- Fabrications techniques
- Microdevices for sensing and actuation
- Integrated microsystems

Center for Advanced Computing and Communications

- High speed networking
- Reliable fault-tolerant systems
- Digital communications
- Distributed systems
- Image analysis

Area Coordinators

Typically, one faculty member is designated coordinator for a center program area. While responsibilities vary, the role of a coordinator is that of a facilitator. The responsibilities of the area coordinator might include fostering communication and collaboration among projects, stimulating and facilitating development of new projects within the area, representing the area's research (current and proposed) to outside groups including the IAB and prospective industrial members. In some larger centers, an area coordinator might be responsible for some duties typically assumed by the director including monitoring project progress.

Research Projects and Virtual Teams

A typical project is carried out by a small team of researchers including one or several principal investigators (PIs) and researchers. Most PIs are tenure-track faculty or post-doctoral research associates. Most of the research is carried out by talented graduate students and frequently constitutes the student's thesis or dissertation.

Although center projects tend to be staffed like university research-as-usual, the highly interactive process used to develop, refine, and manage projects is designed to lead to a very different product. First, project ideas are developed based on intensive interactions between investigators and industry and other university researchers, not by an isolated faculty member. These virtual teams are invariably multidisciplinary in composition. Further, funded projects have all passed the scrutiny and addressed the concerns of a team of industrial sponsors. In addition, projects are subject to at least semi-annual, if not ongoing, review by the same group of individuals, with refinements made as necessary. (See Chapter 5 for a more detailed description of the steps and transactions involved in project planning and management.)

Center projects sometimes involve actual bench-level collaboration with industrial colleagues. Such arrangements can work well and can be very profitable for both sides. Unfortunately, bench-level collaboration is rare because of a reluctance by industry to encourage their researchers to take visiting scientists positions, lack of resources at centers to subsidize these arrangements, day-to-day pressures within industry which undermine part-time collaborations, and concerns about how to handle proprietary interests in shared projects. In spite of this, the rewards of such arrangements are great.

Principal Investigators and Researchers

Most university PIs make technical decisions consistent with the research plan, supervise or carry out the research, operate within an established budget, and prepare reports. Centers ask more of their PIs. The PI is also the key member of the virtual research team, which includes industrial partners. As a consequence, center PIs communicate and cooperate with industrial sponsor representatives during every stage, from proposal development to post project completion to feasibility testing. As members of the center's research team, PIs also have responsibility for communicating and coordinating with other investigators within their program area and within the center. Finally, because most centers operate with a very lean administrative function, PIs also become actively involved in administrative duties like retention and recruitment efforts.

EXTERNAL LINKAGE FUNCTIONS

Centers exist in order to conduct industry-relevant research within the university and to facilitate transfer of the fruits of this work to industry. However, accomplishing both these objectives within the context of a center is complicated by the fact centers involve a relationship with a consortium of firms rather than a single firm and often involve sponsorship by one or several government agencies. Not surprisingly, balancing the needs and interests of individual stakeholders can be a challenging task. As a consequence, the external linkage function of a center is probably the most critical and challenging element of its organizational structure. Within I/UCRCs, these challenges are met through the Industrial Advisory Board and through the roles of industrial member, industrial monitor and government member.

Industrial Advisory Board

The IAB is a board of directors with one voting representative from each sponsor organization[4]. The IAB meets twice-a-year and makes recommendations on policy and research. IAB decisions are not binding on the university. However, because industry provides the vast majority of the center's financial support and because the areas in which industry can express its voice are clearly spelled out in the center's bylaws, IAB recommendations are usually upheld.

Although industry wields considerable influence over a center's research program, this has not meant applied, narrow, and short-term projects. Research on two different NSF-sponsored cooperative research models has shown that industry consortia give significantly higher priority to fundamental research and significantly lower priority to patents and product development than firms involved in one-on-one arrangements with the university (Gray, et al., 1986). Firms are reluctant to disclose specific short-term problems to their competitors. In doing so, they may divulge proprietary or embarrassing information. Even if this were not the case, industrial sponsors avoid sharing resources to solve a problem specific to one of their competitors.

Industrial Advisory Board Members

IAB members represent the interests of their organization within the center. The typical IAB member is a manager in R&D, engineering, manufacturing, or similar function. They are responsible for reviewing and evaluating proposed and ongoing research proj-

---

[4]Some centers have affiliated members at a lower membership fee. Affiliate members may or may not have voting rights.

ects, and acting as a gatekeeper for information and technology developed within the center. They are also responsible for casting the sponsor's vote on matters which affect policy or the center's research program. Since IAB members must periodically evaluate the value of center membership, it is desirable to have a board member who is an advocate for center membership.

The IAB selects a chairperson who runs the executive session of the IAB meeting and represents the IAB interests between semi-annual meetings. Chairs are elected from volunteers or are selected on some rotation scheme. Volunteers usually do the best job. Chairpersons can become very active in recruiting new members or in stimulating interest in projects.

Industrial Monitor

Even the most motivated and technically talented IAB member has difficulty keeping up with all of the research projects covered by a typical center. As a consequence, most centers allow members to designate and send as many industrial monitors (usually bench-level scientists) to meetings as they like. Some centers have found it useful to designate one or several monitors as project mentors. These individuals take a more active role in project guidance and knowledge and technology transfer. Since monitors are likely successors to your current IAB member, their interest and involvement should be a top priority.

NSF/Government

While government agencies who join a center usually have all the rights as industrial members, NSF serves as an ex-officio (non-voting) member of the IAB. Within the I/UCRC program, the NSF representative plays a much more active role. The responsibilities of the NSF representative include promotion and dissemination of the I/UCRC model, technical assistance on management and operations, and advocacy for the center to the university and industry.

FORMALIZATION: GOVERNANCE, POLICIES AND PROCEDURES

The final element of structure is formalization. As we noted, formalization can make a center predictable and reliable; it can also make it rigid, inflexible, and bureaucratic. I/UCRCs have addressed this paradox by varying the amount of formalization by function and job. Specifically, formalization for I/UCRCs typically is high at the university-center interface, high at the sponsor-center interface for some matters (e.g., intellectual property), moderate within the administrative function and low within the research and research linkage functions.

University and Center Interface

Most universities tend to be highly formal, but the degree and type of formality differs across institutions. For instance, state and land grant institutions tend to have a more formal structure than private institutions, and will have detailed rules on issues like extension activities other universities rarely address. Each center must develop an approach to formality which is consistent with that of the host institution.

Most centers have little or no discretion over university policies and procedures that cover personnel appointments, budget, ownership of equipment and facilities, intellectual property, etc. The same is true for individual scientists who participate in a center. Center scientists are also university faculty and must comply with applicable rules governing their appointments.

This does not mean that center researchers inevitably must comply with every university rule and procedure. In order to serve as true boundary-spanning units, faculty and students working in centers must be unfettered by some of the more onerous constraints imposed by the university. In some instances, centers have actually been a vehicle for changing university rules or policies. For instance, many universities have changed or clarified their rules on publication delays in order to accommodate the needs of centers and their sponsors. In other instances, most I/UCRCs have been given significant cost sharing.

Centers can improve their bargaining position in two ways. Centers are more likely to negotiate change in university rules when they report high within the university hierarchy. Since departments and colleges impose their own formalities, the higher a center reports within the university, the more discretion it has. Second, use NSF or other government agency guidelines as a lever within the university. A variety of institutional changes have occurred because NSF required or expects certain policies to be in place.

"Don't ask for permission, if the person you're asking only has the power to say 'no'."

IAB and Center Interface

As boundary-spanning organizations, centers require commitments from outside stakeholder groups. Since these commitments involve legally binding transactions such as exchange of money, completion of research projects, hiring of personnel and commitment of resources to projects and the creation and protection of intellectual property, many of these issues must be covered in a very formal, legally binding manner. Government-University-Industry Roundtable (1993) has published guidelines for developing such agreements. Reams (1986) has examined a number of university and industry contractual agreements and has identified 65 issues which can be covered in such a contract (see Appendix 3-1 for a complete list). Fortunately, most I/UCRCs and their sponsors have found it necessary to address only a subset of all of these issues. They get at the heart of center governance and are usually addressed in the Membership Agreement and the Bylaws.

Membership Agreement

The membership agreement is a formal legal contract between the university and industrial sponsor and is signed by officers representing each. Developing this document can be time-consuming because a center must develop a single agreement upon which all parties can agree. While a membership agreement can and should be tailored to the needs of the industrial member involved in a particular center, most membership agreements are similar. Elements covered in a standard I/UCRC Membership Agreement are shown in Figure 3-5; Appendix 3-2 contains a sample membership agreement and Appendix 3-3 shows how one center has used the reverse side of the agreement to re-state benefits of membership. Additional aspects of these agreements are discussed below.

Membership Requirements

Although antitrust concerns related to center membership have all but disappeared since the passage of the National Cooperative Research Act in 1985, centers must avoid limiting or restricting membership arbitrarily. Centers can, however, limit membership to firms incorporated in the U.S. which have significant R&D or manufacturing operations located within the U.S. Centers may want to register as a Cooperative Research Venture with the Department of Commerce. This will provide members additional protection from antitrust concerns.

Figure 3-5   Elements of typical center membership agreement.

Parties: Specifies legal entities signing the agreement.

Purpose: Simple statement of the purpose of constituting the center.

Participants: Identification of other parties, like the National Science Foundation, involved in the center.

Membership Requirements: Criteria organizations must meet to be considered for membership.

Membership Fees: Description of the cost of membership, manner of payment and schedule of payment (full or associate membership).

Length and Terms of Commitment: Number of years agreement will be in force and conditions for terminating agreement.

Organization and Operation: Usually references bylaws for these details.

IAB Role. General statement of the role, responsibilities and rights of IAB members (with additional details covered in bylaws).

Publication Policy: Description of the procedures for reviewing publications and the circumstances and length of permissible publication delays.

Intellectual Property Policy: Description of the ownership and rights to all intellectual property discovered through center research.

Indemnification: Each party holds the other harmless.

Official Signature: Signatures of designated representatives.

Membership fees. Membership in an I/UCRC involves paying a fixed annual membership fee. The average membership fee within the NSF I/UCRC Program is currently $35,000 per year. Approximately 25 percent of I/UCRCs encourage membership by smaller firms by offering an associate membership at an average $18,000 per year. Associate members have limited rights (e.g., voting privileges; access to research areas or reports and intellectual property).

New centers should set their fees carefully. In spite of inflation, it's difficult to raise membership fees once a contract has been signed. At least one center has overcome this problem by having periodic fee increases reflected in the membership agreement. (See Chapter 11.)

Length and term of commitment. The typical I/UCRC agreement is for three years with a cancellation provision of 90-day notice. This arrangement appears to work. It allows firms which are operating under budgetary uncertainty to make a moral commitment to a center for several years but allows termination of membership if circumstances change. Requiring notice of termination of the agreement warns the center that its budget will change for the next fiscal year and gives an opportunity to reverse the decision.

Publication policy. Research which results in intellectual property is a relatively small part of a center's total output, yet a great deal of time and effort go into negotiations over publication delays and patents. Although variations exist, all NSF I/UCRCs provide some mechanism for delay of center publications. A typical arrangement allows members to request a 3- to 12-month publication delay in order to permit filing of patent applications (see Figure 3-6). Many centers routinely follow this procedure. If the delayed publication involves a student's thesis or dissertation, the student can complete his or her degree but the thesis is withheld from the library for a limited period. According to our research, few faculty have experienced significant publication delays under this system (Gray and Meyer, 1994).

Intellectual property issues. In virtually all I/UCRCs, patents and copyrights belong to the university. NSF waives all patent rights but retains "march in rights[5]" in PL98-620, and industry sponsors

Figure 3-6	Typical publication procedure in center bylaws.

1. Submits copy of center-funded manuscript for review by the IAB prior to publication with an approval form.

2. IAB member must request publication delay within 30 days or the manuscript is approved.

3. To delay publication, the IAB member must ask that a patent disclosure be pursued.

4. University must file a patent disclosure and pursue patent or license.

5. All industry members will be asked to support patent filing cost.

6. Only IAB members who agree to support filing cost will retain non-exclusive royalty-free license.

---

[5]If a patent is granted and is not utilized for a number of years, the government may go to court to determine if it is in the public interest to utilize it. No such action has been initiated in the 24-year history of NSF I/UCRCs.

receive royalty free non-exclusive license to practice and use the invention. Policies vary on who pays for the patenting costs, whether rights are retained if a firm chooses not to share filing costs, and the ability of a sponsor to transfer patents to subsidiaries and non-subsidiaries. Since some IAB members have argued that requiring non-exclusivity of all intellectual property undermines technology transfer (see discussion in Chapter 9) some centers have negotiated mechanisms which allow exclusive but royalty-bearing licensing arrangements under certain circumstances.

Bylaws

Bylaws relieve the membership agreement of important but overly complex procedural details. Bylaws also describe structural or procedural issues which require a fairly high level of formality. The level of detail in the bylaws depends upon the needs and comfort level of the various stakeholders. Some centers and their IAB members prefer to have all major organization and operational issues detailed in the bylaws, others prefer no bylaws, and some want bylaws that address only a few issues and provide much less detail.

As Figure 3-7 illustrates, most I/UCRCs take an intermediate approach by describing all organizational chart functions, mentioning significant operational issues, and providing details only where needed. Significant operational issues include membership rights and privileges, different types of center research and the mechanisms for supporting single or multiple-firm enhancement projects or proprietary contracts, a schedule for required reports and regularly scheduled meetings, and other procedures. The by-

---

Figure 3-7 Elements of typical center bylaws.

Organization: Where center reports within the university, authority for decisions, descriptions of functions, committees, roles, and research areas projects.

Categories of Membership: Rights and privileges of different membership levels.

Operating procedures: Schedule, expected reports, meetings (semi-annual, strategic planning), types of research projects, technology transfer mechanisms, center sabbaticals, financial and budgetary guidelines, fees, and rights related to use of equipment and testbeds.

Appendices: An organizational chart, a description of the research areas, and calendar of regular events.

laws or membership agreement should specify a procedure for amending them.

Internal Center Operations

Centers may be able to take a minimalist approach to explicit formalization of internal operations for at least two reasons: centers tend to be small organizations and have personnel with a high level of professionalism. Nonetheless, all centers must be consistent and predictable with a myriad of complex commitments and transactions. Since functions and activities vary considerably, the challenge is which functions and activities can benefit (and which will not) from formalization and by which mechanisms.

Role Descriptions

Active participation in center tasks by departmental faculty members and managers in industry are critical to the center's success. Unfortunately, it's easy for busy faculty or industry representatives to forget or neglect these responsibilities. Faculty should contribute to recruiting efforts and industrial monitors should transfer technology. When they don't, written role descriptions can be a very effective vehicle for reinforcing specific responsibilities. Descriptions of responsibilities provided in this Chapter may be the starting point for developing these descriptions.

Policies and Procedures

Policies (general guidelines) and procedures (sequential steps for accomplishing work) standardize organizational behavior. They are appropriate for use with at least two kinds of activities: activities which can and should be routinized and made as predictable as possible; activities where there is a proven and effective way—a best practice. They can be informal or understood and still be best practices. Unfortunately, a significant number of centers and staff either never hear or misunderstand when policies and procedures are left undocumented. This is part of the motivation behind this volume. We recommend committing instrumental policies and procedures to writing and publishing them in a center policy and procedures manual. This manual should be widely circulated in an easily accessed notebook. Care should be taken to ensure that the contents be critical to center efficiency and effectiveness, and that they avoid needless bureaucracy. (See Figure 3-8.)

| Figure 3-8 | Suggestions for center policies and procedure manual. |

Routine University Procedures

- Travel Approval
- Changes in Budgets
- Equipment Acquisition
- Release Time Approval

Routine Center Procedures

- Development of Enhancements and Contracts
- Publication Approval
- Patent Disclosure
- Succession and Appointment of Directors

- Record keeping for Research Projects, Research Notebook
- Programming Language and Documentation Levels
- Proposal Submission (format, deadlines, etc.)
- Reports Preparation (format, deadline, etc.)

I/UCRC Best Practices

- Meeting Agenda
- Soliciting Feedback on Proposals
- Proposal Screening and Selection
- Recruitment Protocol
- Technology Transfer

SUMMARY

For a variety of reasons industry and universities find it difficult to engage in intense and ongoing research cooperation. Fortunately, I/UCRCs can serve as a bridge between actors in these two sectors, opening the doors to meaningful interaction. However, designing organizational bridges between industry and universities, two very different and often conflicting organizations, is a challenging assignment for I/UCRCs. Like their physical counterpart, organizational bridges depend upon their structural integrity. In this chapter we've tried to provide the reader with a blueprint and some contingency for developing and implementing a sound infrastructure for cooperative research.

The I/UCRC prototype is a relatively simple yet organic structure. Its success depends upon responsive and appropriately coordinated administrative, research, and external linkage functions, fulfilling many roles and decision-making systems tailored to local circumstances.

In spite of the fact that we've presented a prototype structure, it's worth reminding our readers that the most important rule of organizational design is structure and must be tailored to local circumstances. Clearly, the reader is encouraged to take our recommendations and "reinvent" our prototype. If this is the case, why even offer a prototype? There are several reasons. First, and

most importantly, most universities will confront similar circumstances and the I/UCRC model has been successfully replicated
over and over. Over 75 universities, at last count. Clearly, the core
features of the model are both robust and effective. In addition,
this model provides a good foundation for creating more complex
and sophisticated structures. We discuss structural variations on
the basic I/UCRC model in Chapter 11.

REFERENCES

Government-University-Industry Research Roundtable. *Intellectual Property Rights in Industry- Sponsored University Research*, Washington, D.C.: National Academy of Sciences, 1993.

Gray, D. O., and Gidley, T. *Evaluation of the NSF University-Industry Cooperative Research Centers: Descriptive and Correlative Findings* (No. P.T. 34,04 K.W. 1000000 0600000). Washington, DC: National Science Foundation, 1987.

Gray, D. O., Johnson, E. C., and Gidley, T. R. Industry-University Projects and Centers: An Empirical Comparison of Two Federally-Funded Models of Cooperative Science. *Evaluation Review, 10,* 776-793, 1986.

Gray, D. O., and Meyer, D. C. *National Science Foundation Industry-University Cooperative Research Centers: 1993-94 Process Outcome Survey Results,* Raleigh, NC: Department of Psychology, North Carolina State University, 1994.

Gray, D. O., Stewart, M., Gidley, T. R., and Blakley, C. *Self-Sustaining Industry-University Centers: Is There Life After NSF Funding.* Washington, D.C., National Science Foundation, 1991.

Hall, R. H. *Organizations: Structure and process.* Englewood Cliffs, NJ: Prentice-Hall, 1997.

Matthews, J. and Norgaard, R. *"Managing the Partnerships Between Higher Education and Industry."* Boulder, CO: National Center for Higher Education Management Systems, 1984.

Reams, B. S. *University-Industry Research Partnerships: The Major Legal Issues in Research and Development Agreements.* Westport, CT: Quorum Books, 1986.

Robbins, S. P. *Organization Theory: Structure, Design, and Applications* (3rd. ed.). Englewood Cliffs: Prentice Hall, 1990.

Tornatzky, L. G., and Fleischer, M. F. *The Processes of Technological Innovation.* Lexington, MA: D.C. Heath, 1990.

Walters, S.G. *Special Briefing, the Interfunctional Management Program,* 1971-1987, Graduate School of Management, Rutgers University, Newark, NJ, 1987.

APPENDIX 3-1

Issues Addressed in Typical Industry-University Legal Agreements[6]

1. Number of projects.
2. Administrative structure of projects.
3. Time period of agreement.
4. Provision for continuation of agreement.
5. Extension of projects if contracts are not continued.
6. Method of selection and approval of projects.
7. Ratio of basic research to applied research.
8. Provisions for interaction between scientists.
9. Independent review of research projects.
10. Formula for adjustment of corporate funding for inflation or deflation.
11. Title to equipment purchased with sponsor's funds.
12. Publication restrictions on university researcher.
13. Ownership of patents and technical developments.
14. Protection provided for university proprietary information.
15. Protection provided for sponsors proprietary information.
16. Obligation of sponsor to commercialize research results.
17. Sponsor to monitor research for patentable and novel inventions.
18. Prompt reporting and filing for patentability by sponsor.
19. Prompt reporting of possible results by university sponsor.
20. Who files for patent.
21. Who files for foreign patents.
22. Who pays cost of patent filings and prosecution.
23. Is prosecution beyond patent office rejection required.
24. May university use independent patent counsel.
25. Royalty to university adjusted, based on contribution of sponsor.
26. University to provide records for patent application.
27. University to assure title to all technical developments.
28. University waiver of patent claim against sponsor.
29. Individual inventor waiver of patent claim against sponsor.
30. Indemnification clause for claims arising from patent claims.
31. University agrees to grant licenses to sponsor.
32. Exclusive license on patentable inventions to sponsor.
33. Licenses on non-patentable technical developments to sponsor.

[6]Adapted from Reams, 1986.

34. Licensing of non-program patents by university to sponsor.
35. Licensing requirements specified in agreement.
36. Reasonable attempt to be made by sponsor to market research results.
37. If reasonable attempt not made by sponsor to market results, the non-exclusive sublicense results.
38. Industry sponsor required to submit marketability schedule during period of exclusive license.
39. Sponsor permitted to sublicense.
40. Royalty payments by sponsor to university.
41. If no royalty rate agreement, arbitration is provided.
42. Law to be applied to agreement.
43. Action to be taken in event of infringement.
44. Who may sue infringer?
45. Infringement suit cost recovery.
46. Has university right of approval prior to sponsor bringing suit?
47. University may assign title to sponsor bringing suit.
48. Right of university to license elsewhere if sponsor does not elect to license.
49. Termination of agreement for breach or default.
50. Termination for insolvency of a party.
51. Patent and license rights survive termination of agreement.
52. Indemnification of university by sponsor for liability arising from use of products.
53. University warrants sufficient insurance and workers' compensation for its employees.
54. Sponsor to hold university harmless for sponsor's employees injured at university.
55. Assignment of rights and obligations by either party.
56. May university subcontract.
57. Use of university or sponsor's name with publicity.
58. Research participant non-disclosure agreement.
59. Distribution of product by university for research only.
60. Third-party competitor distributes similar product, significantly affecting sponsor's business, then royalty payment to university may cease.
61. Repayment of sponsor's costs required at termination of agreement.
62. Provision for alternative funding to university.
63. Contract funding stated.
64. Designated director of research or principal investigator.
65. Provision for resolution of disputes.

APPENDIX 3-2

Sample I/UCRC Membership Agreement.

Industry/University Cooperative Research Center for _____

This agreement is made this _____ day of _____, 19__ by and between The University of _____ (hereinafter called "UNIVERSITY") and _____ (hereinafter called "COMPANY").

WHEREAS, the parties to this Agreement intend to join together in a cooperative effort to support a Industry/University Cooperative Research Center for _____ (hereinafter called "CENTER") at the UNIVERSITY to maintain a mechanism whereby the UNIVERSITY environment can be used to perform research to _____ _____.

The parties hereby agree to the following terms and conditions:

A. CENTER will be operated by certain faculty, staff and students at the UNIVERSITY. For the first four years the CENTER will be supported jointly by industrial firms, federal laboratories, the National Science Foundation (NSF), the state and the UNIVERSITY.

B. Any COMPANY, Federal Research and Development organization, or any Government-owned Contractor Operated laboratory may become a sponsor of the CENTER, consistent with applicable state and federal laws and statutes. Federal Research and Development organizations and Government-owned Contractor Operated laboratories may become sponsors of the CENTER on terms and conditions other than those in this agreement upon approval by UNIVERSITY and two-thirds of the Industrial Advisory Board.

C. COMPANY agrees to contribute $_____ annually in support of the CENTER and thereby becomes a sponsor. Payment of these membership fees shall be made to the University of _____ as a lump sum effective _____, or in four equal quarterly installments on _____, _____, _____, and _____ of each year of sponsorship. Checks from COMPANY should be mailed to _____ and made payable to _____.
Because research of the type to be done by CENTER takes time and research results may not be obvious immediately, COMPANY

should join CENTER with the intention of remaining a fee paying member for at least two years. However, COMPANY may terminate this Agreement by giving UNIVERSITY 90 days written notice prior to the termination date.

UNIVERSITY agrees to contribute indirect charges related to the membership of industrial and federal members of the CENTER. The results of CENTER research will be made equally available to all sponsoring companies. Ownership of patents and copyrights that result from CENTER research will remain with UNIVERSITY, as per the terms of this Agreement.

D. The organization and operation of CENTER will be specified by CENTER bylaws that will be adopted at the first Industrial Advisory Board meeting. The bylaws, when adopted, will become part of the Agreement.

E. There will be an Industrial Advisory Board composed of one representative from each member. This board makes recommendations on (a) the research projects to be carried out by CENTER, (b) the apportionment of resources to these research projects, and (c) changes in the bylaws. The operation of this board is specified in the bylaws.

F. UNIVERSITY reserves the right to publish in scientific or engineering journals the results of any research performed by CENTER. COMPANY, however, shall have the opportunity to review any paper or presentation containing results of the research program of CENTER prior to publication of the paper, and shall have the right to request a delay in publication for a period not to exceed one (1) year from the date of submission to COMPANY, for proprietary reasons, provided that COMPANY makes a written request and justification for such delay within sixty (60) days from the date the proposed publication is submitted by certified mail to COMPANY.

G. All patents derived from inventions conceived or first actually reduced to practice in the course of research conducted by the CENTER shall belong to UNIVERSITY. UNIVERSITY, pursuant to chapter 18 of title 35 of the United States Code, commonly called the Bayh-Dole Act, will have ownership of all patents developed from this work, subject to "march-in" rights as set forth in this Act. COMPANIES that were sponsors at the time of disclosure and wish to exercise rights to a royalty-free license agree to pay for the costs of patent application. UNIVERSITY agrees that all such CENTER sponsors are entitled to a nonexclusive royalty-free license. COMPANY will have the right to sublicense its subsidiaries and affiliates. If only one COMPANY seeks a license, that COMPANY may obtain an exclusive fee-bearing license through one of its agents. COMPANY has the right to sublicense its subsidiaries and affiliates.

H. Copyright registration shall be obtained for software developed by CENTER. COMPANY shall be entitled to a nonexclusive, royalty-free license to all software developed by CENTER. COMPANY will have the right to enhance and to re-market enhanced or unenhanced software with royalties due to CENTER to be negotiated, based on the worth of the initial software, but not to exceed _____% of a fair sale price of the enhanced software product sold or licensed by COMPANY.

I. Any royalties and fees received by UNIVERSITY under this Agreement, over and above expenses incurred, will be distributed as follows:

(1) _____% to inventor, or in accordance with UNIVERSITY royalty-sharing schedule,

(2) _____% to the University of _____, and

(3) _____% to CENTER operating account, or to the College of _____ in the event that CENTER is no longer in operation.

J. Neither party is assuming any liability for the actions or omissions of the other party. Each party will indemnify and hold the other party harmless against all claims, liability, injury, damage or cost based upon injury or death to persons, or loss of, damage to, or loss of use of property that arises out of the performance of this agreement to the extent that such claims, liability, damage, cost or expense results from the negligence of a party's agents or employees.

	UNIVERSITY	COMPANY
Name	_____	_____
Title	_____	_____
Signature	_____	_____
Date	_____	_____
For	_____	_____

MEMBERSHIP

HOWARD LEVINE, *California College of Arts and Crafts, San Francisco*

S. GEORGE WALTERS, *Professor Emeritus, Rutgers University, NJ*

DENIS O. GRAY, *North Carolina State University, Raleigh*

RECRUITING, SUSTAINING AND RETAINING IAB MEMBERS

Like the proverbial elephant and a group of blind men, I/UCRCs can be described differently. They can be research and development centers, subunits within a university, graduate training facilities, bridges between theory and practice, or nodes in a government program. Each requires the successful Center Director to demonstrate a different management skill including conducting a research program, coexisting and flourishing within a large university bureaucracy, cooperating with existing graduate programs, disseminating and diffusing research results, and meeting federal program requirements.

However, a different part of the I/UCRC "elephant" is yet to be described in detail: I/UCRCs are organizations that span the boundary between research and commercialization, between education and industry, and between non-profit and profit-making institutions. Many of the challenges posed by this dual identity have been addressed in other chapters (e.g., the research program, communications), and they are, at the least, consistent with academic management skills. But this cannot be said of the indispensable need to recruit new members. This marketing and salesmanship function is necessary for a successful center; yet it is not the type of competence that is synonymous with academic skills and training. In fact, the recruiting of new members (either at the center's inception or as part of the ongoing process of center growth and renewal) is often described as the most time-consuming and frustrating of a Center Director's tasks. While there is no magic recruiting formula, we believe the material in this chapter will help the Center Director make the best use of his or her time and deflect frustration by giving an understanding of the process, ultimately leading to more recruiting successes.

No Members Means No Center

Most partnership-based government programs require a minimum level of industry support. National Science Foundation policy requires industry membership in I/UCRCs: "The NSF will not endorse a proposal to establish an NSF I/UCRC, or continue to fund it, unless a 'critical mass' of companies are committed to a center." This is defined as at least six members, or a combined total of company membership fees equaling at least $300,000 yearly. A strong membership base is critical for other reasons.

I/UCRCs are designed to be true partnerships between universities and industry. Corporate membership involves much more than paying a fee. The philosophy of the I/UCRC concept includes a role for member firms to help the Center Director identify unfilled research needs and to help match those needs with the center's research strengths. The IAB is responsible for working with the Center Director to shape the center's goals and programs.

Membership fees are the largest single source of income for the average center. Membership fees, unlike direct grants and contracts, are untargeted monies; that is, membership fees provide the flexible funds that may be used to study good ideas at very early stages of development and to begin new initiatives without delay.

IAB members are important sources of other funds. They may provide additional funding to pursue specific, targeted research. The center and IAB may submit grant proposals to any of the various governmental agencies seeking to foster university-industry cooperation. Recently, membership fees in the typical center have been dwarfed by the supplemental support provided by firms and firm-government partnerships.

There is another description of an I/UCRC that may help to put the recruitment process into focus. Centers are non-profit businesses marketing knowledge and services through memberships to their customers. The wise Center Director should keep Peter Drucker's (often quoted) words in mind while planning and executing the recruiting strategy: "There is only one valid definition of business purpose: to create a customer."

THE MARKETING MODEL

Successful recruiting occurs through the wise application of a long-term marketing model coupled to the dogged short-term employment of coherent sales procedures (Ohame, 1993). Although marketing is a rich discipline with numerous variations, every model contains:

- Development of the company's "story."
- Development of the products it wishes to market.
- Determination of the targeted customer base.
- A plan for reaching those customers with a marketing offer.
- A method for monitoring the marketing effort.

Corporate Vision

Marketing an I/UCRC should start with an organization vision. I/UCRCs are in a fierce competition for corporate research dollars. Potential recruits may choose to spend those dollars on in-house research, or on targeted, contract research, or they may join other university-based centers. While it is true that customers always purchase a specific product or service, savvy corporate heads know that vision, or image, plays a key role in that purchase decision. There are many reasons for this: consumer psychology (i.e., the desire to purchase from a recognized company), brand loyalty (i.e., the phenomenon of cognitive dissonance enforces repeat purchases), and promoting corporate image may be a cost-effective way of advertising a complete line. Center Directors need to make the case that the special structure and vision of their center allows it to best any competition. While a corporation may join a center because of a specific line of research, keeping them as a long-term member will involve selling them on the I/UCRC concept; cooperative, consultative research; and access to well trained graduate students. I/UCRCs are as much a way of doing business as they are the business they are doing, and the marketing strategy must reflect this.

Corporate Products

Very few businesses have as easy a time identifying their product as the legendary *Saturday Night Live* skit in which the store sold nothing but scotch tape. Most companies sell multiple product lines, and there is always pressure to expand the line or add new products. Firms that deal in services have a much more difficult task in specifying their products. I/UCRCs are in much the same position. However, there are many different services that a center may provide, e.g., current research, consultative assistance, access to trained personnel. The marketing plan must make potential recruits aware of these services and convince them that such services meet their needs.

Customer Base

Put somewhat crudely, who will buy what I/UCRCs are selling? Once this initial question is answered and a customer base established, growth comes in only three ways: (1) sell more to existing customers, (2) win competitors' customers, or (3) create new customers. Each of these options requires a different marketing strategy. Selling more may involve new products or services, or it may be the result of superior performance and burgeoning good will. Winning competitors' customers demands incomparable performance. Creating new customers requires convincing potential customers that your products and services meet their needs. I/UCRCs face the same marketing problems. In the formative stage, they need to focus on a core list of potential firms who clearly stand to benefit by membership, but mature centers lose an average of 10 percent of their members per year. Centers must constantly apply these three marketing strategies. Chapter 10 discusses strategies for expanding a center's customer base.

The Marketing Offer

All the strategizing must result in a marketing offer, advertising or promotion that explain the corporate vision and products and services to the potential customer. All offers, from the simplest ad for a can of peas to the most complex thousand page prospectus for a start up company have three elements: (1) the benefits to the customer, (2) the price or cost, and (3) the reason the benefits are worth the price.

While each I/UCRC will have its own unique benefits, membership in an I/UCRC does come with generic benefits: enhancement of corporate image and cost-effectiveness of leveraging the research budget. While each I/UCRC produces its own marketing materials, the I/UCRC program has a video and a center folio that explain the benefits of belonging to a center.

Monitoring

No firm that expects to stay in business can launch a marketing plan and fail to monitor it. Their marketing efforts are monitored by three measures: profit, volume, and awareness and satisfaction. Some of the steps involved in monitoring membership are discussed in Chapter 7.

MARKETING THE I/UCRC

Applying the five-step marketing model to an I/UCRC requires knowledge of a particular center's research strengths and targeted applications as well as a general knowledge of the I/UCRC concept. Of necessity, this chapter deals primarily with the marketing potential of the concept (Kotler, 1994). Suggestions concerning the best strategies for marketing individual centers are also made.

I/UCRC Vision

If one is part of the NSF program, it's important to remember that I/UCRCs do not stand alone. They are links in a web of some 55 centers supported by over 700 memberships, conducting almost $70 million dollars of research each year. A useful metaphor is to think of an I/UCRC as a franchise. As in the corporate world, the franchise concept is one important method of maintaining quality control: I/UCRCs begin with the NSF "seal of approval." No center may begin operation until it meets strict NSF standards regarding operating plan and industrial membership. Additionally, each center has an independent evaluator funded by NSF who assesses progress and helps support continuous improvement.

The I/UCRC model ensures that industrial sponsors have access to resources far beyond a single university. About one-third of all I/UCRCs are involved in some form of joint operation with other universities (e.g., consortia, satellite centers) and this trend is increasing. NSF's TIE-grant program allows several I/UCRCs to work together on different aspects of the same research problem. In other words, a single I/UCRC membership is a passport to a vast array of resources.

I/UCRCs started without NSF involvement can capitalize on much of the "halo" associated with the NSF program. The I/UCRC governance model gives industrial sponsors a distinctive and significant role. IAB members play a substantial role in planning and overseeing the research program. An IAB member advises, submits research ideas, co-designs, and develops the research activities. In short, I/UCRCs are collaborative research centers in which university and industry share the responsibility and the benefits. This industry role is unique to the I/UCRC structure, ensuring the "customers" that their needs will be met.

I/UCRC Products

According to Dorin Schumacher (1992), there are eight major reasons why companies sponsor university research:

- A window on current advances in science and technology.
- Help in solving specific problems.
- Cost-effectiveness in leveraging the research budget.
- Access to trained personnel.
- Access to specialized resources.
- Corporate responsibility.
- Community relations.
- Enhancement of corporate image.

Not surprisingly, each of these reasons corresponds to an I/UCRC product. The first five loosely are technology transfer. They may be subdivided further into transfer of ideas and transfer of people. Transfer of ideas includes: patents and licenses, early access to publications, consultative services, visits to center member firms, firm visits to the center, short courses, the center's Internet site and IAB meetings. All of these are available on a cost-effective basis. The typical membership fee buys access to a research enterprise 20 times larger than their contribution. Transfer of people includes early recruitment of the best graduate students working on center projects, having I/UCRC university researchers spend substantial time working in an industrial laboratory, and industrial researchers spending extended time periods in center laboratories.

Individual centers can improve their marketing position by offering more. For example, many centers provide their members with quarterly newsletters and provide publications and materials for no fee. Other centers maintain computer databases or programs that members may download. Still others make specialized laboratory equipment available on an as-needed basis. Others expose members to national experts outside the center community. Successful centers understand that the best way to develop new products is in consultation with existing or potential members.

The final three items on Schumacher's list are ways to enhance a corporation's image or meet non-research goals. Marketing an I/UCRC may involve more than contacting a research department. Contact should also be made with offices of community relations or development, or human resources. A firm's office of human resources may see membership as a cost-effective way to provide professional development services to their research department staff.

Other marketing strategies trade on the prestige of an I/UCRC membership. If a few firms are competing in the same technology-driven market but only one is an I/UCRC member, it may be possible to approach top management of the non-member firms with the argument that they cannot afford to be left behind. I/UCRCs have much more to market than research results and many more potential customers than industry researchers. Wise marketing plans need to cast nets as widely as possible.

I/UCRC Clients

Inspecting the list of more than 700 NSF I/UCRC members provides insight into typical I/UCRC members. They are U.S.-based corporations, multinational corporations, governmental agencies at both the federal and state level, and governmental laboratories such as the Department of Energy (DoE) national laboratories. While the majority are large corporations, a significant number are small businesses. Furthermore, some are members of as many as a dozen different I/UCRCs. This is important. It demonstrates that potential members do not have to be sold on the I/UCRC concept, but only on the merits of a specific center.

Of course, applying this information is always a local matter. Compiling lists of potential members is almost always a matter of personal contacts. While it may be useful to engage in researching corporations through their SIC [Standard Industrial Classification] codes, annual reports, and Dunn and Bradstreet credit reports, successful recruiting invariably begins with a personal contact. There are several sources of such contacts: IAB members, Center Directors, faculty, graduate students, contract lists, alumni and school contacts.

IAB Members

Many new members are suggested by firms who are already committed to a center or by existing IAB members. There are many reasons for this. To increase research funding and leverage, original equipment manufacturer (OEM) firms may look for visibility or they may simply want to hear their customers think out loud. Member firms in niche markets may seek out new colleagues. Whatever their reasons, Center Directors need to develop strategies to encourage organizations who are already sold on membership to become actively involved in recruiting.

Center Director Contacts

Center Directors generally are quite well known in their fields and usually serve on various national organizations and panels, which provides numerous contacts with potential member firms. After meeting at a conference and exchanging business cards, there should be a follow-up phone call within a week. An information package should be sent along with an invitation for a site visit or IAB meeting. This personal contact should lead to discovering who can actually make the decision to sponsor the I/UCRC. No matter how the contact is made, two factors are constant: first, a procedure for tracking all contacts, and second, follow-up communication as necessary until membership is secured.

Center Faculty

The typical center has ten faculty researchers from four different departments which should result in dozens of personal contacts during the year. At the very least, these faculty should be screening their professional and industrial contacts for interest in center membership and listing their name, firm, reason for contact, brief summary of discussion, and points to stress in pursuing membership to the Center Director. At least one I/UCRC has set up a new member incentive system. If a faculty member brings a new firm into the center, then the first year fee is targeted for research of special interest to the company and conducted by that faculty recruiter. It may not work at every center, but it shows how flexible recruiting schemes can be.

Graduate Students

Most universities have summer intern programs for graduate students and many who are affiliated with I/UCRCs spend their summers interning for IAB members. Others intern for firms that are not members, and these are potential members. Perhaps more importantly, students are eventually hired by these same firms. In order to take advantage of these personal contacts, Center Directors should enlist the help of their graduate students and graduates in identifying contacts in these firms.

Information Requests Leads to Members

Responding to requests for center products can also be a way to recruit. Centers' materials, workshops, short courses, summer courses, technical reports, published research, brochures, and newsletters advertise the I/UCRC to potential new members. They should always acknowledge center support. These contacts should also be recruited.

Each of these products may serve multiple purposes, but one purpose they all serve is to provide the center with a list of names of individuals and organizations who are interested in what the center is selling. It will probably take a substantial amount of work to secure memberships from this mailing list, but such a list must be treated as a prospect list.

Retention and Research Competitors

Centers that lose their core IAB members cannot expect to remain viable. I/UCRCs are competing with IAB member in-house research, or IAB contracts for research outside the center structure. Every Center Director needs to understand competition and develop strategies to overcome it. As centers mature and grow, their original research focus may change or expand. As part of the annual management and control review, ascertain new directions and potential new membership markets.

The Marketing Pitch

The I/UCRC's marketing pitch should sell potential members at three levels. First is the I/UCRC concept. If a center is part of the NSF I/UCRC program, this may be conveyed through a canned 20-minute video, *Catalysts For Change: NSF Industry/University Cooperative Research Centers* (available from the NSF Program Manager) that explains the I/UCRC concept, many of its benefits, and includes three case studies of successful technology transfer. A number of NSF-produced print materials, including *Industry/*

University Cooperative Research Centers Program NSF 93-97, also demonstrate the I/UCRC concept.

Second, center-specific materials introduce and explain its vision and its products. Many centers have a standard marketing packet that includes items such as a list of benefits, abstracts of projects, lists of publications, newsletters, technology transfer successes, awards and honors, lists of patents, a message from the IAB chair, and videos.

Third, the membership agreement detailing the benefits of membership, particularly intellectual property, the rights and duties of both the university and the members, and the membership fee.

Throughout the offering process, it is crucial to recognize that the hard materials (e.g., brochures, videos, membership agreement) are only one way that the offering is communicated. Equally important is the constant person-to-person contact that must be maintained. Remember, one vital aspect of the center concept is the continuing dialogue between the Center Director and the members regarding everything from center vision to individual research projects. It is imperative that potential members are not only told this, but shown as well through an offering approach that listens to their concerns and attempts to accommodate them. As explained in the next section, each membership sale is a unique transaction that must speak to the unique concerns of each potential member.

THE SALES MODEL

One of the best methods to create customers is to adopt a customer-oriented approach to selling. Such an approach is built on three assumptions:

1. customers have latent needs that constitute opportunities for the sales or recruiting representative

2. customers appreciate good suggestions that help them focus and meet their needs

3. customers will be more responsive to firms and sales representatives who are interested in long-term relationships.

Within this basic framework, selling proceeds through seven steps.

- *Step 1. Prospecting and Qualifying.* Generating leads is often easy. Screening those leads so that one doesn't waste time with unqualified customers is more difficult. The previous section stressed the need for person-to-person contact in the I/UCRC context. This generates leads and is a first screen in the qualifying process.

- *Step 2. Preapproach.* The goal is to learn as much about the prospective customer as possible and to shape the sales strategy. For example, the objective of the initial approach is either introduction, to gather information (e.g., on who the decision-maker is), or set up a visit.

- *Step 3. Approach.* As the old maxim says, you only make a first impression once. Good sales people also know that they seldom get a second chance with a potential customer. These rules emphasize the need for a prompt, business-like approach that stresses the customer's interests.

- *Step 4. Presentation and Demonstration.* A general rubric for a sales presentation is the AIDA formula: get their Attention, hold their Interest, arouse their Desire, and obtain Action. Given the I/UCRC emphasis on collaborative sales, the best presentation is one based on satisfying the potential member's needs. Rather than launching into a canned sales pitch, the emphasis is on listening and responding accordingly. (See Chapter 6.) Directors will need to be prepared to make presentations to individual prospects. However, group sales meetings attended by multiple prospects and current members can be very effective (see section titled *The Pre-planning and Recruiting Meetings* in Chapter 2).

- *Step 5. Handling Objections.* Effective sales people don't wait for potential customers to recognize their own needs, they work with the customer to identify needs that their firm can meet. Working with the customer they identify the needs and demonstrate the I/UCRC as the low-cost provider of the best of the available options. Presentation must be exceptional, objections must be clarified and met, and competitor's shortcomings must be magnified.

- *Step 6. Closing.* This is the payoff. Everything up to this point has been preparatory. The first rule is only deal with the ultimate decision-maker. By now, that individual should not only be identified, he or she should have been part of the process for some while. The second rule is keep the deal moving forward; don't revisit old objections. The final rule is be prepared to make a final concession to seal the deal. Both parties will win if the deal is properly structured. The effective sales person subjugates his or her ego for the good of both the customer and the firm.

- *Step 7. Feedback and Follow-up.* More business is done with customers than potential customers so sales people are in the business of long-term relationships. No successful business can afford to treat its customers as disposable.

CONSULTATIVE, COLLABORATIVE SELLING

Successful Center Directors must be able to recruit members, but that does not mean that they need to face the customer with "nothing but a shoe shine and a smile." When Arthur Miller penned that phrase for *Death of a Salesman,* sales people were viewed either as mere order-takers or as high-pressure hucksters. Today, there is a third model of the salesperson's craft—consultative or collaborative selling—which, by emphasizing clients' needs and partnerships, is an excellent fit for a center's modus operandi.

In collaborative selling, sales people never dictate solutions (Cespedes, 1989;1995). Rather, they form partnerships in which prospects play an active role in the search for best solutions. This team approach to problem solving helps to insure that prospects are committed to proposed solutions and reduces the stress of closing by allowing the prospect to commit to the deal when all their buying criteria are met. Collaborative selling puts a decidedly interactive and cooperative face on the seven selling steps.

THE SIX MAJOR STEPS IN COLLABORATIVE SELLING

Targeting

The greatest source of leads is always personal contact. The Center Director, IAB members, faculty, graduate students, administration should list their network of contacts as potential customers. Because the typical membership takes between six months and two years to secure, centers must keep track of potential members. Such a system might begin with a master list of anyone who has ever expressed an interest in a center product. If communication continues, a separate folder should be established listing every communication, questions asked, and materials sent.

While there is no magic buzzer that goes off to signal a hot prospect, the best indicator seems to be the willingness to make a personal visit.

Contact

The goal here is building a foundation for a cooperative working relationship. Emphasis should be put on exploring needs and opportunities, and explaining competitive advantages, rather than on any preset presentation. Because of the stress on personal contacts in the targeting stage, someone affiliated with the I/UCRC will already have had contact with the potential member. Therefore, the objective during this step is to smoothly transfer the contact to the individual responsible for recruitment. This may be accomplished through personal introduction, conference calling, or letter of introduction.

Explore

Two way communication is key. Potential customers are encouraged to express their needs and how they hope to benefit from the partnership, while sales people learn as much as they can about the potential customer and begin to suggest ways that the partnership can help meet the expressed needs, the customer should do most of the talking at this stage. Information exchange and answering questions should lead to a visit. Identifying the decision maker at the firm who is responsible for authorizing the membership is the goal. Few memberships are secured without a visit; none are secured without the approval of the decision maker.

Collaborate

Once the potential customer has a complete picture of the services being offered and the sales person fully understands the customer's needs and reservations, what remains is working together, collaborating, to produce singular solutions. This is the unique strength of the I/UCRC concept. A successfully operating center is constantly engaged in a dialogue with its members designed to refine the research agenda so that it matches those members' needs. Bringing in a member firm to explain how the center helped it to solve a problem is appropriate at this stage. Remember that even though you are interested in a long term relationship, getting the firm to sign the membership agreement now may require a solution to a specific problem. Identifying such a problem and the center's role in its solution may be the deal clincher. The Center Director can show the decision maker that the membership fee is justified because it will solve a singular research problem and also solve problems that may be shared by human resources, or community relations, or marketing.

Confirm

If all goes well, confirming the sale is a logical conclusion to the collaborative process. Customers commit to the sale when all their questions are answered and their buying criteria are met. Unfortunately, "confirming" may be too passive a verb to close a deal as novel and complicated as an I/UCRC membership. Be aware of the potential member's budgeting cycle and push to confirm when new funds have just been committed, or at the end of a cycle when funds must be expended. Be flexible regarding payment schedule; it may be easier for the firm to make smaller, multiple payments. If possible, accept equipment or other non-monetary compensation in lieu of the membership fee (if approved by the IAB). Try to put together a membership fee package funded by research, human resources, marketing, and other departments within the firm. Appeal to the ultimate decision maker. If necessary, add a sweetener such as reduced fees for center run short courses. Keep asking "What can we do to consummate the membership?"

Assure

The level of communication after sale must intensify, not diminish. New members must be assured that their satisfaction is not just part of the sales pitch, but center philosophy. IAB members are encouraged to communicate any concerns. The center evaluator can conduct an entry interview to give new members an opportunity to express their needs, and the Center Director should schedule a visit to the member's facility within one year of membership.

Listening, communicating, determining needs, and problem solving are all competencies that many academicians have in rich abundance. Recruiting may never be a Center Director's fondest task, but it need not be viewed with alarm. Recruiting by collaborative selling plays to their strengths.

RETENTION

A bird in the hand is worth two in the bush. Two-thirds of a business's income comes from current customers. It is also true of I/UCRCs. Funding from members for targeted research and university-industry competitive awards exceeds the funding from membership fees. This means that creating a customer is only half the battle; retaining that customer is equally important. Broad range strategies are used to ensure current customer loyalty, longevity, and profitability. Such strategies are often thought of as the five A's.

Acquainting

I/UCRCs need to identify their members and to understand their needs and behavior. Of special interest is recognizing high-value customers with the potential for increased business. The major strategy at this step is maintaining an accurate and complete member information file. Because of the recruiting process, the Center Director is well acquainted with new members from the moment that they join. But this level of acquaintance needs to be understood as a floor, not a ceiling. In particular, the relationship with the new member firm needs to be both broadened and strengthened. Broadening entails searching out other parts of the firm that might have an interest in sharing the center relationship. In this way, the center will be perceived by the firm's decision maker as adding extra value and such value may eventually lead to additional funds for contracted research. The formal I/UCRC relationship is between the university and a corporate entity, but the strength of the relationship lies in the relationship between people. One major reason for firms leaving a center is that the initial center advocate is reassigned or leaves the firm. In order to avoid this, Center Directors need to cultivate several advocates within the firm.

Acknowledging

Responding to each and every communication is essential. It is also an important source of information. Further, many I/UCRCs conduct member satisfaction surveys to ascertain current levels of performance and to determine new research needs. Promptly acknowledge all member-initiated communication. Make certain that any complaint is handled in a timely fashion.

The director may keep a separate file for each member containing the contact sheet, correspondence, notes regarding conversations and informal meetings, and memos from others in the center concerning their communications with the member. This documents how well the center is serving each firm.

Appreciating

I/UCRCs must let their customers know they are appreciated. In-house publications, premiums ranging from key chains to videos, open-houses acknowledge the customer and engender loyalty and good will. There are many ways that centers can convey appreciation. These may range from superior food service at the IAB meeting and responding to any special dietary requirements, to distributing a professionally produced newsletter and securing multiple copies of publications in which members may be interested. Centers need to go the extra mile in meeting member's needs and in fulfilling their requests.

Analyzing

Two-way communication between an I/UCRC and its members keeps members satisfied, and also provides an opportunity to learn member opinions and feelings. Understanding the member is a cardinal rule of success, and analyzing their communication is one good method of doing so. The I/UCRC program requires an annual process questionnaire and exit interviews. We suggest two more: entry interviews and keeping contact logs. We have counseled how to use IAB meetings as an important source of member information to measure the overall health of the center and for judging each member's level of satisfaction. Center Directors need to be sensitive to failure to attend IAB meetings, a decline in ratings on the LIFE and/or process questionnaires, and take immediate, corrective action.

Acting

Successful I/UCRCs must act on member information by showing a willingness to listen and a readiness to change operating procedures or products to better satisfy their needs. I/UCRCs are fortunate in this regard. The evaluation process provides the center with a mechanism for identifying needs and concerns. Centers must demonstrate a track record of handling these problems.

However, often the reason for dissatisfaction is lagging communication. While there is no doubt that the key to retention is a high quality, industrially relevant research program, it is also clear that centers may measure the health of their relationship by the frequency of communication.

LEARN FROM FAILURE

The reality is that losing members can show how to get new ones. Successful I/UCRCs need to analyze what went wrong and re-approach the potential customer emphasizing both all their strengths that initially won the customer as well as new procedures and products designed to overcome the reasons the customer left.

REFERENCES

Cespedes, F., Doyle S., and Freidman, R. *Teamwork for Today's Selling*. Harvard Business Review, March-April, 1989, pp. 44-54, 58.

Cespedes, F. *Concurrent Marketing: Integrating Product Sales and Service*. Harvard Business School Press, 1995.

Kotler, P. *Marketing Management*. Eighth Ed., Prentice Hall, 1994, pp. 602-5, 706-7.

Kotler, P. and Armstrong, G. *Principles of Marketing*. Sixth Ed., Prentice Hall, Englewood Cliffs, NJ, 1994. pp. 192-3; 535-9.

Ohame, K. *The Strategic Triangle and Business Unit Strategy*. The McKinsey Quarterly, Winter, 1993.

CHAPTER 5

PLANNING THE COOPERATIVE RESEARCH PROGRAM

LOUIS TORNATZKY, *Southern Technology Council,*
Research Triangle Park, NC

DENIS O. GRAY, *North Carolina State University, Raleigh*

ELIEZER GEISLER, *University of Wisconsin, Whitewater*

STRATEGIC PLANNING

There are several good reasons to bring some degree of disciplined strategic planning to cooperative centers. Strategic planning communicates an organization's intentions and elicits feedback which promotes coordination. Cooperative research centers are much more complex than the typical academic research project. Centers include dozens of participants, stakeholders, and long-term, multi-year project initiatives. Without strategic thinking I/UCRCs are likely to fail.

Plans also serve a public relations and marketing function. Centers need to communicate with and influence a variety of outsiders. For instance, plans help inform the public and prospective members about organizational intentions and persuade them to support I/UCRC efforts. Well articulated plans often become the basis for recruitment presentations, press releases, articles in alumni magazines, and presentations to community or scholarly audiences.

Academic culture is often at odds with industrial culture. Planning can bridge the gap between industry's need for using proven technology and keeping proprietary information secret, and academia's need to publish and innovate.

Most important, strategic planning leverages the available resources of a program. One can easily have a $1 million center program in which $500,000 is wasted on poorly selected projects and in foolish thrust areas. Industrial participants will not tolerate a chaotic research program for very long. In fact, data collected as part of I/UCRC process/outcome assessment confirms this. The strongest single predictor of intention to renew membership is satisfaction with research program planning!

Although strategic planning is relevant to recruitment, budgeting, staffing, diversification, etc., this discussion concentrates on the center's research program. First some background on how planning is approached conventionally and how this approach can be tailored to the unique characteristics of an industry/university cooperative research center is presented. Then behaviors and products used by successful centers for strategy formulation and programming are discussed. In a companion chapter (see Chapter 6), we discuss how to implement center research plans.

Planning and the Industry/University Relationship

At an operational level, planning of cooperative R&D relationships that involve university researchers and industrial supporters and 'customers' in fast changing research areas may appear contradictory. At the outset, it should be acknowledged that we will not rely much on the practice and wisdom literature of R&D management. That literature is indeed vast (Clarke and Reavley, 1993). Unfortunately, less than one percent of it is even remotely applicable to the situation that concerns us: the case of multiple academic researchers involved in a cooperative relationship with multiple industrial partners.

There are good reasons why this might be so. Most academic research programs neither are planned nor managed in the same way as industrial research. The university culture of academic freedom promotes relative autonomy for professors and graduate students to pursue their research projects with minimal outside supervision. In contrast, industry research teams are subject to frequent management review.

Cultural diversity on the research-performer side is matched by many degrees of freedom on the industrial participant side. A consortium-based cooperative research center is likely to involve as many as 25 companies active in a rapidly changing business environment with international markets and corporate operations, necessitating careful and quick changes in corporate R&D priorities. Each I/UCRC company member wants to maximize the business and technology interests of its firm, but frequently cannot be forthcoming about preferences or priorities because of proprietary concerns. Often, company representatives will only be candid during one-on-one dialogues with center management or individual researchers. Accurately assessing research needs of I/UCRC members under these circumstances is challenging, to say the least.

When these factors are taken into account, there is reason to believe the university-industry cooperative research center cannot be planned in a traditional sense. Nor probably should it be. Planning is necessarily much more dynamic, informal, participatory, and approximate.

What Is Planning?

Henry Mintzberg (1994) defined planning as "a formalized procedure to produce an articulated result, in the form of an integrated system of decisions." It is a highly formalized, deliberate, analytic, quantifiable reductionist decision-making process.

Unfortunately, the results of conventional planning have often fallen far short of their promise for several reasons. Many planners have become too single-minded in their approach to planning. Strategic planning requires both strategy and planning. However, planners often ignore or short-change strategy formulation. The results are a well-executed plan with little direction.

Further, planning is effective in circumstances of stability, industrial maturity, large size, elaborate structure, simple operations and external control, but is ineffective in dynamic and less structured environments. Again in the words of Mintzberg (1994): "Managers don't always need to program their strategies formally, sometimes they must leave their strategies flexible, as broad visions, to adapt to a changing environment" (p. 112). Planning and all its formalities may impede or obstruct strategic thinking or promulgate an incomplete strategy.

Does this mean I/UCRCs, which operate in a dynamic and unstructured environment, shouldn't plan? Certainly not! However, they might want to adopt what Mintzberg labels a soft approach to planning, with emphasis on creative and strategic thinking; collection, analysis and reconnaissance about emergent strategies; loose and flexible targets and milestones; and implementation which emphasizes organizational learning. This is the planning approach Mintzberg recommends for project-driven adhocracies like NASA, and it is the approach we recommended for I/UCRCs. In the next section we will try to flesh out some of the important characteristics of this approach.

Defining a Soft Planning Approach

Conventional planning generally is described as a process which involves a series of tasks, often arranged in a linear manner as steps. Models of varying detail have been used to describe that process. Figure 5-1 presents a simplified center planning process: strategy formulation, strategy programming, and implementation.

Figure 5-1	The center planning process simplified.
Stage	**Activity**
Strategy Formulation	Visioning and Mission
Strategy Programming	Defining Program and Thrust
	Defining Goals and Objectives
Implementation	Developing Research Projects
	Review, Evaluation and Selection
	Project Management

While this schema provides a useful model, it also provides a simplistic and misleading picture of how planning is and should be carried out within an I/UCRC. While the best-in-class programs tend to cover most of the key issues and do certain things before others, we would argue that the tasks and characteristics of planning in a cooperative center are much too dynamic to permit such an ordered approach.

A soft planning approach will differ in a number of respects. First, the process will not be linear (see Figure 5-2). For instance, some centers must implement their research program before they have an opportunity to articulate their vision and strategy, but conducting and getting feedback on their research program may allow them to find rather than formulate a strategy that makes sense.

Another way in which a soft planning approach (Figure 5-2) differs is the regularity of the tasks performed. Planning can include a one-time organizational event or task like launching a new center, or regularly occurring events or continuous tasks. Conventional planning is dominated by tasks performed in one to three-year cycles. Soft planning gives greater emphasis to continu-

Figure 5-2   The soft planning process.

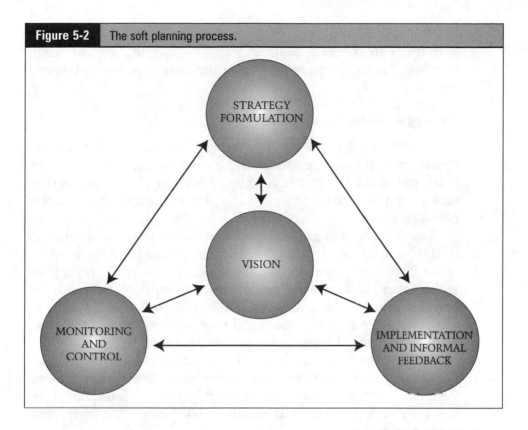

ous tasks. Concomitantly, the time frames covered by cyclical tasks will be much shorter. In addition, the formality of activities and products, at least with respect to strategy formulation and programming (but not implementation), will be much lower when engaged in a soft planning approach.

The traditional distinction between strategic planning and operational planning also loses its salience: in conventional planning, strategic planning tends to be long-term, conceptual, general, and more important than operational planning. Operational planning tends to be short-term, detailed, and subordinate to strategic planning. Because the time frames are so much shorter in a soft planning approach, these distinctions tend to be blurred, with tactical plans often leading to strategic insights and changes in direction.

Finally, soft planning will involve different center functions. Conventional planning activities primarily involve top management. Soft planning, particularly in a customer-driven organization like a center, tends to be broader in scope with many planning tasks involving everyone including the customer and affecting everything.

While all this might seem a bit abstract, and perhaps chaotic, planning can be made more concrete by focusing on the basic building blocks of planning: planning activities and planning products.

Planning Activities and Behaviors

Good planning depends upon a strategy, and creative strategy formulation requires integration and synthesis. Learning how to think out of the box and envisioning possibilities that do not currently exist is perhaps the most important element of a center's planning process.

Planning involves gathering information external and internal to the organization. Information relevant to soft planning may include facts, data, opinion, beliefs, and myth. It may encompass technical or market trends, outcomes, competitive intelligence, or political events. It provides the intellectual grist that undergirds other planning activities. Consolidation, documentation, aggregation, or analysis of information is also assumed.

Planning involves deciding. Information in itself is useless unless participants prioritize which outcomes or directions are more desirable, or which activities need to be linked and coordinated. In soft planning, decision making will involve short time-cycles and greater participation.

Planning involves communicating. Planning demands a huge amount of discussion, debate, writing, presenting, and revising. Center leaders who are not comfortable communicators in these ways will be at a distinct disadvantage.

Planning Tasks and Products

Planning products vary in formality from a formal written mission statement or project plan to a presentation overhead or a motto on a business card. While these products will be addressed in more detail in the balance of the chapter, some of the more important include a center name, a technical vision or mission, defined research areas, goals and objectives, proposal solicitations, project research plans, and project evaluations.

The Planning Process

When most people think about planning, they think about an orderly process that starts with Step 1 and proceeds in a lockstep manner to Step n, and involves conventional boundaries and responsibilities. While this process might work well in some organizations, typically it will not suit the needs of dynamic boundary-spanning organizations like centers. Based on I/UCRC experience, centers will benefit most from using a soft approach to planning. It is a highly recursive process, which is very heterogeneous in nature, involves shorter feedback cycles, emphasizes continuous improvement, requires a catalyst more than a programmer, and results in products that often are quite informal in nature. In spite of these differences, it is planning nonetheless.

The next section describes how to formulate and program a soft research strategy for your center. Later, in Chapter 6, we will discuss strategy implementation; recruiting investigators; and developing, refining, and prioritizing projects. Some cooperative research center directors may find that implementing an informally articulated plan is a more pressing need for them at this particular time. We recommend that these individuals skip ahead to the next section and return here when time and circumstances permit.

FORMULATING AND PROGRAMMING A RESEARCH STRATEGY

Most industry-university cooperative research centers follow a similar strategy of marketing pre-proprietary research to a consortium of industrial members. However, each center must also devise a unique research strategy and develop a portfolio of research projects tailored to their capabilities and the needs of a specific segment of industry.

The following section provides practical advice on how to formulate and program a strategy for developing a successful research portfolio including creating a vision, information gathering, defining research areas, goals, objectives, implementation, and products. While we will cover these topics in a conventional sequence, there is no rule for the order of stages.

Vision and Mission

A vision, an idea of a possible future to achieve, is probably the most important ingredient in a successful strategy. I/UCRCs should spend some creative energy on it and an associated mission statement. Vision and mission statements should be reviewed and recast periodically in the evolution of a center program. In fairness, it should be noted that many cooperative research centers may neglect to do so and may develop a mission statement only after three to four years of operation.

Vision and mission statements:

- Define what is in bounds and what is not.
- Define a future to attain.
- Facilitate easier external communication about what the center is and does.
- Drive strategy development.

The boundary-spanning, multi-stakeholder nature of a center dictates that one approaches this process in a participatory manner. This does not mean vision and mission statements are written by committee, but all stakeholders must be given an opportunity to shape the technical direction the center will take.

Vision

Words influence behavior and effective leaders are able to paint "word pictures" of a vision for a desired future. A center vision describes a future scenario or an optimal or highly desirable set of hypothetical events. Vision may predict technical accomplishments or research. It usually depicts a scenario that extends outside an affected industry or regional economy.

HYPOTHETICAL VISION STATEMENT

A ceramics composites industry in which the volume of use is 100-fold greater than current levels, and in which products extend beyond high temperature application into structural materials and high volume consumer goods. Ceramic composites will be characterized more completely through a robust body of theory and empirical knowledge. Design and development of new applications routinely will be accomplished via simulation and the computerized application of design algorithms. The Center for Ceramics Composites will be a preeminent university-based research center with an annual volume of research that exceeds $10 million and with 40 member companies. It will on average yield annually ten patents and have a highly diverse portfolio of funding sources and research relationships.

One of the more useful features of vision statements is that it is often extremely enlightening to dig these out every few months and assess how current developments compare to what was projected.

Techniques for Developing Vision Statements

The various ways in which vision statements can be created include developing a draft to solicit feedback, building on existing models, storyboarding, and other group-based, including computer-mediated techniques. It is not clear whether any of the more intensive or expensive approaches are significantly better than the more commonplace approaches discussed above. In all of this, the key is to not over-program the process and to have knowledgeable and creative people involved.

Solo Draft

Center Director drafts statements which are then reviewed and refined by members of the core planning team.

Build on Existing Models

Assemble sample vision statements from existing R&D centers, or from corporations as good models. Corporate members of the core team are often excellent leads for identifying samples.

Storyboarding

The core team, in a one to two-hour session, composes sentences and sentence fragments which are then pieced together. Typically these fragments are pinned or stuck to a board. A facilitator rearranges, eliminates, and enhances the fragments into a meaningful whole which everyone can support. (See Kuhn, 1988, for a more detailed discussion of this methodology.)

Group and Computer-Mediated Techniques

Computer-based groupware and other interpersonal approaches foster new associations and new ideas (see Tornatzky and Ostrowiecki, 1994).

The Mission Statement

Writing a mission statement or establishing goals is relatively easy once there is a vision statement. A good mission statement rarely

> ### Hypothetical Mission Statement
>
> *To advance the field of glass science and engineering through research, education, and technology exchange among academe, industry, and government.*

exceeds two to three sentences. It is pithy, straightforward, and easily understood.

Mission statements contain four elements:

Who: Center for Glass Research.

What: Advance the field of glass research.

Means: Through research, education and technology exchange.

Participants: Academe, industry, and government.

More complicated and lengthy mission statements are counterproductive, confuse the reader, and send a message to industry that the center doesn't have its act together.

Some useful addenda to mission statements can be free-standing chunks of prose. A statement of organizational philosophy or values is an example. These can convey to readers (both external and internal to the center) a powerful statement about the organization.

> ### Hypothetical Agenda
>
> *The Southern Technology Council serves a regional constituency in a style that is hands-on, action-oriented, businesslike and practical. The emphasis is on cooperation and collaboration in accomplishing the mission.*

Interestingly, many corporations have developed fairly involved value statements which cover not only how they deal with customers, but how employees and managers treat each other. It might be overkill for a university-based research center to go this far, but some expression of philosophy or values will be well-received by corporate partners.

Finally, it is often useful to boil down the mission into four to six-word motto or credo, e.g., *better living through chemistry* for business cards, stationary, and marketing materials.

Strategy Programming

Once a research vision and mission is articulated it is time to figure out how to get there. This is where, as Mintzberg (1994) labels it, strategy "programming" comes in. We begin by discussing information gathering.

Information Gathering

All planning-related tasks can be strengthened by thoughtful information gathering and analysis. Most information gathering will be focused on a few major questions including the state of the science, needs, trends, opportunities, and threats. As a boundary-spanning organization, an I/UCRC must be aware of needs and developments in both the academic and industrial communities. This might involve what is going on in one's discipline and related disciplines and in your industry and related industries. Since this can be an overwhelming task, centers must focus on local environment, faculty, and current or pending members. Then, if warranted, extend to the proximate environment, faculty at other institutions, knowledge in related fields and firms, and knowledge from the same industry as your members. And finally to one's distal environment or faculty, knowledge, and firms, and from unrelated disciplines or industries. (See Figure 5-3.)

Informal Information Gathering

Valuable information about local environment can be gathered informally from the center's faculty, industrial members, and their associated networks. This information can often be collected *on the fly* from IAB members, new prospects and other stakeholders in the context of other business. For instance, in the course of reviewing and prioritizing new proposals, members often point out unmet needs and new directions. (See "Formulating and Programming a Research Strategy" for a more detailed discussion of how to capitalize on this opportunity.) This information can provide a basis for midcourse corrections and adjustments or a new plan.

| Figure 5-3 | Center data-gathering environment. |

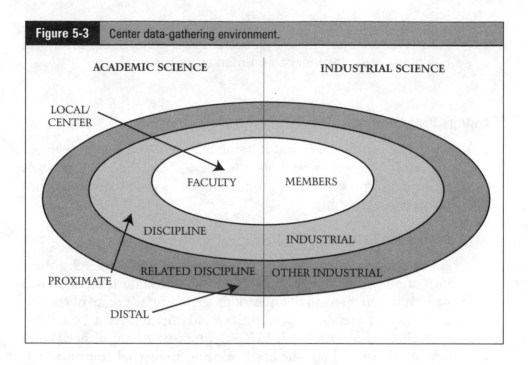

In order to benefit from informal information gathering, it is important that such data be documented. Much of this information will be gathered during project review, evaluation, and new project selection, and during informal meetings and phone conversations. Center Directors should make a habit of jotting down notes during or after these events, and collating member LIFE forms. These notes can simply be stuck in a folder or filing box or kept in a computer file, and then examined every few months. They often yield interesting themes or common issues.

Another valuable setting for informal data gathering is conferences and meetings. Attendance at conference industrial meetings or meetings for other disciplines often has the biggest payoff.

Primary Data Gathering Via Surveys and Structured Interviews

Surveys and phone interviews are quite time-consuming but can prove valuable if one has the resources. It should involve only key informants in your local environment, such as members of industrial advisory boards. Some of the data collected by NSF I/UCRC evaluators provide a useful example of this kind of data (see Chapter 8).

There also is some utility in conducting a limited series of one-on-one interviews with members of the planning team or external stakeholders. These might be conducted by the Center Director, or by someone who has responsibility for facilitating the planning effort. A typical format is to have three to six open-ended questions in the context of a half-hour interview (see Chapter Appendix 5-1). The interview may be conducted in person or by phone. It is important to take good notes or ask permission to record the session. Such sessions often uncover strategic issues (or solutions!) that may not be expressed in a group meeting session. They can confirm or reject conclusions reached in a group setting. An important role for the interviewer is to extract either common or novel themes and share them with the planning team.

Mining Reports, Data Bases, and other Secondary Sources

When trying to gather information about one's proximate or distal environment, as one must during the start-up phase or when one is engaged in a major change of directions, the most efficient approach involves reading the work of others. For instance, one might want to find out the number of firms in a sector or R&D expenditures. A particularly rich source of reports is the federal government. NSF, the National Academy of Sciences and its constituent organizations, the National Academy of Engineering and the Institute of Medicine, various professional organizations and associations, e.g., Electronic Industries Association, Association for Manufacturing Technology, U.S. Bureau of Economic Analysis, and Bureau of the Census, publish industry-specific trends, economic analysis, and research data.

Electronic data-bases are also available (Figure 5-4). Since the information gathering needs of each center are likely to vary considerably, center staff are urged to consult an appropriate librarian. Internet browsers are another tool. The more thought and time spent on the front end of the information gathering process, the more useful the mining of secondary sources.

In summary, there are a variety of ways to gather information and an almost unlimited number of sources of information that may be relevant to your planning needs. While center staff should consider all of these options, our emphasis on a soft planning approach argues for heavy but not exclusive reliance on informal data gathering from one's local environment. In other words, keep your eyes open and your ears to the ground.

| Figure 5-4 | Electronic business and technology databases. |

ABI/Inform. Worldwide literature in business and management, accounting economics, finance, taxation, marketing, etc. Abstracts of principal articles from over 1,000 journals (full text from over 550).

American Business Disc. A compilation from the Yellow Pages, selected portions of corporate annual reports and SEC filings.

Automated Patent Service. A full-text database consisting of U.S. patents from 1971 to the present.

Applied Science and Technology Index. Indexes over 300 English language technology and engineering publications.

Business Index. Indexing and abstracts for 850 business, management, and trade journals, plus citations to business-related articles in more than 3,000 other publications.

Compendex Plus. Indexing and abstracts covering engineering and technology. Corresponds to print Engineering Index.

Disclosure. Detailed records for more than 16,000 public companies, and selected records for foreign companies traded on major American exchanges.

Lexis/Nexis. Offers access to full-text databases that cover business, company, financial, legal, and news information.

Predicast's F&S Index. Abstracts, excerpts, and full text of articles dealing with information on companies, industries, and markets.

Defining Research Thrusts

At some point, planning for a center needs to get down to cases. That is, develop a portfolio of research projects which maintains member interests and entices prospective members to join. A research portfolio might be structured in any of the following modes: (1) a supermarket or menu approach, (2) the use of clusters or thrusts, or (3) some combination of both.

The supermarket or menu approach includes something for everyone. It is a selection of programs and projects which appeals to all the companies (or at least a majority) supporting a center. This approach may be preferred for a center with only a few member companies, perhaps early in the life of a center, when it is still sorting out its core competencies and how the interests of companies coalesce, or operating in a very dynamic field. While this approach has its pluses, it also has some serious shortcomings. Most prominently, it can lead to a dilution and fragmentation of a center's research program.

Another approach assumes that projects can and should be clustered into a few discrete themes, each of which tends to draw the attention and interest of a sub-group of companies. In fact, a few companies may have exclusive interest in one or two projects, and zero interest in others. On the other hand, some draw the interest of virtually all member companies. In fact, research on the I/UCRC program demonstrates member firms are highly interested in and closely monitor about 40 percent of all center projects.

Figure 5-5 illustrates some I/UCRC research themes. Experience suggests that defining discrete research themes or clusters will satisfy more members, most of the time.

Figure 5-5	Sample I/UCRC research themes.			
CENTER	*Process Analytical Chemistry*	*Ceramics Research*	*Software Engineering*	*Materials Handling*
Research Themes	Chemometrics	Processing science	Development tools	Manufacturing systems
	In-line sensors	Surface science	Maintenance methods	Warehousing systems
	Spectroscopy	Electro-ceramics	Distributed environment	Logistics systems
	Flow chemography	Structural	Modeling and metrics	Flexible automation
	Process monitoring and control			Information systems

Participants

Like most of the planning covered up to this point, defining research themes should include researchers in the host university, with specialties that pertain to or complement the general area being addressed by the center; researchers from partner institutions; IAB members or prospective IAB members; and representatives from potential state or federal government funding agencies. A professional facilitator might be appropriate when defining research themes in a large gathering.

Generating Ideas

There are several ways in which research themes can be generated. Participating university researchers raise roughly defined research questions and then cluster them into themes, or the Center Director extracts themes from the raw data of research ideas. A second approach is to have the core planning team take on the task. A third option is to have the group of participating researchers brainstorm research themes with help from a neutral facilitator.

The problem with all these approaches is that they are done in relative isolation from industry and defeat the concept of a industry/university cooperative center.

A way to involve industry in developing research themes is ask each company for two to four pages identifying research of a basic science nature that are of critical importance. It is useful for faculty members to identify research they believe should be of interest to industry. It is often enlightening to compare and contrast these different perspectives.

A final approach is to hold a more interactive strategic planning meeting which incorporates some of both of these approaches. This approach is described in some detail in "Pulling It All Together: The Strategic Planning Meeting."

It is hoped that these methods will lead the center to identify three to five research themes that can be described in a few sentences or paragraphs (see Figure 5-6). As these examples illustrate, depending upon the focus of the center, a given thrust might range in specificity from a major subdisciplinary topic (e.g., surface science), to a general methodology (e.g., simulation), to a topic of specific industrial interest (e.g., out-of-plane dynamics on web machines).

In all of these approaches a critical chore involves eliminating projects/themes from your nominated list. This can easily be handled by establishing criteria for evaluating and selecting candidates. These criteria might include: converges with faculty expertise and industry needs; complementary to other areas; doesn't represent a dilution of effort.

The latter two represent the all-important element of focus.

Goals and Objectives

Once research themes are defined I/UCRC goals and objectives are defined and redefined periodically over the life of the center.

| Figure 5-6 | Sample research descriptions. |

Center for Ceramics Research
Surface Science: Molecular dynamic computer modeling of bulk and colloidal surface and interface phenomena; physical surface analysis using atomic force and scanning tunneling microscopy; chemical surface analysis using x-ray photoelectron, Auger electron ion scattering, and secondary ion mass spectroscopy.

Center for Analog-Digital Integrated Circuits
Simulation: Developing methodologies to evaluate, test, and characterize new and existing circuit simulators; improving speed and efficiency for analog-digital simulation through use of hardware accelerators with hierarchical simulators using parametric yield optimizers.

Center for Web Handling Research
Out-of-plane dynamics: Web flutter is a serious obstacle to high-speed operation of web machines. Flutter can lead to breaks or wrinkling in machines that handle paper and register errors in printing presses and damage on polymer sheets. Research in this area focuses on predicting the critical operating conditions in which flutter starts and predicting flutter amplitude if a machine is operated above the flutter threshold.

The difference between goal and objective is that the latter quantifies or specifies the former. Each objective should articulate a technical need or obstacle. (See Figure 5-7.)

Goals must harken back to the mission or vision statements, and related planning products. It is probably better if a center has a few meaningful goals with measurable objectives rather than dozens of goals with no implications for the participants in the

| Figure 5-7 | Sample statement of goals and objectives. |

Goal: Basic and applied industry research to ensure high quality color images are provided to customers.

Objective: Provide information necessary to define standard protocols for transferring color data accurately among many users at different sites using different display devices.

Specific sub-objectives: More accurate color scanning methods, reproduction and color correction; improved coding and compression methods for both single and sequential color images; more accurate models for the complex color printing process by use of nonlinear systems theory; and methods to obtain more accurate color reproduction among a large variety of printing devices having different color gamuts.

program. Since new findings may modify their relevance they should be reviewed and revised much more frequently than vision and mission statements.

Most centers will find goals and objectives adequate for planning, but some centers prefer more detail (see Figure 5-8). They create a roadmap in block diagram form of the current state of science and technology, the vision of the future, and road blocks and research activities to resolve them. The power of the technical roadmap is not only its visual appeal, but also the ability to identify the order of action, such as which research activities and questions are on the critical path for another set of questions, and thereby ought to be addressed first. Unfortunately, technical roadmaps may sometimes serve as an obstacle to attempts to revise or re-invent a research area.

PULLING IT ALL TOGETHER: THE STRATEGIC PLANNING MEETING

How can centers tackle the planning activities described in this section in a systematic and coherent fashion? A one or two-day strategic planning meeting can be a useful vehicle for broadening information gathering, analyzing future needs and opportunities and for resetting a center's course. The meeting will require a great deal of time, thought, and preparation. Many centers will find it difficult to convene more frequently than every few years. As a consequence, some centers may prefer to set aside a few hours at their semi-annual review meetings and address one or two planning issues as discussed below.

It is extremely important to manage carefully the focus and agenda of such sessions. Time will be limited and it is critical that participants get a sense of tangible accomplishment.

Guidelines for a Successful IUC Strategic Planning Meeting

Develop Consensus about the Need for a Meeting

Before scheduling a planning meeting be sure there is a broad-based consensus among potential participants, particularly from industry, on the need to formulate or re-evaluate the center's mission, goals, objectives, etc. Never schedule a planning meeting just for the sake of having one or because you haven't for awhile! If the costs are an obstacle consider combining your planning meeting with your semi-annual research review.

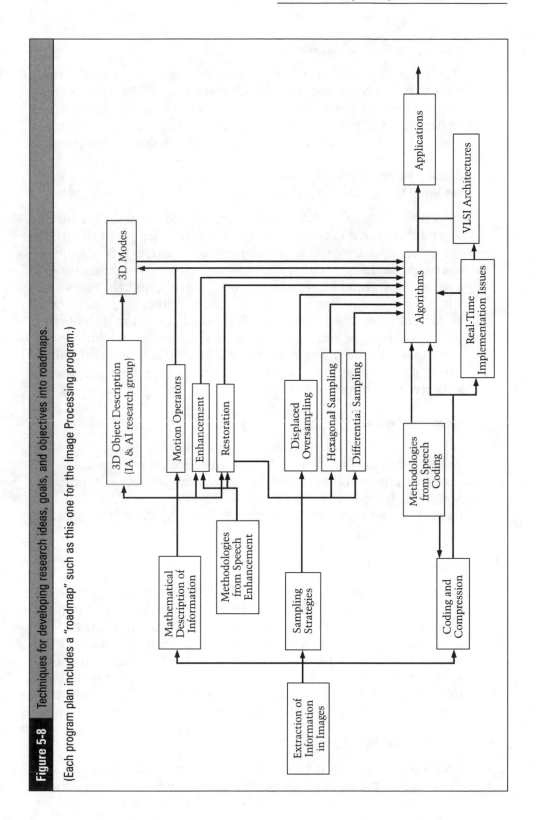

Figure 5-8 Techniques for developing research ideas, goals, and objectives into roadmaps.

(Each program plan includes a "roadmap" such as this one for the Image Processing program.)

Specify the Goals of the Meeting

The meeting planner needs to specify and describe the likely products that will come out of a planning session. It is also important not to be overly optimistic about what will be accomplished. It is better to get closure on a manageable agenda than feel that the meeting failed to accomplish an unrealistically ambitious agenda.

Make a Formal, Timely, and Structured Request for Work to be Done BEFORE the Meeting

Experience suggests that participants should be assigned homework before the meeting. For example, if the purpose of the meeting is to redefine goals or objectives, the participants should be asked to read the current statements and come up with new or improved ones. In addition, some centers have found that it is useful to ask industrial participants to poll their key staff and managers via written questions distributed several months before and again right before the meeting (See Appendix 5-1 for sample questions). While a few participants may still arrive with notes scribbled on an airplane cocktail napkin, experience has shown this strategy promotes high-quality input.

Have an Agenda

Like any meeting, an effective strategic planning session needs to be orchestrated. That means having an agenda that is organized in terms of topics and time blocks, as well as identifying those responsible for participating. This should be circulated ahead of time if possible. Chapter Appendix 5-2 provides a typical one-day planning agenda.

Spend Time on History

Unless this is the first-ever strategic planning meeting for a center, every participant will have different knowledge about prior planning efforts. It is very useful to circulate materials on various components of a center's plan before the meeting. Time should be allocated during the meeting for a brief review of them. In most organizations there will be one or two individuals who have been participants in the early years of development. Ask them to provide an oral history for the newer members.

Request Input from Every Participant

Social science research has demonstrated repeatedly that valuable input is lost via bashfulness or the dominance of a few individuals when others have to volunteer their ideas in a group setting. Special efforts should be made to go around the room and ask each member company to share their written or verbal comments. Faculty should also be asked through a faculty representative.

Consider Using Outside Technical Experts

A nationally respected expert who is not part of the center can be asked to address the strategic planning meeting or scheduled periodically as part of your IAB meeting. Some centers have even engaged in forecasting technology in which a number of national experts are interviewed about where a field or industry is heading.

Anticipate Follow-Up and Document Action Items

Anticipate that the meeting will end with a series of action items for follow-up by appropriate individuals or committees. It is useful to draft a memo at the meeting which summarizes follow-up actions and responsibilities and have it read before the meeting adjourns.

SUMMARY AND CONCLUSIONS

Centers need to plan their research program to avoid chaos and organizational decline. However, the highly formalized and linear approach to planning practiced in many large, stable organizations is not suited to I/UCRCs' innovative, fast paced, dynamic environments. As a consequence, we advocate a soft approach to planning.

A soft approach to planning requires the planner to be more catalyst than programmer. It emphasizes the importance of developing a technical vision appropriate to the center's environment, faculty, and industry stakeholders. Reaching a vision requires creative and strategic thinking and broad-based participation by various stakeholders. Programming a strategy for this vision requires data gathering from your IAB. Like conventional planning, this process should result in traditional planning products but they may not be addressed in a conventional order and may not crystallize until after the research program has been in place for several years. Even then they typically will be stated less formally.

While a soft approach to planning may appear messy and chaotic, it should not be mistaken for seat-of the-pants management. Rather, research planning in the context of a center must emphasize organizational learning and continuous improvement.

REFERENCES

Clark, C.H. *Idea Management*. American Management Association, NY, 1980.

Clarke, T.E. and Reavley, J. *Science and Technology Management*. A bibliography. Ottawa: Stargate Consulting Ltd., 1993.

Mintzberg, H. The Fall and Rise of Strategic Planning. *Harvard Business Review*, 72, 1994, pp. 107-115.

Kuhn, I. *Handbook of Creative and Innovative Managers*. NY: McGraw-Hill, Inc., 1988.

Rawlinson, J.G. *Creative Thinking and Brainstorming*. London, England: Gower Publishing, 1981.

Tornatzky, L.G. and Ostrowiecki, B. "Technical Needs: The Art and Craft of Identifying and Communicating." In S.K. Kassicieh and H.R. Radosevich. *From Lab to Market: Commerce of Public Sector Technology*. New York: Plenum Press, 1994.

APPENDIX 5-1

Information Gathering for Planning

Sample Questions for IAB Interviews

1. What challenges will your organization or industry face over the next five years which are related to <center name>?

2. What are the major technical, regulatory and competitive obstacles that your organization or industry must overcome to meet these challenges.

3. Of these which is <center name> best positioned and equipped to help you with?

4. Based on your answers, which area(s) (at least two) of research and specific topics, problems and issues within those areas (at least five) do you feel <center name> should emphasize during the next five years?

5. Given current funding and membership constraints, are there any areas of research or specific topics <center name> should stay away from, at least for now?

APPENDIX 5-2

Sample Agenda for Strategic Planning Workshop

Welcome and Introductions (15 minutes; director or IAB chair)

Review of Goals (15 minutes; director or IAB chair)

Opportunity to review purpose of meeting and outcomes and deliverables expected. Try to state outcomes in terms of various planning products to be created or revised: vision, mission statement, program or research areas, goals, objectives.

Center History (30 to 45 minutes; director)

Opportunity to review where the center has been over the past x years. Review could focus on: current mission, goals, areas, previously and currently funded projects organized by research theme, major technical outcomes of the program, e.g., students trained.

Future Needs and Opportunities—National Perspective (30 minutes; director; resource person; optional)

Opportunity to present formally collected data on center environment and technical needs and opportunities. See section titled *Strategy Planning* in this chapter.

Future Needs and Opportunities—Local Perspective (15–20 minutes per presenter; 1–4 hours; IAB members and faculty)

Presentations by each IAB member; one speaker to represent faculty perspective. See Appendix 5-1. Someone should be assigned responsibility for taking notes and summarizing them for immediate distribution.

Future Needs and Opportunities—Discussion (1–2 hours; director or group facilitator)

Opportunity to review and discuss the key points made during presentations. This process would be facilitated by posting major points made by each presenter. Discussion and comment on major issues or surprises, agreement and disagreement. Goal should be to reach a consensus on key technical needs and opportunities for the future. Might include a prioritization of needs and opportunities.

Review and Revision of Appropriate Planning Products (varies depending goals of workshop; director or facilitator)

Opportunity to write or revise mission, goals, etc. based on results of previous discussion. Session needs to be structured to avoid unproductive digressions. Goal should be to reach a general consensus on the wording of various planning products without getting into "word smithing." If some issues need more detailed discussion, might involve break-out sessions.

Overview and Closure (½–1 hour; director or IAB chair)

Opportunity to review what was accomplished during the meeting. Focus should also be on action items and individuals assigned to carry them out.

IMPLEMENTING THE COOPERATIVE RESEARCH PROGRAM

DENIS O. GRAY, *North Carolina State University, Raleigh*

LOUIS TORNATZKY, *Southern Technology Council, Research Park, NC*

INTRODUCTION

A plan is merely words. In order to have any impact, words must be translated into deeds. This involves implementation. Implementing a center's research involves project development project review, evaluation and selection; and project management. In contrast to planning activities described in Chapter 5, many of the implementation activities described in this chapter occur regularly, in a relatively set order and by established procedures.

In many industrial settings implementation means assigning people and resources to carry out projects defined and prioritized in a highly detailed strategic plan. Centers can't work that way. Implementation in an I/UCRC involves identifying, informing, and motivating talented, unobligated researchers to develop and submit high-quality research proposals. It also requires decision-making processes that allow marketplace competitors to reach consensus on a research program. We discuss these and related issues in this chapter. Since planning and implementing the research program are so closely intertwined, readers are encouraged to also read Chapter 5.

Recruiting Colleagues: Soliciting Proposals

The first step in implementing a center's research plan is soliciting from faculty a manageable number of high quality, member-relevant proposals to review. Strategies to solicit proposals vary (see Figure 6-1).

Solicitation can be targeted at specific individuals, usually based on their reputation, previous track record, or prior working relationships with the individual, or it can be open, in which case anyone from a defined population (e.g., all Electrical Engineering and Computer Science faculty) will be offered an opportunity to develop a proposal.

Second, the approach itself can be a personal phone call or a formal letter and request for proposal (RFP). The personal approach

Figure 6-1	Advantages and disadvantages of proposal solicitation strategies		
Dimension	**Option**	**Advantage**	**Disadvantage**
Focus	Targeted solicitation	■ Concentrate on proven reputations ■ High percentage positive contact	■ Miss people outside network ■ Center perceived as closed club
	Open	■ Efficient ■ Keeps door open ■ Encourages new blood	■ Shotgun approach ■ Quality can vary ■ Must screen
Approach	Personal	■ Interactive ■ Allows persuasion	■ Time-consuming ■ Message can get garbled
	Formal RFP	■ Information communicated accurately	■ May be ignored
Scope	Narrowed to one faculty community	■ Reinforces local commitment ■ Money stays close to home	■ May not meet IAB member needs
	Broaden to outside	■ Diverse perspectives ■ Enhanced ability to meet IAB member needs ■ Creates opportunities for multi-university center	■ Money goes off campus ■ Local faculty may get discouraged

allows some preliminary discussion of research ideas, while formal written RFPs may be ignored.

Since talented and creative faculty and graduate students are the life blood of a center, and since all of these options have their advantages and disadvantages (see Figure 6-1), we advocate an eclectic approach. Center Directors and IAB members need to personally solicit proposals from the best and the brightest. This is best accomplished by targeting and directly contacting, and sometimes working with, faculty who possess specific interests or expertise. On the other hand, centers also need to send a message that they welcome new ideas and researchers. This is most easily accomplished by posting and circulating formal announcements and RFPs to relevant departments and individuals.

Directors should solicit proposals from all relevant departments on their campus. As a center matures it should consider targeted and even open solicitation at other institutions. This becomes a practical necessity if a center is unable to meet its members' needs on its own campus. While such arrangements sometimes raise the ire of local administrators, they often have led to multi-university arrangements which have produced a bigger pie. At least one I/UCRC has taken this approach and become a virtual center which accepts proposals from around the country (see Figure 6-2).

Figure 6-2	Center for Innovation Management Studies (CIMS)—A Center Without Walls.

CIMS is an I/UCRC located at Lehigh University. It is devoted to the study of the management of technological innovation and its focus is on management disciplines rather than science or engineering disciplines. Like other I/UCRCs, CIMS is supported by a consortium of members. However, since its inception, CIMS has operated as a 'virtual center' soliciting and supporting proposals from investigators (faculty and graduate students) from across the country. Over the past 12 years, CIMS has funded 75 projects at 40 different universities and 12 institutes. Most projects are relatively small (under $20,000 per year) and require investigators to make a presentation of results at semi-annual research reviews. Investigators and their home institutions must agree to abide by all CIMS policies.

The Request For Proposal (RFP)

A formal written RFP is a very efficient way to communicate information. An RFP can be a letter or a flyer, and should include center name, contact person, deadline, where to send proposals, the type of proposals being requested, budget guidelines or restrictions, timeline and mechanism for review, and expectations of personal presentations to a review group. The RFP package should detail I/UCRC needs and priorities.

Needs/Priorities

Your ability to enlighten prospective researchers about center needs and priorities depends upon the center's investment in its planning process (see Figure 6-3). A center that has produced planning products that accurately reflect IAB members needs will be in a better position to inform.

Proposal Format

The RFP in a center should call for three to four pages written in clear language following a specified format (Appendix 6-1). Respondents should follow a standard executive summary form, organized into sections with white space for a brief response (see Appendix 2-2). These guidelines can be modified for a preliminary concept paper or pre-proposal.

RFP selection criteria should be specified. For example, relative amounts can be assigned to proposal themes:

- Relevance to industrial needs and priorities—40 percent.

- Clear and workable methodology and work plan—20 percent.

- Potential deliverables and products—10 percent.

- Contribution to scientific understanding—20 percent.

- Qualifications of the research team—10 percent.

Figure 6-3	Information provided by planning products.
Product	**Information**
Center Name	Research related to center name
Vision and Mission Statement	Research mission boundaries
Themes or Programs Defined	All of above, plus high and low-priority themes
Goals and Objectives	All of above, plus topics and goals
Roadmap	All of above, plus specific technical obstacles to be overcome or requirements to be met

DEVELOPING VIRTUAL RESEARCH TEAMS

Formal planning and its by-products (e.g., mission statements) can and should be used to inform would-be proposers. However, centers should not rely completely on formal planning because needs and priorities change rapidly. Members sometimes are reluctant to disclose them in public, and a consensus-based planning process may suppress unpopular views. Further, it would be a mistake to assume that a two-year old statement of goals and objectives, no matter how well conceived, necessarily reflects current needs and priorities of IAB members.

Thus, the Center Director can and should compensate for the shortcomings inherent in formal planning products by constantly updating these products or informally briefing faculty based on real-time reconnaissance. Comments and feedback disclosed during the proposal review process provide a rich source of current needs and priorities. However, directors cannot fulfill this role on their own. Faculty also must shoulder the responsibility.

Center proposals and projects should represent the work of virtual industry-university teams. One strategy for achieving this goal involves encouraging and facilitating direct one-on-one interaction between proposers and IAB members perhaps as early as the idea generation phase of new proposals. Unfortunately, because of past experiences many faculty believe they are supposed to develop a research proposal in a hermetically-sealed room with no feedback. Such an approach is anathema in a cooperative research center. Directors can use a number of techniques to avoid this.

- **Consultation.** Faculty can be encouraged or required to consult with at least one IAB member before submitting a proposal. Some centers designate IAB mentors for certain themes or topics. Other centers schedule informal pre-proposal meetings to encourage a collaborative process.

- **Pre-Proposals.** Short informal pre-proposals are an efficient way to test, circulate, and get feedback on ideas. A center may request, usually in the form of a letter, a one-page concept paper or pre-proposal. This is a good way to quickly surface new ideas from investigators. A pre-proposal that doesn't garner at least one champion is a poor bet. Conversely, pre-proposals may spark interest among a few industrial participants and lead to full-fledged proposals. Poster sessions can also be used for this purpose.

■ **Industry Initiated Proposals.** Centers should allow and even encourage industry to submit proposals for projects they would like faculty to pursue.

Motivation

How can a center motivate faculty to follow through and develop proposals? Personal solicitation, opportunities for quick and early feedback on ideas, and minimal proposal documentation should all help motivate proposers. The strongest motivation must be the center concept itself.

It has been suggested that closer university-industry ties may result in faculty being coerced into doing research they would otherwise shun (e.g., Brooks, 1993), but the truth is that faculty are diverse and are not easily coerced. Some faculty are totally curiosity-driven. They get a great deal of satisfaction out of solving theoretical puzzles, enjoy following a question wherever it leads, and typically like to work solo. Other faculty like solving or contributing to the solution of real problems. They respond to a larger mission, are willing to reshape their personal interests in pursuit of a challenging problem, and relish the idea that their work will be put to use. Many enjoy the give and take involved in team research. Thus, some faculty will gravitate toward or away from your center.

The most important thing you can do to motivate appropriate faculty is to create a setting that is ripe with interesting and challenging problems that reinforce problem-driven but theoretical informed research, possesses ample resources, and encourages collaboration and teamwork. Experience shows, if you build it, they will come.

Summary

Good, high quality proposals are the life blood of a center. Centers lacking them must re-evaluate information provided by their formal and informal planning products, ability to communicate this information, nature of solicitation efforts, and organizational culture regarding teamwork.

REVIEW, EVALUATION, AND SELECTION

The overarching goal of the review, evaluation, and selection stage should be to reach an agreement, hopefully a consensus, about allocating resources to research projects. This is undoubtedly the most critical and organizationally challenging stage of the implementation process.

This stage is critical for several reasons. First, this is the point at which members find out if they are in a workable partnership. Review, evaluation, and selection transactions help answer questions like: Will my advice and counsel be heeded by the university? Do the interests of other members converge enough with mine that I will realize the benefits of financial leveraging and technical synergy?

Review, evaluation and selection, if managed correctly, provides a wealth of information about current and future needs and priorities. Information obtained can help keep a center's research relevant. Most important, a center's plans or intentions become reality. Dollars are allocated to projects. The value and success of projects selected during these steps will ultimately determine the success of the center.

Unfortunately, for review, evaluation, and selection to be effective, it is necessary to meet the needs of a diverse group of stakeholders and to conduct constant communication, feedback, and decision-making within a one or two-day time frames. The semi-annual meeting is discussed in more detail in Chapter 7. Because the stakes are so high and the social and interpersonal dynamics so complex, a relatively structured decision-making process is advised. Review, evaluation, and selection are discrete steps (see Figure 6-4) in what should be a sequential decision-making process. Specifically, review provides an opportunity for interactive feedback between proposers and members; evaluation provides an opportunity for members to share their observations with each

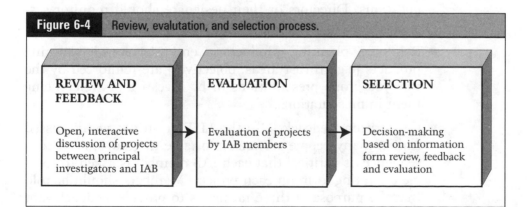

Figure 6-4 Review, evalutation, and selection process.

REVIEW AND FEEDBACK	EVALUATION	SELECTION
Open, interactive discussion of projects between principal investigators and IAB	Evaluation of projects by IAB members	Decision-making based on information form review, feedback and evaluation

other (and hopefully begin to achieve a consensus); and selection involves making decisions about allocating limited resources to projects. Since each step in this process serves a different purpose and requires different conditions, we will discuss each separately.

Project Review and Feedback

The review process should promote candid interactive communication and feedback between individual investigators, IAB members, and other stakeholders. Most of the exchanges will tend to be along paired opposite groupings—between individual faculty and IAB members. Faculty will want an opportunity to communicate ideas and plans, and respond to questions and concerns. Industry, to ensure industrial relevance, will want an opportunity to seek clarification and resolve questions and concerns. The following format has been used extensively within the I/UCRC program and have proven very successful:

- Distribute written proposals in a timely fashion. Nothing irritates IAB members more than to be asked to review and prioritize proposals they haven't had sufficient time to read. Centers should distribute new proposals two to three weeks prior to the semi-annual meeting.

- Schedule oral presentations at semi-annual meetings. Oral presentations are an effective way to promote two-way communication between investigators and IAB members. Faculty and especially graduate students should be encouraged to practice presentations.

- Communicate and enforce time allotments. Since members have already read the written proposals, these sessions should be short, 15- to 20-minute overviews and audience questions. Directors or their designate should monitor sessions to ensure they keep to the time allotted.

- Reinforce planning products. Center-developed planning products (e.g., thrust areas, objectives) are reinforced by the way you group presentations or by investigators referencing them in presentations.

- Get written feedback. Use the LIFE Form. As we discussed earlier, many people are uncomfortable in groups. As a consequence, it's critical that each IAB member is asked to complete a rating form on each project. Members should be told that the purpose of these ratings is to provide feedback (not for selection). Many I/UCRCs use a LIFE form (Level of Interest and Feedback) for this purpose. It is a relatively simple form which includes a single rating scale (interested, interested with change, not interested) and two or three open-ended questions. Setting aside time to complete this form after each presentation (and prompting same) is an effective way of ensuring a high response rate and timely feedback. Instructions and sample forms are presented in Appendices 2-3 and 2-4.

- Share copies of LIFE forms immediately with researchers so they can respond to IAB concerns. Some I/UCRCs facilitate feedback by using multi-copy carbon forms.

- Provide ample opportunity for informal interactions between researchers and IAB members. It's important that sufficient breaks, poster sessions, cocktail hours, and dinners be included on the meeting agenda to permit informal discussions and mutual lobbying activities.

Evaluation

The evaluation process should facilitate consensus within the IAB about the quality and relevance of individual projects. In order to achieve this goal, one must promote candid, interactive (multi-party) exchange of information and opinions. Sometimes the ratings provided during review are so clear-cut, Center Directors are tempted to skip formal evaluation. This is a mistake! If handled correctly, the processes that occur during this stage should allow members to gain a sense of where each other is coming from and also provide the Center Director with a veritable gold mine of information about current and future member needs, desires and priorities. These inputs constitute high-quality, real-time reconnaissance. As we have discussed elsewhere, they can and should be used to shape the center's emergent plan.

This kind of evaluation requires a group format and facilitator. The following procedures have proven very successful in the I/UCRC program.

Procedures for evaluating proposals:

- Summarize and share LIFE feedback. Someone, often the evaluator, should take responsibility for producing a hard copy summary (newsprint or handouts), aggregating ratings (simple frequency counts) and transcribing open-ended comments on each project. The process has also been automated (see Figure 6-5). The summary should list the total budget requested for each project. IAB members should be given an opportunity to review the ratings and comments for each project.

■ Reinforce the center's plan. There's no reason to have a plan if it isn't used when you're preparing for project prioritization and resource allocation decisions. This is particularly true if you've invested time and energy in soliciting proposals and PIs based on your plan! As a consequence, this is as good a time as any to refer the members back to your center's mission, goals, thrust areas, etc.

■ Select a discussion leader. Someone must act as the discussion leader during the project evaluations, probably the Center Director. However, evaluators and IAB chair people have also filled this role. The Center Director should leave the room when his or her own project is evaluated to avoid conflict of interest.

■ Promote a thorough discussion of each project. The facilitator ensures evaluation not selection takes place and encourages discussion of the merits and shortcoming of each project. One tactic is to recite comments, questions, and concerns from the transcribed LIFE forms and invite clarification and discussion from the IAB. Another tactic is to ask: "What makes this project so 'hot'?" "Why isn't anyone interested in this one?" "How could we improve this project?" The director can comment and provide relevant background information.

■ Encourage real-time project revision. Be particularly attentive to IAB requests for project changes. An IAB member vote

Figure 6-5	The Graphic Program for LIFE, and meeting effectiveness data.

The Graphic Program (GP), developed by the evaluation team at Texas A&M University, provides evaluators with pre-formatted data entry spreadsheets which are auto-linked to chart templates. Using the GP evaluators are able to quickly and easily format spreadsheets and graphics, adapting them to their individual center's needs. With the GP, at IAB meetings evaluators can quickly compile LIFE and meeting effectiveness data, and graphically present this data (either on a paper handout, computer projection screen, or transparency-overhead projector), along with previous meeting data, immediately following entry of data. Also included in the GP are MSWord® files containing LIFE and meeting effectiveness survey questionnaire form templates.

may be influenced positively if the facilitator declares immediately that the investigator will accommodate them. Obviously, some changes (a merger of two related projects) may require active consultation, extensive revision, or re-submission that cannot be settled immediately.

■ Make sure someone takes copious notes. Comments about needs or priorities which don't relate to current projects probably have implications for future projects!

Selection

Project selection methods discussed in standard textbooks (Martino, 1995) are complex, and highly quantitative and inappropriate for the more informal I/UCRC planning and implementation process.

A center's selection process should meet two fundamental criteria. First, it should provide a process for allocating resources to thrusts and projects in a way that is consistent with the center's formal plan (e.g., goals, objectives) and at the same time is responsive to the center's emergent plan. The foundation for achieving this goal should have been laid in the discussions held during this review and evaluation stage.

In addition, the selection process must meet the strategic and psychological needs of IAB members. For most members, the ability to prioritize research projects and to shape the center's research portfolio is the single most important privilege they get from their annual membership fee. Because it can help create a sense of participation in the center and ownership of the research program, it can have great personal and psychological significance for the IAB member. Experience indicates that an IAB member who doesn't get the opportunity to participate actively and personally in the selection process, will soon lose interest in attending semi-annual meetings, resulting in an inevitable loss of commitment to the center.

Preliminaries

A few preliminaries to selection must be handled.

Review financial, staff, and capital resources. Before the IAB allocates resources to projects, they need budget and resource information. At a minimum, the total amount of funding available for projects, approximately how many projects can be supported, need for specialized equipment, current project commitments within each research area, and any external factors against committing support should be provided.

Decide on format. Some IAB members prefer that no staff is present during selection. This allows them to discuss projects and personnel candidly. On the other hand, experience shows that IABs often need to clarify certain points while they are making their decisions. The IAB should be asked if the Center Director is to sit in on their deliberations or be available. Most I/UCRC centers that go into a closed executive session allow the NSF representative and the evaluator to sit in as observers.

Informal Approach: Reaching a Consensus

When an IAB is small, homogeneous, and cohesive, and project evaluation is relatively clear cut, discussion held during the evaluation stage can approximate the selection discussion. In these cases, often the selection moderator, usually the IAB chairperson, can achieve a consensus by following the steps described below. This approach has the advantage of avoiding conflict within your board.

- Review and revisit LIFE project ratings. Since ratings may have changed because of the evaluation discussion, it's wise to ask if there is interest in revising the LIFE forms.

- Reach decisions on the tail ends of the rating distribution. Generally, there is little debate about the highest rated and the lowest rated projects. The goal of this step is to approve a few of the highest rated projects and to eliminate a few of the lowest rated projects.

- Select among remaining projects. The IAB selects from remaining projects after a brief review of the strengths and weaknesses of each project, including how they fit into the center's plan or complement other projects, and how they meet the needs of specific members. This usually leads to a real-time revision of ratings. Members are asked if the failure to fund a particular project would affect negatively their ability to maintain their membership. One benefit of this approach is it sometimes results in one or several members agreeing to provide enhancement support for projects that fall below the funding threshold. (See section titled *Research Enhancements* in Chapter 11.)

Structured Approach: Allocating 1,000 Points of Light

If your IAB is large, diverse, not particularly cohesive, or demonstrates significant disagreement during evaluation of various projects, a formal voting or rating procedure to select projects is advised. Projects can be rated, ranked, and approved until there is no more money. However, with most rating systems minority interests are put at a severe disadvantage. Members with interests or needs out of synch with the majority won't have the votes to get funded. In fact, this is one reason for reluctance to join a center[7]. The following weighted voting scheme mitigates this concern.

- Provide voting points. Each member is given the same number of points. The number of points is arbitrary. Some centers give members 1,000 points. Other centers have found that members like the symbolism of getting one point for every $1,000 of membership support.

- Members allocate points across projects. Members express their priorities by dividing points among top projects. A member may allocate points equally among top projects (e.g., 250 points each). A member who is only interested in two projects might allocate points to two projects (e.g., 500 points each).

- Tally points and select projects. Similar to the procedure described above, support is allocated to the projects with the most points.

This approach is effective in producing a research portfolio everyone can support, but it is only a temporary solution to a board with divergent interests. A center made up of nothing but outliers will not survive very long. A lack of leveraging and a mishmash of projects with little synergy will seal its fate. When using this approach the goal should be to bring outliers into the mainstream or add more members who share similar interest.

PROJECT MANAGEMENT: BACK TO THE FUTURE

While it is inappropriate in a chapter on implementation to delve into issues that are strictly management, there are some aspects

---

[7]At least one center has avoided this problem by letting new members assign their first year's membership fee to a specific project.

of project management that have implications for planning. As a project unfolds and is implemented, does it remain "true" to the original project proposal and, by extension, to its place in the overall plan of the center? Project management in the context of a university-industry cooperative research center does not have the same meaning that it has in an industrial setting. Teams of faculty and graduate students tend to be autonomous, and at best a Center Director can provide some informal oversight and guidance. This is, of course, supplemented by the project reviews that take place at the periodic IAB meetings, and by special committees that the IAB may establish. Whatever the processes of project management that are in place, the following are the important issues and questions from a planning perspective.

Projects and Critical Paths on the Roadmap

Some projects may be more critical than others. A project addressing a key question may force redrawing the road map and revising planning goals. By the same token, a project yielding positive or revolutionary results may also demand revising the roadmap and plan. As each project moves along to completion the center leadership needs to assess its effect on other projects.

Projects, Structure, and Partnerships

One of the planning issues that often becomes acute during project execution is the need for additional or complementary research capacities. A project or research area outcome may be more satisfactory if the team has access to special equipment or experts. These observations should not be ignored. They have implications for planning strategic partnerships or personnel that the center should develop. A center which is launched from one university may need to evolve into a multi-institutional structure, with greatly enhanced research capacities and industrial participation.

Termination of Projects

One result of project management LIFE evaluations and oversight may be a decision to terminate a project. This is always painful, but should be done when it appears that continuation of an effort will not benefit the program. Sometimes a project is terminated when a key principal investigator or graduate student leaves the university. This has implications for planning to disband this line of work or to acquire, directly or through partnership, new human resources. A project may be terminated when preliminary results or findings indicate that a line of inquiry is an unpromising blind alley or effort has been lacking[8]. In all cases of project terminations, there will be decisions about how to reinvest resources.

SUMMARY AND CONCLUSIONS

In some respects, implementation in an I/UCRC resembles conventional R&D implementation. Decisions should be guided by the by-products (e.g., goals, thrusts) of the planning process. Implementation is approached sequentially: project development; project review, evaluation, and selection; and project management. However, the process deviates from industrial R&D implementation in a number of respects. First, it depends heavily on a Center Director's ability to identify, recruit, and motivate talented researchers. Second, the selection process must produce a viable research portfolio balanced on the needs of market-place competitors. Finally and most important, because soft planning requires short feedback cycles, directors must capitalize on the information gathering opportunities inherent in the implementation process and use this information to make appropriate adjustments in the center's research plan.

REFERENCES

Brooks, H. Research Universities and The Social Contract for Science. In Branscomb, L.M. (Ed.) *Empowering Technology*. Cambridge, MA, MIT Press, 1993, pp.202- 234.

Martino, J.P. *Research and Development Project Selection*. New York: Wiley 1995.

---

[8]NSF/I/UCRCs always ensure graduate student thesis plans are not affected by termination decisions.

APPENDIX 6-1
Sample Standard RFP Format

- Investigators name, departmental and institutional affiliation.

- Industry need, problem or theoretical issues.
  Length: half-page maximum.

- Review of Relevant Existing Research. Should be clear and draw from non-academic sources as well as patent literature and member company reports.
  Length: one-page maximum.

- One or two goals and a few attainable objectives should be stated in behavioral, operational terms.
  Length: half-page.

- Work plan organized into research tasks specifying approach and methodology, level-of-effort and expected products and deliverables.
  Length: one to two pages.

- Budget for the project by major categories.

- Relevance to center plan research themes, goals and objectives, and specific IAB member company interests.
  Length: half-page to one page.

- (Specify font size, margins, number of words, an overall page limit, and *curriculum vitae* to be attached.)

CHAPTER 7

COMMUNICATIONS

HOWARD LEVINE, *California College of Arts and Crafts, San Francisco*

VIRGINIA SHAW-TAYLOR, *Evaluator Emeritus, Consultant, Golden, CO*

COOPERATION REQUIRES COMMUNICATION

Scientists and university faculty members are often caricatured by stereotypes inimical to good communication: The wooly-headed, white-coated scientist who is totally self-absorbed and speaks a language understood only by seven other colleagues studying the same arcane problem, and the absent-minded professor who rarely remembers the day of the week and rambles on so long that he forgets the question half way through the putative answer. While we all may know someone who exhibits a few of these traits, the stereotypes are counterproductive in the arena of modern scientific research, which is very much a cooperative process. Cooperation puts a premium on the scientist's ability to communicate with other scientists and with funding agencies, administrators, technicians, graduate students, and editorial boards. Add to that list the industrial representatives at I/UCRCs and it becomes clear that today's successful scientists (and scientific administrators) must be well versed in the art of communication.

Communication theory—the study of systems and techniques that encourage or impede the transfer of information and understanding—is both a science and an art. As a science, communication theory began in the 1940s with the work of Shannon, Weaver, and Wiener. To a great extent, the information society, with its computers, satellites, and coming super highway, is built on their work and the realization that information may be mathematically modeled. But these discoveries have little to do with successful communication between individuals or within organizations, which relies much more on the art of communication. Today, social scientists are rigorously studying all aspects of interpersonal communication in order to determine the best methods for conveying information and understanding (Werner, 1995). The section titled *Cooperation Requires Communication* in this chapter surveys that work. It is presented as a series of questions and checklists that the reader may use to assess the communication environment within his/her organization, and to improve personal communication skills. The section titled *Requirements for Internal Communications* in this chapter details formal communication tasks faced by a center.

In addition to a matrix that catalogs these tasks along with their rationale and the party responsible, sample letters, lists, outlines, and agreements are included.

Communicating Within an Organization

Center Directors are responsible for more than their own personal communications; they also are responsible for establishing a center culture that facilitates effective communication. To be sure, corporate culture has become something of a meaningless buzzword, but it masks an underlying truth: all organizations have both stated and unstated values which form an organization's culture. The I-We-Them-It Principle is a way to understand an organization's culture.

I   How are individual staff regarded by the organization? Is there a premium put on individual initiative or is the premium put on organizational unity?

We   How do individuals relate to each other within the organization? Is the structure hierarchical (authoritarian) or interpersonal (democratic)?

Them How does the organization view its "clients?" Are they seen as part of an extended family or as customers whose needs must be met?

It   How does the organization perceive its major task. What does it do? Is the job to produce the best product possible or is it to help clients make the best possible use of its products?

There are, of course, no right or wrong answers concerning which values to choose. While most centers will want to embrace and communicate I/UCRC values like industry relevance, cooperation, and teamwork, there are successful centers with authoritarian management styles just as there are successful centers with democratic management styles; there are successful centers that treat their industrial members as part of an extended family and there are successful centers that view their industrial members as a customer base. It is the communication of the chosen values, rather than the values themselves, that is the hallmark of a successful center, and that communication must begin with the Center Director. This position must communicate what the center stands for to both the center staff and the outside world. What are its core values? While there are many means for accomplishing this, three rules (or opportunities) seem foremost.

Use the Socialization Process to Communicate the Corporate Culture

This is a key example of watch what we do, not what we say. New staff and graduate students will learn more about center values from observing how their colleagues interact, how the industrial members are treated, and how students and the professional staff relate than they will from speeches. Centers are high turnover organizations; students, faculty, and IAB members are continually joining and leaving the center. Research indicates that the initial weeks of contact are a critical period for the manager to exert influence and that this influence wanes after the first month or so. This means that recruiting contacts, semi-annual meetings, the hiring process and early training are especially vital in transmitting the center's values.

Link Specific Behaviors with Center Values

By definition, values are abstract concepts, but they can be made concrete by linking them with specific behaviors that model the value. For example, a center that believes itself to be run democratically needs policies and procedures that allow everyone to have his or her voice heard. A center that is committed to seeing its research commercialized might have a checklist that contains all the steps it will take once the research result is transferred out of the center to the IAB firm. A center which believes in team work will set aside some funding for multi-investigation projects. Once again, communication need not always be in the form of words.

Maintain an Open Door Policy

The easiest way to stifle communication is to let word get out that top management isn't interested. An open door policy doesn't mean that literally, but it does mean that the organization has a procedure (e.g., suggestion box, anonymous e-mail, specific times) that allows all staff, and in the case of centers, members, to make suggestions and vent their frustrations. The evaluation system described in Chapter 7 and elsewhere is an example of this approach. All successful organizations know that good ideas can come from any member and many corporations have employee incentive programs designed to encourage communication of ideas.

Information Flow Within the Organization

Perhaps the most efficient way to conceive of an organization's paper flow is through a table or matrix. The I/UCRC Information Flow Matrix presents a detailed listing of task categories with its producers and recipients (Figure 7-1). It provides a quick overview of a center's information flow. More detailed tables may be produced for each subtask.

However, communication involves more than routing patterns. A Center Director also must understand factors which facilitate or impair the flow of information. The following five strategic principles are rules of thumb for managing that flow.

The More Links in a Communication Chain, the More Likely That the Message Will Get Distorted

This argues for shorter chains or feedback mechanisms to ensure accuracy. For example, I/UCRCs may want to communicate directly with bench level scientists at their member firms while such communications may typically be transmitted through IAB representatives or managers. In order to avoid the distortions that such communication links may generate, centers might encourage IAB firms to send bench scientists to the semi-annual meetings, request that center researchers give at least one symposium a year at each member facility, secure distribution lists from member firms so that research reports can be mailed directly, or make reports available via computer bulletin boards.

The Form in Which the Information Is Presented Can Be As Important As Its Substance

In order to encourage high standards for both quality and presentation, Appendix 7-5 contains guidelines for preparing technical

Figure 7-1	Information flow matrix.			
	Semi-Annual Meeting	**Formal Reports**	**Internal Communications**	**External Communications**
Center				
Staff	P	P	P/R	P
Faculty	P/R		P	
Students	P/R		P	
University				
Administration	R	R	R	R
Financial	P/R	P/R	P/R	
Departments	R			R
Public Relations				P
Membership				
Technical Reps	R			R
Management	R			R
Scientists	R			R
Sponsoring Orgs.				
NSF	R	R		R
State	R	R		R
Other	R	R		R
Public				
Other Centers				R
Member				R
Public Media				R

Key: P = Producer of Communication   R = Recipient of Communication

presentations. Unfortunately, the rule governing form and content is uni-directional: splashy graphics and typesetting cannot turn poor results into award winning research, but unintelligible graphs and an illegible typeface can fail to communicate even the best research.

The Message Is Never Independent From the Source

Communication is a social act; as such, knowledge of the sender's identity is usually a vital piece of information for our interpretation of the message. The successful manager must know how to manipulate that context, (e.g., the differences among a communication from the Center Director, Professor Smith, or Jack although all are the same person) and when it must be masked entirely (e.g., blind reading of proposals, frank personnel appraisals).

The Quality of Information

The quality of information in a message decreases as it moves further away from the sender's expertise and experience. Professor Smith may be the ranking expert on chemical lasers, but is there any reason to think that his memo on the office's new mailing equipment deserves to be given expert status. Do not confuse the message with the messenger. As Center Director, you need to be aware of your staff's qualifications and expertise.

Be Aware Of Each Individual's Information Load
And His or Her Ability To Handle It

Cases of information overload can often be ameliorated by answering a few specific questions: Does the organizational structure create information bottlenecks? For example, must all reports from PIs to the IAB go through the Center Director? Does everyone on routing lists really need the information? Can the decision-making process be streamlined? Can a decision regarding allocating new funds be handled by conference call or fax vote instead of arranging a meeting? Are reports being generated for which there is no real audience? Can reports that are being prepared for different audiences (e.g., NSF and University administrators) be merged to prevent duplicated effort?

Unfortunately, following these principles does not ensure a well-oiled communication machine. Yet, failing to heed them will almost certainly guarantee an organization that does a poor job of communicating.

REQUIREMENTS FOR INTERNAL COMMUNICATIONS

Even if an organization's values and information flow design support quality communication, defining that quality remains. Too often, we focus solely on the message itself. If we prepare a memorandum, or talk, or proposal we assume effective communication is bound to occur. Unfortunately, this fails to acknowledge the interactive nature of communication.

The following seven clusters of suggestions that correspond to the seven numbered steps in Figure 7-2 are designed to help you maximize your communication opportunities. No one has the

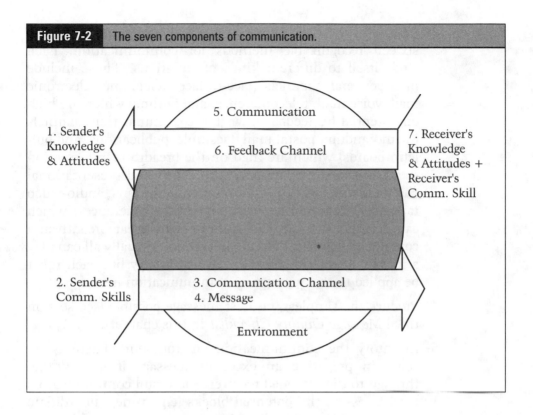

Figure 7-2   The seven components of communication.

5. Communication

1. Sender's Knowledge & Attitudes

6. Feedback Channel

7. Receiver's Knowledge & Attitudes + Receiver's Comm. Skill

2. Sender's Comm. Skills

3. Communication Channel
4. Message

Environment

time to review all the steps every time they need to communicate. Awareness of their existence, as well as explicit referral for those critical communication chores, especially when you're having a communication problem, will help ensure that you've maximized your messaging abilities.

1. Inventory your own knowledge and attitudes regarding the information you wish to communicate. Before beginning "external" communication, have an internal dialogue: What is the purpose of my message? Why am I communicating? Is my purpose to simply convey information (e.g., report to NSF), persuade someone of my point of view (e.g., sell a new recruit), begin a dialogue (e.g., refine a research program)? Do I understand all the ramifications of these ideas?

2. Inventory your ability to formulate and send messages. Given the type of message you need to send, which medium do you feel most comfortable using. In considering your communication strengths, you also need to consider the suitability of different types of communications channels.

3. Choose the best medium to express your message. There are sixteen recognizable methods for communication. Each lends itself to different kinds of situations. These include inter-personal channels (face-to-face, telephone, electronic mail, voice mail, teleconference, and hotline) which are high on potential for feedback, written communication channels (memorandum, postal mail, facsimile, publications, and bulletin boards) which are high on the breadth of information they can transmit and their scanability, and presentational channels (group meetings, formal presentations, audio-video tapes, computer conferences, and video conferences) which can be expensive but can accommodate great breadth and complexity and allow group interaction. Virtually all can play a role in a center's communication strategy but each must be applied to the appropriate communication need.

4. Produce the simplest, clearest message possible (see section titled *Message Quality Checklist* in this chapter).

5. Inventory the communication environment. There is no sense in preparing an excellent message if it can't get through to the intended receiver. Successful communicators need to assess the potential blocks (e.g., time, subordinate screening, delays in feedback) in the environment and devise strategies for avoiding them.

6. Leave a communication channel open for feedback. This may be the most important and overlooked aspect of effective communication. Good communicators are good listeners. At its simplest level feedback lets you know that your message was received. Feedback shows the receiver that you are open to ideas, and it gives you an opportunity to learn how the ideas contained in your message might be improved and how you may be able to improve your communication skills. This principle is just as important for written communication as it is for face-to-face oral communication. There are many opportunities for centers to demonstrate that they are listening and open to suggestions.

7. Understand the receiver's ability to receive your message. The biggest mistake a communicator makes is to think that just because he has created a simple, clear message, his work is done. Effective expression is not equal to effective communication. Successful communicators understand that the receivers of their messages are really interpreters of their

messages. For example, pitches to prospective corporate members must take into account the roles that different individuals play at the corporation: opportunities for technical information exchange may be what the research staff is interested in, while financial managers may be more interested in tax and overhead benefits.

Message Quality Checklist

The following are tried and true ways of avoiding distortion of your message. Reviewing these guidelines (and sharing with center staff periodically) should help improve your communication efficiency.

Decide Your Real Purpose in Communicating

Try to make the message and the intent consistent. Is the purpose simply to convey information (e.g., the results of a study) or persuade someone (e.g., convince a firm to join the I/UCRC) or begin a dialogue (e.g., what direction should we take in the future?). Each purpose dictates a different tone and content to the message. As described above, purpose will also affect the choice of communication channel (i.e., formality vs. personal warmth).

Reduce the Number of People Through Whom a Message Must Travel

It is better to spend some time deciding who is the best person to receive your message than just sending it to a large firm and hoping it gets to the right individual. Distributing reports directly to a member's technical staff may ensure valuable information gets to where it can do the most good.

Orient Your Message to a Particular Receiver

Many faculty are used to making presentations to other academics who may be interested most in theoretical results. Alternatively, industrial scientists may be interested more in the tools embedded in a research project. Good communication requires being able to understand the receiver's motivations and needs.

Limit the Amount of Information in Your Message

Most I/UCRCs get good results using short report and presentation formats.

Preview and Review the Material in Your Message

Practice the rule of three: Tell them what you're going to tell them, tell them, and tell them what you told them.

Simplify Your Messages

Distinguish between important and unimportant information. You cannot tell your audience everything you know about a research project in 15 minutes. Who is the audience? What will be of most interest to them? What's changed since the last time you spoke?

Report Details In Order

Use some form of consistent organization such as chronological, spatial, or cause-effect sequencing. Place important information at the beginning or end of your message, never in the middle.

Highlight Important Information

Use headlines, type sizes, and key phrases to make the key points.

Use Visuals for Oral Presentations

When making oral presentations slow down, use handouts, and make sure that all slides/overheads are visible and understandable from the back of the room.

Consider the Consequences of Your Communication

What if everything you propose is attempted? How will it affect you? the organization? Never "open the door" unless you are willing to take suggestions seriously. For instance, don't solicit input on the center's research agenda unless you're willing to follow it.

Summary

Up to this point we have tried to convey some of the general principles of effective communication and how they might apply to a cooperative research center. In the remainder of the chapter we will discuss strategies for improving critical I/UCRC communication transactions in four areas: the semi-annual meeting, formal reporting, internal communications, and external communications. Each section will include a table which lists significant communication transactions or tools. Where appropriate, copies of tools or communication specimens are included in the appendix.

For instance, Appendix 7-1 is a master calendar of communication commitments.

THE SEMI-ANNUAL MEETING

The semi-annual meeting focuses interaction between the university researcher and the IAB member. Since most industry and university communication takes place at the IAB meetings, it is natural to conclude that IAB meetings are the single most important communication opportunity for a center. In order to maximize this opportunity, we have identified the aspects of a successful meeting. Figure 7-3 provides a list of meeting communication transactions and related tools.

Planning and Preparation

Good meetings just don't happen, they are the result of meeting logistics (time and location, facilities, materials and supplies) and advance communications. Formal letters of invitation signed by the Center Director should be sent to IAB members, representatives of outside agencies, university officials, and guests, eight to ten weeks before the meeting. One month before the meeting, an interim information package containing a final meeting agenda, a sheet detailing transportation and lodging options, a membership update, and any briefing papers that attendees are expected to read before the meeting, are sent to attendees.

Preparation of the agenda is crucial (see Figure 7-4). All IAB meetings should give members a status report on the center's operations and technical information and ask for feedback on the current and proposed research problems, opportunities and initiatives.

Technical Presentations

The major reason for semi-annual meetings is the technical presentations. The appendix provides suggestions to make certain they are optimal. As the Center Director, you need to establish a format and ensure enough lead time so that all presentations are polished by the time of the meeting. One large center suggests that presenters and schedules must be finalized six weeks before the meeting to print the program in time. Hard copy materials are due to the Center Director three weeks before the program is finalized. Mail presentation materials two weeks before the meeting.

Figure 7-3	Semi-annual meeting communications matrix.	
WHAT	**WHO**	**WHY**
Meeting Checklist (7-2)*	Center Staff	Account for all meeting details.
Facility Checklist (7-3)	Center Staff	Detailed list for venue.
Supplies Checklist	Center Staff	Detailed list for material and supplies.
Meeting Agenda	Director	Overall meeting plan and objectives.
Research Proposals (7-4)	Faculty, Students	New initiatives for IAB consideration and selection.
Presentation Guidelines (7-5)	Faculty, Students	Report status of ongoing research.
LIFE Forms (2-5 and Chapter 5)	All	Assessment of new and ongoing research.
Poster Feedback (7-6)	IAB	Feedback to student presenters.
Closed IAB Meeting (7-7)	IAB, Eval., NSF	Overview of center administration and research.
IAB Business Agenda (7-8)	Dir., IAB, Eval, NSF	Center status, select new projects, IAB feedback.
IAB Minutes	IAB Chair	Record of meeting.
Additional Activities	All	Meetings may include scheduled activities such as workshops, demonstrations, and special talks designed to facilitate the transfer of information.
Informal Meeting	All	Successful meetings include unscheduled time for networking and exchange of information.

*Appendix references in parenthesis.

Videotaping rehearsals are scheduled two weeks prior to the meeting. Finally, posters are due the day before the meeting begins. A map showing the location of individual posters is distributed at the morning IAB meeting.

A 15-minute technical presentation for all projects before the entire group is not written in stone. While we recommend brief

| Figure 7-4 | Typical semi-annual meeting outline. |

FIRST DAY:

Morning Session

Welcome, Introductions, Opening Remarks, Review of Schedule

Technical Review

Reports of On-going Research
(Allow between 10 and 20 minutes with time for questions and written comment.)

Brief break mid-morning, Networking

Noon

Lunch and Networking

Afternoon Session

Presentation of new proposals and/or research reports
(Allow for completion of LIFE forms, analysis, and posting.)

Brief break mid-afternoon, Networking

Poster Session, On-going Research and/or New Research Proposals

Evening Session

Dinner and Networking
(Some Centers have special speakers.)

SECOND DAY

AM Session

Closed Meeting with IAB and NSF program manager and evaluator
(Held before IAB meeting.)

IAB Business Meeting

Note: Some Centers meet for longer than a day and a half, depending on size of the Center, the number of research projects, etc.

one page executive summaries for all projects, many centers have experimented with projects presented as tutorials, sessions run in parallel, poster sessions for projects for which there is no time or reason for a full technical presentation, videos, presentations by IAB members about their firm's research, and non-I/UCRC speakers. In principle, there is no restriction on presentations except that they communicate what needs to be communicated, by whom, for whom, and for what purpose.

Operational Activities

Business meeting topics include budget; personnel including center staff, faculty researchers, and graduate students; research status and direction; and any changes in the bylaws. Because the business meeting is an established part of every semi-annual meeting, it should be possible to routinize the reporting of information beforehand to allow for decision making at the session. For example, a summary overview of the source and application of funds and revenue available for new project support should indicate to the IAB how much funding is available for allocation to new research. Likewise, a chart of center statistics showing past performance and current status (e.g., inputs—members, faculty, graduate students, staff, and outputs—articles, patents, conferences) is useful. Mailing a version of the Evaluator's Annual Report well in advance of the meeting and allowing the center evaluator to make a brief presentation regarding the process questionnaire results also helps. Orientation of new IAB members can be facilitated by early mailing of materials and arranging for new members to arrive half a day early to meet with center staff. Assigning a knowledgeable person to stay with the new member during the meeting is advisable. Business meetings should be short and simple. Meeting time is too valuable to waste.

Industry Feedback

Good meetings require formal and informal industry feedback. Of course, the most obvious is industry reaction to technical presentations. I/UCRCs have developed a Level of Interest Feedback Evaluation (LIFE) form and process for assuring such communication (see Chapter 6). The appendix has a LIFE form that may be customized for poster or technical presentations. Using the forms (see Chapter 6) to track levels of IAB interest may be a good way to determine their commitment to your center.

Less formal, but no less important, is the opportunity at meetings to receive industry feedback regarding new policies, research directions, and funding initiatives. Listening is important. If you are doing more than a quarter of the talking, you're not doing a good job of listening. Do not monopolize the meeting explaining your ideas, proposals, and initiatives. They should be written out and distributed prior to the meeting. The focus of the meeting should be answering questions and exploring alternatives.

Finally, the entire meeting must be seen as an opportunity to swap ideas. The savvy Center Director knows that sometimes presentation structure can get in the way of conversation, so good meetings have plenty of unscheduled time built into them. Unscheduled does not mean unproductive.

Conducting the Meeting

An agenda is like a road map, but it doesn't tell you how smooth the trip will be. The quality of the meeting is a function of the interactions that occur.

- Don't deviate from the pre-meeting agenda. Participants arrive with expectations. The interim information package gives them time to plan which sessions to attend and which to skip; so avoid changes. At worst, many changes can torpedo the whole meeting by creating confusion.

- Consider various modes of presentation. Sitting for more than a day and being talked at is a prescription for listener burn-out. Are there presentations that can make use of different communication media? Even if most of the presentations must be lectures, how can feedback be ensured? A passive listener is often a bored and ineffective listener. Consider questions, discussion groups, bulletin boards to solicit interactive participation.

- Practice, Practice, Practice. While every meeting has its own unique dynamics, the typical IAB meeting is a series of research presentations. Each of these presentations should be prepared, rehearsed, video taped if possible, and polished. Use the information for effective research presentations.

- Effective Chairperson. Effective chairing of a meeting requires attention to both tasks and human relations. Starting on time and keeping to the agenda are the bare bones tasks. Participation can often be facilitated by making a clear, initial statement of the meetings goals, emphasizing that all contributions are valuable and probing to clarify ideas or concerns.

Use the final session to come to closure by restating the objectives, synthesizing the key accomplishments, explaining the next actions, and thanking everyone for their participation and reminding them when the next meeting will be held.

The Informal Meeting

Of course, as with most meetings, quite a bit of the important business is the result of one-on-one conversation between formal sessions. Centers must program as much informal time as possible (pre-meeting cocktail hours, coffee breaks, PI-IAB networking sessions, and group dinners) and try to capitalize on the communication opportunities. This type of informal communication puts a premium on listening skills. Whether you are talking to the IAB chair or a first-year graduate student, effective listening is important. The following principles should help ensure you receive the most information from each communication opportunity.

Keep an Open Mind

Remember that thought is faster than speech so it is always possible to jump to erroneous conclusions. While difficult, try to suspend judgment until you've heard and understood the speaker's main point(s). Fight against stereotypes and past, unpleasant associations. The IAB representative from Universal Widgets may generally be a cranky complainer but he may have something very valuable to say.

Listen for Ideas

In reading, we've taught ourselves to skim the passage until we reach the central idea. Listening has no skim button, therefore it is essential not to get bogged down in anecdote or embellishment. When in doubt, always ask politely, "What's the most important idea you want me to take way from this conversation?"

Resist Distractions

IAB meetings can be like three ring circuses. There is always some distracting noise, or activity, or interruption. Part of being a good listener is putting co-conversationalists at ease, letting them know that they have your undivided attention. This probably means that conversations will have to be short. Give each person you talk to your maximum attention and offer to speak with them at a future time if it is not possible to conclude the conversation in the time allotted.

Use Summary Notes

The faintest writing is sharper than the brightest memory. Take notes during the conversation that include the speaker's name and a one line summary at the end of a conversation to allow for follow-up.

Meetings are complex functions that can take on a life of their own. Experience has shown that early planning, paying attention to details, rehearsing presentations, facilitating feedback, and listening are the important keys to a successful IAB meeting.

FORMAL REPORTING REQUIREMENTS

Formal reporting requirements need to be filed according to a well-established schedule. The key to these communication tasks is to develop a system for routinizing them (see Figure 7-5). In the NSF program, the Evaluator Annual Report, Process Questionnaire, and Exit Interview are the center evaluator's responsibility. The Director's Questionnaire and Proposal Renewal are the responsibility of the Center Director, Evaluator, and staff. Other government programs will have their own reporting requirements. Keep to a defined annual schedule. Begin collecting process data in the summer so the report will be ready for inclusion in the renewal proposal deadline. Review last year's reports, the Center

Figure 7-5	Formal reporting communications matrix.	
WHAT	**WHO**	**WHY**
Evaluators Report (8-1* and Chapter 8)	Evaluator	Progress, challenges, opportunities facing center.
Process Questionnaire (Chapters 6, 8)	Evaluator	Data from faculty and IAB, expressing their views of center operation.
Enter Interview (7-9)	Evaluator	Establish baseline expectations for new member.
Exit Interview (Chapter 6)	Evaluator	Ascertain reasons for leaving.
Director's Report	Director	Basic data regarding center operation.
Proposal Renewal	Director, Evaluator	Continue NSF funding. Add yearly evaluator report.

*Appendix reference in parenthesis.

Director's report should not fluctuate much year to year. Prepare important documents for IAB meetings with enough lead time to ensure a proper review, revision, and production cycle. Maintain a distribution list so that all relevant parties receive the required reports.

INTERNAL COMMUNICATIONS

Budgets, personnel evaluation, and progress reports are internal communications with which every organization must comply. These communication tasks present no special problems (see Figure 7-6). However, other internal communication tasks are complicated by the fact that the I/UCRC has faculty members from many departments, its ultimate goal is the commercialization of research, and its audience is both the research community and the IAB.

On most college campuses, departments are autonomous. They make independent hiring and tenure decisions, secure outside funding from different sources, and often report to different ad-

Figure 7-6	Internal communications matrix.	
WHAT	**WHO**	**WHY**
Proposal Summary (7-10)*	Researcher	
Quarterly Report (7-11)	Researcher	Monitor research progress report.
Annual Report (7-12)	Researcher	Present project results, opportunities to IAB.
General Administrative	Center Staff	Budgets, contact lists, lists of publications, general record keeping, reports.
Informal Contacts	All	Complete record of contacts with member firms (visits, correspondence, e-mail, phone, conferences).
Variance Analysis	Director, Assoc. Dir., Evaluator	Significant variances in budgets operating and research targets, must be examined and appropriate action taken.

*Appendix reference in parenthesis.

ministrative units. The successful I/UCRC must conduct meaningful interdisciplinary research despite academic autonomy and competition. Center culture should emphasize that all ideas, from any quarter, are valued and that research itself takes precedence within the I/UCRC over more parochial concerns. One method for doing this is brainstorming. Brainstorming adheres to these rules: (1) ideas are generated, not evaluated, (2) the more ideas the better; (3) building on the ideas of others is encouraged, and (4) far out ideas are welcome. Additional strategies include seminars, co-authoring papers, guest lecturing in colleagues classes, shared responsibility for theses committees, and assigning graduate students from different disciplines to the same research project. Judicious use of a research tracking report should also help. In an interdisciplinary world, the isolation of autonomous university departments has long outlived its usefulness. I/UCRCs communicate that message.

Since I/UCRC research supports the field and commercialization efforts, two communication strategies are necessary. First is the formal communication that takes place between the IAB and the university researcher: the initial research proposal, the use of LIFE forms at the meetings, the preparation of research reports. Each of these is designed to inform the IAB of progress and intentions, and to elicit comments about how to proceed in order to best meet industry's needs. Second is I/UCRCs' informal communication regarding research: talks at the industrial site, site and reverse site visits, industry staff spending an extended time on campus, short courses, and, of course, poster sessions. The wise Center Director realizes that informal communication need not be haphazard communication. Taking informal communication seriously by regularly contacting each IAB member each quarter, keeping a record of that communication, and being responsive to queries is one good way to avoid unpleasant, formal communication. These communication activities make sure that I/UCRC research is cooperative research.

EXTERNAL COMMUNICATIONS

External communications transcend a given center and the I/UCRC program. It includes administrative reporting to the university, newsletters, press releases, videos and public outreach (see Figure 7-7).

The development of a center newsletter is an important communications decision (Figure 7-8). It serves to inform readers

| Figure 7-7 | External communications matrix (university, other centers, institutions, prospective sponsors) |

WHAT	WHO	WHY
Administrative Oversight	Director	Status of center within the university.
Patents and Legal	Director	Status of Intellectual Property, IAB membership.
NSF TIE Grants	Researcher	Coordination of projects between centers.
NSF Debriefing	Director, NSF	Feedback following semi-annual meeting.
Newsletters, Brochures (7-13)*	Staff	Center accomplishments, plans.
Technical Publications	Researchers	Research accomplishments.
Public Education, Publicity	Staff, Director	Center accomplishments.

*Appendix reference in parenthesis.

| Figure 7-8 | Contents of a typical newsletter. |

Basic
- The name of the center—the address/phone.
- The name (and logo) of the university.
- Listing the center as government sponsored (e.g., NSF I/UCR) center.
- Listing of sponsors—their locations/phones—the names of the IAB members.
- Listings of the center faculty, students and staff.

News
- Information about center publications and instructions about how to obtain them.
- Brief summaries of center research projects.
- Topical articles by center faculty.
- Invited articles by sponsor representatives.
- Listings of recent publications and Center patents.
- A calendar of center events—listing of professional meetings and conference notices.
- Recent activities of the research faculty and student researchers.
- Announcements about new center sponsors and center personnel.
- Information about special center educational programs and workshops.
- Feature articles about technology trends and breakthroughs in the field.
- Messages from the Center Director.

about both highlights and progress of center research and activities. A newsletter can be circulated easily by the sponsors' representatives to internal work groups or teams, etc. and/or via a regular mailing list. The center newsletter also provides a series of concise measurement of the research accomplishments and activities of the center that might not be communicated in any other way. A newsletter can be used to promote the center to potential sponsors, the university and the public in general. It may also enhance a feeling of belonging among center students, staff, etc. who may not otherwise be aware of the big picture. Typically, newsletters are published semi-annually or quarterly. The frequency depends upon the needs of the center, the resources available, and the complexity and length of the newsletter. Also to be considered are the downside concerns about a center newsletter. Will the benefits of publishing a regular newsletter pay off relative to the effort and resources required? Is the center newsletter a duplication of effort? Will the center newsletter find enough new information or articles after the first few editions? A newsletter that peters out may cast a negative image on the entire center.

Public education and relations are the things with which the average Center Director has the least experience. Fortunately, most universities have full-time public relations staff and their job is helping you to get your message out.

Campus public affairs officers and video production offices know how to write press releases, informational stories, and produce videos. They also know how to work with researchers. Publicity is a matter of having both the proper material and the proper outlet. Such campus offices have the technical expertise to help you produce the best message possible; they also have the contacts to see that your information gets into the local newspaper or on the local news. But your job is to be clear about your message. Hopefully, the principles discussed in the section titled *Cooperation Requires Communication* in this chapter will help you address this challenge.

SUMMARY

Unlike budgeting, evaluation, or research, which we tend to think of as skills requiring special training, few of us ever bother to study communication. It is simply a given; after all, we've been communicating for as long as we can remember. Yet, if we are honest, we realize that many of our problems (with the Dean, PI, or IAB member) arise from a failure of communication. Sometimes we

fail to make ourselves clear; sometimes we fail to properly interpret another's message, sometimes the communication never
happens. The underlying premise of this chapter is that with a little work each of us can become a better communicator. Part 1 has
presented some basic strategies for improving overall communication skill levels. Part 2 has harnessed those strategies to the particular needs of an I/UCRC Director. We believe that both parts,
together with the appended samples, form a cohesive communication package, and that improved communication will improve
center operation.

REFERENCES

Clampitt, P. G. *Communicating for Managerial Effectiveness*, Sage
Publications, 1991.

Corsten, H. "Technology transfer from universities to small and
medium-sized enterprises—an empirical survey from the stand-
points of such enterprises," *Technovation*, 6, pp. 57-68, 1987.

Page, S. B. *Business Policies and Procedures Handbook: How to Create
Professional Policy and Procedure Publications*, Prentice-Hall,
1984.

Schumacher, D. *Get Funded!*, Sage Publications, 1992.

Watzlawick, P. *How Real is Real? Confusion, Disinformation, Communication*, Vintage, 1976.

Werner, D. *Managing Company-Wide Communication*. Chapman and
Hall, 1995.

APPENDIX 7-1

Communications—Master Calendar

JANUARY

- NSF Director's/ Evaluators Meeting, D.C.
- Complete IAB Oct. Minutes
- Develop Meeting agenda for IAB Apr./Dir. Report
- Give ideas for new research to faculty
- Make arrangements for IAB meeting location, etc.
- Submit Questionnaire data to NSF
- Center Budget Review

FEBRUARY

- Prepare research reports
- Faculty develop new research proposals
- Newsletter preparation
- Advise Administration of IAB mtg.
- Center Budget Review

MARCH

- Mail new research proposals to IAB
- Mail research reports (30 days before IAB meeting in April)
- Send April meeting agenda to all parties
- Mail minutes of Oct. Meeting to IAB
- Meet with Center students about plans and presentations for April IAB meeting

- Meet with students about plans and poster session for April IAB meeting
- Sponsors prepare for IAB meeting
- Center Budget Review
- Evaluator report to Director & NSF

APRIL

- Hold IAB meeting, technical reviews: select new research (L.I.F.E. form)

  Center students make presentations and student poster session is held
- Hand out Center Newsletter to IAB
- Report NSF questionnaire results
- Center Budget Review
- Process Outcome data / evaluator's report
- Submit NSF Renewal Proposal

MAY

- Main Marketing/Visits to Sponsors
- Write draft of Minutes of IAB Mtg. April
- Center Budget Review

JUNE

- Main Marketing/Visits to Sponsors
- Old budget year ends
- Center Evaluator's meeting (D.C.)
- Center Budget Review

JULY

- New budget year begins
- Main Marketing/Visit Sponsors
- Submit History to NSF
- Make arrangements for IAB meeting location, etc.
- Center Budget Review

AUGUST

- Prepare research reports
- Complete IAB meeting minutes (Apr.)
- Develop new agenda for IAB Oct./Dir. report
- Newsletter preparation
- Advise Administration of IAB mtg. date
- Center Budget Review

SEPTEMBER

- Send October meeting agenda to all parties
- Mail minutes of April Meeting to IAB
- Mail research reports (30 days before IAB meeting in October)
- Meet with Center students about plans and presentations for October IAB meeting
- Meet with students about plans and poster session for October IAB meeting
- Sponsors Prepare for IAB meeting
- Center Budget Review

OCTOBER

- Hold IAB meeting technical reviews, request ideas for new research from Sponsors.
  Center students make presentations and student session is held.
- Hand out Center Newsletter to IAB
- Administer NSF questionnaires
- Deliver History to IAB
- Center Budget Review

NOVEMBER

- Write NSF Grant renewal (or on anniversary date)
- Write draft of minutes of IAB meeting
- Center Budget Review

DECEMBER

- Deadline for new research ideas from sponsors (mid December)
- Center Budget Review

APPENDIX 7-2

Center Semi-Annual IAB Meeting Checklist

Note: Some tasks will vary.

Category	Item/task	Deadline/By Whom
Meeting items	date and location	
Meeting items	day 2 date and location	
Meeting items	arrange for mike, amplifier, ext. cord	
Meeting items	arrange parking / obtain parking pass	
Invitations/letters	send 1st ltr of invitation to paid members	
Invitations/letters	send early ltr notifying payment status	
Catering	reserve dinner facility	
Rooms	reserve meeting rooms	
Invitations/letters	verify payment status of members	
Research reports	send researchers notice re: Research Reports	
Research reports	obtain center statistics for meeting booklet	
Research reports	prepare budgetary info. for meeting booklet	
Catering	arrange break/lunch catering	
Posters	obtain poster materials for researchers	
Catering	arrange payment of caterer	
Catering	request entertainment expense permission	
Research Reports	complete projects chart for meeting booklet	
Invitations/letters	send invitations to Center faculty/other	
Research Reports	make meeting booklet of reports/send to copy cntr	
Research Reports	edit research reports	
Newsletter	obtain copy from director/s	
Certificates	arrange for printing	
Invitations/letters	obtain RSVPs from faculty and students	
Invitations/letters	send second letters w/agenda and reports	
Newsletter	edit articles, prepare camera-ready copy	
Presentations	arrange rehearsals and send reminders	
Catering	finalize faculty and students RSVPs/dinner	
Certificates	arrange for framing	
Newsletter	copy newsletter/send to copy center	
Misc.	make hotel reservations as requested	
Misc.	update center publications list	
Certificates	finalize membership certificates/framing etc.	
Posters	posters due from students	
Late news	material due from students	
Presentations	research presentation material due	
Posters	arrange for set up	

Category	Item/task	Deadline/By Whom
Misc.	assemble binders	
Misc.	compile list of attendees	
Name tags	prepare from list of attendees with extra blanks	
Packets	assemble packets	
IAB meeting	prepare copies of minutes of prev. IAB mtg.(confidential)	
Report	prepare directors report for IAB meeting	
Posters	copy posters	
Posters	set up at meeting location	
Misc.	prepare maps, pads, pencils, packets for mtg.	
Forms	prepare LIFE forms/feedback forms	
Meeting	prepare late list of attendees	
Meeting	prepare receipts for attendees/deposit checks	
Meeting	set up signs for meeting if needed	
Meeting	set up name tags, packets etc. for pickup	
Meeting	collect unused parking permits/name tags	
Meeting	collect materials and prepare for next cycle	

APPENDIX 7-3

Facility Checklist for IAB Meetings

Space Check Out

___ size and shape of space
___ electrical outlets
___ microphone outlets
___ acoustics
___ doors
___ bathrooms (where,
    number can accommodate)
___ stairs
___ elevators
___ heat/cold regulation
___ ventilation
___ parking facilities (number
    and access)
___ registration area
___ location
___ transportation, access
    to facility
___ room set-up arrangements

___ access to meeting room(s)
___ lighting
___ name of custodian, engineering,
    where to be reached
___ telephone access for messages
    and calling out
___ exhibit space
___ wall space for newsprints, etc.
___ emotional impact (color,
    aesthetics)
___ access to photocopier
___ others
___
___

Materials and Supplies

___ name tags/tents
___ small tip felt pens
___ large tip felt pens
___ paper clips
___ crayons
___ pins
___ scissors
___ stapler
___ glue
___ newsprint paper
___ scratch paper
___ carbon paper
___ reprints of articles
___ copies of reports
___ books
___ posters/charts

___ pamphlets
___ visual aids
___ masking tape
___ resume of resource people
___ directional signs (to meeting)
___ chalk (various colors)
___ file folders
___ others
___ display materials
___ instruction sheets
___others
___

APPENDIX 7-4

Presentation Guidelines and Checklist for Graduate Students

The opportunity to make a technical research presentation before a group of industry representatives is not afforded to all graduate students. **When you make your presentation about your research which is the primary goal,** you are also presenting and selling yourself. Even though you may not be hired by any one firm in the center, you are practicing for the future and the contacts you make may be very valuable. Don't sell yourself short or fail to recognize the opportunity.

___ **Outline your talk with the guidance of your faculty advisor.** (Appendix 2-5)

- For your **talk** and your **overheads or slides,** include: Your **name** and your **advisor's** name; **Title** of the research; **Goals/objectives; Relevance** to industry, and to center goals, plans or road maps of technology in your field of research; **Progress** to date or since last time; **Difficulties** encountered; **Results; Plans** for the future; **Acknowledgments,** e.g., the center for supporting the work, individuals or company or companies for providing assistance, materials, etc. Be sure that your talk can be given within the time indicated. Allow for questions. (See presentation feedback sheet.)

- At the end of your talk, **ask if there are questions.** This question and answer interaction is very important for both your research work and yourself. It is helpful if you arrange with someone to take notes for you on the questions for future reference.

___ **Preparation of your slides or overheads.** (Use information which is applicable.)

- Check for readability in the place you will make the presentation.

- Keep the phrases short and to the point. Minimize the use of complicated formulas.

- Check the sharpness and readability of the slides or overheads from where the audience will be siting.

- Provide **copies** for distribution to the audience before your talk or according to center deadlines.

- Watch for dark slides. If it is necessary to reshoot your slides, "bracket' them first to save time. It is helpful to the projectionist to have a brief description of slides available if, during the questioning, you need to instruct the projectionist to switch to it.

- It works best to advance your slides yourself with a hand held control.

- Experience has shown that it is best to use a microphone especially in large settings; the voice does not tend to drop off when speakers turn to look at their slides or overheads if a microphone is used.

- Check to see if others use a consistent graph plot format.

- Ask questions, especially of students who have presented before. Team work is essential.

- Have your name, academic background, research topic and expected date of completing your program up front in your slides/overheads.

___**Rehearsal and Presentation.**

- Complete the dry run in the actual setting if possible; Rehearse 3 times if possible before a critical audience, e.g., professor/peers.

- Use a pointer (metal, wooden or laser) with overhead or slides on the screen. **Do not** use the pointer, your hand, or pen directly **on the overhead screen projector. Use a pointer on the screen.** Position yourself with your best side to the screen and face your audience, e.g., right-handed stand to the right of the screen as the audience sees you. Dress professionally.

___**Technical, Poster and/or Review, Question and Answer Sessions.**

- Have research notebooks available for reference.

- Take notes and write down who asked the questions.

- Ask for business cards at review and poster for future reference.

- Have your name, academic background, research topic, and expected date of completing your program posted.

___ **Debriefing.**

- Meet with your faculty advisor to review the results and make plans for the future. Also obtain feedback and notes from your student partner.

___ **Use of the presentation feedback sheet is suggested.**

- This can be used in both rehearsal and in the actual presentation.

___**Other ideas, add below:**

APPENDIX 7-5

Executive Summary for Technical Presentation*

Executive Summary
for
CPAC Sponsor Meeting

Principal Investigator:

Research Associates:

Goals of Presentation

Highlight Accomplishments
Provoke Pertinent Questions
Encourage Applications & Support
Increase Understanding
Provide Interesting Presentation

Technical Basis of Project

Equations:

Theories:

Previous Accomplishments

Lab established
Grad Students recruited
Equipment ordered
Prototype built
Prototype calibrated
Initial test results

Recent Results

- Graphs
- Charts
- Pictures
- Data
- Illustrate the last six months of research

Implications of Results

Possible Applications:

Impact on Industry:

Future of Project

Short term plans & ideas:

Long range plans & ideas:

---

*Also see Appendix 7-10, which is more generally used.

APPENDIX 7-6
Poster Session Feedback

(For use by Center director faculty, students, IAB members, and industry technical advisors.)

Project Id. Number:_____   Date _____

Name of Researcher: _____   Advisor:_____ _____

Title of Research _____
_____

Research Goals/Objectives presented: Yes_____ No_____

Relevance shown to industry, Center goals, long range plans, or technology roadmaps: Yes_____ No_____

Comment: _____

Progress to date or since last time included: Yes____ No____

Difficulties encountered mentioned: Yes___ No___ Not applicable___

Comment: _____

Results presented: Yes___ No___

Plans for the future included: Yes___ No___

Questions/suggestions/comments about the research:
_____
_____

Name:_____ Representing _____

Phone_____

APPENDIX 7-7

Outline for a Typical Closed Meeting

Introductions and meeting usually conducted by the current chairperson of the IAB.

Questions from Minutes of the previous IAB business meeting.

Review and discussion of Technical Sessions.
> Summary of Comments

Other concerns
> Summary of Comments

Comments from NSF
> Program Officer
> Evaluator

Adjournment

APPENDIX 7-8
Outline of a Typical IAB Business Meeting Agenda

(The length is usually a half day)

Welcome, Introductions, and Opening Remarks

Approve Minutes of previous meeting.

Review and finalize the meeting agenda.

Presentation of the Director's Report:

> Status of the Center since the last meeting:

>> Staffing, activities, center development, review of Technical Sessions, future abstracts for approval, budget review, recruitment—sponsors, students and faculty, etc.

>> Visits to/from sponsors and visitors.

>> Previous action items.

Discussion and approval of report and budget.

Comments from:

> IAB closed meeting

> NSF representatives

> Graduate student representative

> Other

Break—networking

Old business from previous action items

New business as needed and identified.

> Selection of new research

Determine dates for next semi-annual meeting.

Adjournment

APPENDIX 7-9

Outline for New Company Interview

Organization:

Name: Phone:

Title:

1. The Decision to Join

Probe: How did the company find out about the Center?

How was initial contact made?

How did the interviewee get involved?

Is the interviewee a technical representative? IAB member? Describe the company's decision process. How is the Center funded in your Organization? By whom? Is there any mechanism to consider supplemental funding?

Does the company have any formal tracking mechanism to judge the success of its Center membership?

2. Benefits of Joining

Probe: Does the organization have specific objectives (e.g., specific technologies)?

Has any technology been transferred to your organization?

Into any company products?

Personnel goals—use the Center as a means of updating company R & D staff. Use graduates as a recruiting pool?

How important is the contact with other companies?

Are any contacts made/kept aside from the Center meetings?

3. Organizational Dissemination

Probe: Who in your company is involved with the Center? (e.g., outside R & D?, how high up?

Who else in your organization should be included on the dissemination list?

What might the Center do to help you to institutionalize the Center within your organization?

4. **Formative Check**

Probe: Are you satisfied with your Center membership to date?

    Thoughts about the IAB meeting?

    Anything the Center might do in order to be a better resource for your company?

    Have you/are you considering two-way visits? Short courses?

Summary:

APPENDIX 7-10
Project Proposal Form

Program Name: New:_____

Program Manager: Continuation:_____

Description:	
Experimental Plan:	
Related Work Elsewhere:	How ours is different:
Related work in:	Milestones:
Deliverables:	Budget:
Economics:	
Potential Member Company Benefits:	
Progress to Date:	
Knowledge Transfer Target Date:	

APPENDIX 7-11

Quarterly Progress Report Format

TITLE OF PROJECT

(QUARTERLY PROGRESS REPORT)

Principal Investigator, Affiliation

1. Project Summary

This should be a one paragraph synopsis of the project goals and approach.

2. Milestones and Goals

This section will summarize the milestones, goals, and objectives planned for this reporting period and will discuss the status of each. If planned objectives were not achieved, the major obstacles should be sketched.

3. Research Planned

This section will summarize the milestones, goals, and objectives planned for the next reporting period. Unachieved objectives from previous periods should be discussed here.

4. Research Output

This section should list the research products and other evidence of research activity achieved during this reporting period.

5. IAB Contacts

This sections should summarize contacts with IAB members and SIGS during this reporting period.

6. Financial Status

This section should indicate the status and adequacy of current funding levels and the spending progress of the project toward planned levels.

APPENDIX 7-12
Annual Report Format

TITLE OF PROJECT
(STATUS REPORT)
Principal Investigators
Affiliation

1. Long-Term Goals
In this section the main focus and target of the research is presented. This is basically the explicit formulation of the research's core problem. The expected time frame is three years.

This sections should be organized into two parts:
Plan: Describe the original long-term goals
Actual: Describe the changes made to the long-term goals

2. Background for Long-Term Goals
In this section the historical and/or systematic context of the research is described. Why is the problem important? What is its relevance to the IAB? What are the main contributions or position related the this problem? How original is the current approach? Relationships with other projects should also be highlighted in this section.

This sections should be organized into two parts:
Plan: Describe how the original goals were perceived.
Actual: Describe any changes from the original perceptions.

Highlight any new contributions to the research literature or other research developments that may have affected the approach.

3. Intermediate-Term Objectives
In this section the objectives of the current year are presented. These are major phases of the yearly progress toward the long term goal.

This section should be organized into two parts:
Plan: Describe the original stages for the current year.
Actual: Indicate any changes in the staging of research activities

4. Schedule of Major Steps
In this section, concrete steps to achieve yearly objectives are listed. Main entries are dated as major milestones. This enumeration may comprehend the whole year as its focus, or a six-month time frame.

This sections should be organized into two parts:
Plan: What milestones were planned?
Actual: What milestones were actually achieved? What portions of the schedule slipped?

An attached milestone chart should represent the same information in graphical format.

5. Dependencies
This section is optional. It contains the list of materials and products needed for the actual conduct of the research: tools, publications, equipment, etc.

6. Major Risks
This section highlights major concerns related to the proposed research. especially those risks related to the dependencies in Section 5.

7. Budget
This sections should present the planned and actual direct costs required to perform the proposed research. All budget categories should be included.

8. Staffing
This section should list planned and actual scientists participating in the research and should explain their roles.

9. Category of the Current Stage
In this section, the current stage of the research is classified according to whether it is Assessment, Feasibility, Prototype, or Development. Transitions between categories should be noted.

10. Contacts with Affiliates
This sections should discuss the contacts with affiliates and the plans for future interactions.

11. Publications and other Research Products
This sections should describe the planned and actual output of the project in terms of deliverable items such as reports and software.

APPENDIX 7-13

Outlines for Contents of Center Brochure

Center Brochure

Center Name, Logo, University, Location
    Identify as a NSF–I/UCRC Program

Purpose—Center Goals/Objectives

Operation of the Center

Director(s) name(s)

Benefits of joining the Center

Scope of Research

Facilities available to the Center

List Faculty—highlight their special expertise

University Information
    Degree Programs
    Sponsor Opportunities for seminars/workshops, etc.

Contact information/address, telephone, fax, e-mail, and
website (if any)

MANAGING AN I/UCRC:

Control, Budgeting and Evaluation

HOWARD LEVINE, *California College of Arts and Crafts, San Francisco*

DENIS O. GRAY, *North Carolina State University, Raleigh*

ELIEZER GEISLER, *University of Wisconsin, Whitewater*

Effective management may be similar to a naval metaphor: Set the proper course and steer to it. Of course, even a brilliant navigator needs a compass to stay on course. Put into language more fitting to an MBA program: Well run organizations require both appropriate goals and techniques, like the navigator's compass, to ensure that those goals are being met. Those techniques include the control systems we will discuss in this chapter.

Goals give a center a sense of direction and encourage staff and IAB members to communicate about critical issues. However, centers work with multiple and sometimes conflicting stakeholders and in very dynamic environments. A center with goals, but no mechanism for judging progress toward attaining those goals, will quickly find itself adrift, perhaps inviting mutiny by its most important stakeholders—its members.

This chapter provides this mechanism. It discusses tools, techniques, and methodologies such as controls, budgets, evaluations, and some best practice to monitor and ensure progress toward goals. In doing so, we will try to emphasize a pragmatic strategy which meets the needs of small as well as large centers, and recognizes that while control and feedback mechanisms are essential to success, an obsession with formal controls and controlling can drain scarce resources and stifle creativity.

CONTROL

Control is generally defined as regulating organizational activities to achieve levels of performance in conformance with expected standards and objectives. In more common language, controls are means by which we head toward an objective; they keep us from veering off in undesirable directions and help to prevent unwanted outcomes.

In the scientific and engineering world the concept of control is closely identified with feedback. Similarly, the generalized methodology for management control closely resembles an informational feedback loop. Evaluation research also stresses feedback for decision-making.

Control mechanisms serve many purposes in an organization: they help to gather timely information; identify problems, opportunities, and irregularities; cope with uncertainty; and provide credibility for decision making. But even these important purposes do not mandate that every organization have a formal management control system. I/UCRCs, characterized by modest size, multiple clients, and a boundary-spanning operation, present the Director with a wide choice of control mechanisms. For example, talking with IAB members at semi-annual meetings is an opportunity to gather information in a timely fashion and exert *informal control* over the important issue of member satisfaction. Alternatively, the NSF-mandated evaluation protocol (see section titled *Applying Controls for Operational Issues* in this chapter) provides an opportunity for obtaining objective, sometimes anonymous and detailed information from members about center operations and outcomes. The data, in turn, may be incorporated into a *formal, systematic control function* to contact all those who are not "almost certain" that their firms will renew membership to ascertain problems and suggest solutions. Both approaches provide an opportunity for exercising management control. Choosing a formal or informal control strategy is largely dependent upon the variable to be controlled, the resources available, and the personal style of the manager.

There are three types of control systems: at the time of decision (go/no-go control), during project operation (steering control), and at completion (post-action control). Each has a role in an I/UCRC.

Go/no-go control is used whenever prior approval of an action is mandated. For example, the IAB voting the start-up of all new research projects is this type of control.

Steering control ensures that progress is being made and if not, allows corrective actions. For example, a researcher reports to the IAB on progress to date and can solicit advice and suggestions about how best to meet goals and successfully complete the project.

Post-action control determines the success of completed efforts. For example, most centers report end of fiscal year spending patterns. Additionally, in the I/UCRC context, post-action control is an important technique for justifying the center research program to NSF, member firms, other parts of the university. Whether the control is exerted formally or informally, each keeps the center focused toward its mission and objectives.

The primary emphasis of a control strategy must be utility. Control information has value to the extent that it may provide some surprise, causes the decision maker to take action that otherwise would not have been taken, or leads to improved performance. The exception report is such a document. It is prepared only when the variable being controlled deviates far enough from a recognized standard that management needs to be informed and corrective action taken. Control systems which tell you what you already know, provide no impetus for action, and don't lead to improved performance probably are not worth the investment of time and resources.

THE CONTROL MODEL

The control process model (see Figure 8-1) is more descriptive than prescriptive. That is, every control opportunity, particularly informal controls, need not follow it to the letter. Rather, awareness of these steps, as well as explicit referral for formal control functions, should help ensure an effective and efficient I/UCRC.

Select the Control Variables

Control is not abstract; it is a concrete task applied to specific organizational variables. For example, an I/UCRC may wish to institute a formal control system for financial resources for both future revenues and expenditure of funds, membership retention and recruitment, and research quantity and quality.

Define the Appropriate Units of Measure

Specificity is the key. While the meaning of high or low is arguable, numbers are not. For example, a year-to-year comparison

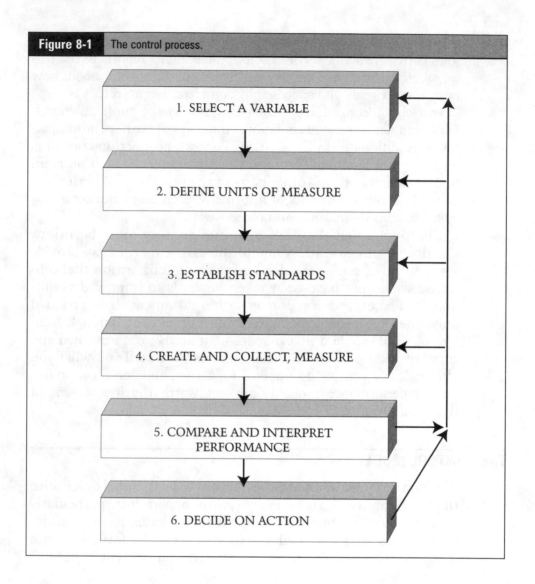

Figure 8-1   The control process.

1. SELECT A VARIABLE

2. DEFINE UNITS OF MEASURE

3. ESTABLISH STANDARDS

4. CREATE AND COLLECT, MEASURE

5. COMPARE AND INTERPRET PERFORMANCE

6. DECIDE ON ACTION

of the number of center members is a specific measure of retention. Recruitment measurements might include the number of new firms contacted, visited, or attending a center function or meeting compared to the number of firms that join the center.

Establish a Performance Standard Based on the Unit of Measurement

Various types of standards have a role to play in center management. One is the floor—sometimes a standard becomes the minimal level of acceptable performance. For example, the National

Science Foundation has established $300,000 as the minimum industrial support for I/UCRC membership. Another kind of standard is norm-referenced—a standard can be based upon the average performance of all I/UCRCs such as comparing the number of IAB members in each center. During the recession of the early 1990s the average mature center lost members. Any center that stayed even was actually performing at a better than average level. Yet another is the fiat—a standard of measurement might be that the IAB require that no single project account for more than 25 percent of the research budget. The last is the goal or plan—certain levels of performance can be specified in the I/UCRC plan, goal, or in RFPs.

Create and Implement the Measurement Tool(s)

This is the step where control information is collected. Some of that information (e.g., number of members, annual budget) is already in the system; no special tools are required. Information on IAB member satisfaction is much more diffuse and care must be given to ensure the best methods are used to collect it. The NSF evaluator is mandated to collect data and has a battery of tools (see section titled *Control and Evaluation Research* in this chapter). The savvy director needs to ascertain how they fit into the I/UCRC's control system by focusing on the previous steps and what additional information gathering tools are required.

Compare Actual Performance to the Established Standard and Interpret the Results

These comparisons can be mundane. For instance, the standard was to generate three patents and the center received five, or the standard was to sustain all members and two resigned. Much more important is interpretation: Is the discrepancy significant? What caused it? What should be done? Trend analysis of the number of patents awarded per year for the previous five years would demonstrate whether the most recent year's performance was normal, extraordinary, or below par. In general, longitudinal data are much more helpful for interpretation. Determining causes may prove simple (e.g., two members were lost because those companies were merged with companies that were also members) or nearly impossible (e.g., company xyz left and they can't really explain why or what might have been done to keep them).

Understanding the cause is not always necessary, but it always widens the scope of proposed action.

Decide on the Action Required and Follow Through

A control system is deficient if the information provided isn't actionable. One appropriate action may be to do nothing at all (e.g., the performance meets standards). A second action may be to investigate what caused the loss in membership; is it a factor under I/UCRC control or the result of a national recession. A third possible action is revising the standard. Trend analysis shows more patents generated, so the standard is increased. Another option is to revise the control system: introduce a new variable to control, design a more sensitive collection instrument, or alter the time frame in which the system works. Finally, perhaps atypically, is to take the indicated action(s) which will reimpose control over a recalcitrant variable (e.g., fire the administrative assistant who can't seem to keep the center budget in accord with university accounting procedures). The key to action to the entire control process is to understand that it is an ongoing process. It is not a decision that is arrived at only once; it is a repetitive cycle that continues over the life of the center.

Summary

The concept of control is central to the management function and directly complements the planning process. Like most small organizations, information for the control process may be informal reconnaissance or formal information collected as part of a systematic data collection effort (collected before, concurrently or after center operations). Regardless of how control information is collected, it always should be a part of an iterative process which provides a basis for action which can improve a center's performance.

FINANCIAL CONTROL: BUDGET DRIVEN MODEL

As Brinckloe et al. (1977) conclude, finances have the favorable characteristic of being driven by explicit cost and expenditure figures, making them convenient for control. Not surprisingly, this is undoubtedly the aspect of organizational control most of us have firsthand experience with. Following the six step process introduced in the previous section, most of the financial control process can be broken down into two major components: budgeting (steps 1 to 3: selecting variables, defining units, establishing standards), and accounting (steps 4 and 5: measuring and comparing performance to standard). Where budgeting can be seen as an art that is inextricably linked to organizational planning and involves forecasting, accounting is a science that must obey generally accepted accounting principles. In our coverage, we will emphasize budgeting for two reasons: budgeting is central to all three kinds of control (go/no-go, steering, and post action), whereas accounting is most frequently associated with post-action control; most Center Directors, because of their responsibility for planning, will need to learn the art of budgeting, but can always delegate or purchase the science of accounting.

PRINCIPLES OF BUDGETING

Because budgeting is an art, there is no one, specific model that all managers should follow. There are, however, *four* desiderata of a practical and useful budgeting system:

- Budgets should be comprehensive, objective public documents available to all interested parties; they should account for all aspects of a center's operation and reflect the choices made for competing futures (e.g., projects and approaches).

- Budgets should be based upon measurable units of responsibility that each researcher and center administration prepares, and for which they are responsible.

- Budgets must be flexible, and capable of adjusting to change. Budgets are only based on certain planning assumptions. When those assumptions prove wrong, or totally unexpected information is received, managers must accommodate the new data by reconfiguring their plans as well as their budgets. Center budgets are always in flux (e.g., grants may be in the pipeline, an economic downturn may cause membership to drop) and the wise director and principal investigator (PI) must be able to plan and budget around these contingencies.

- Budgeting systems should include a comprehensive, integrated information and performance reporting system that provides management with timely reports as to progress and significant variances from the plan. When accounting information is added they are the framework for steering control, measuring at suitable intervals, i.e., bi-monthly, how the plan is actually progressing and taking necessary corrective action.

BUDGETING IN AN I/UCRC

Centers are small organizations in which administration is responsible for preparing a *master budget* that combines all revenues and expenses. In order to accomplish this, the Center Director (or designate):

- Forecasts revenues. This is the most difficult element since recruitment and retention of members and other revenue-generating activities are uncertain.

- Justifies the fixed costs associated with center administration, recruitment and technology-transfer activities. This budget will provide the basis for determining the center's research budget.

- Delegates but not abrogates responsibility to principal investigators to develop and justify operating budgets for research projects. This should include support that is already committed to multi-year projects as well as to new projects.

Information on project budget variances must be available bi-monthly so that the Center Director can utilize the steering control option.

CENTER REVENUE: FUND ACCOUNTS

Unlike most university-sponsored research, a center's revenue budget is neither certain nor simple. The typical center revenue support structure involves multiple sources, often with different overhead rates, which arrive at different times during the year, and with varying certainty. It presents directors with questions about how and when to bill members (see Figure 8-2.) This presents the director with two unique challenges: how to keep various sources of funding with their conflicting structures straight and how to accommodate the uncertainty.

Centers receive support from multiple sources and each source may have different conditions and rules (see Figure 8-3 for a summary of possible differences). Combining all sources of funding into a single account can cause an administrative nightmare for the center and the university (how much overhead should be

Figure 8-2	Billing center members.

It probably doesn't make sense for a center to invoice members for annual dues or enhancement projects. This activity is best left to the university administration, but they should confirm the billing.

Invoices are usually sent out once a year, but most universities will send semi-annual or even quarterly invoices, particularly if a member supports a significant amount of research on your campus.

Figure 8-3	Typical I/UCRC revenue accounts.

NSF/Government Agency

Predetermined overhead rate. Support budgeted into specific line items. Must meet specific rebudgeting and auditing guidelines. Limits on carrying support forward from year-to-year.

Industrial Memberships

Many Centers provide cost sharing by waiving or reducing their negotiated overhead rate on industry membership fees. Funds are not budgeted to specific line items. Great rebudgeting latitude. Support can be carried forward from one year to next.

Government IAB Members—MIPRs

Memberships from government agencies are usually transferred by NSF to a center via Military Interdepartmental Procurement Request (MIPR). These funds will be charged the same overhead as industrial memberships plus a small NSF handling surcharge.

Government Sponsorship

Federal agencies can sponsor a center via a multi-year grant or contract. Overhead and restrictions will depend upon the nature of the award and the requirements of the specific agency.

State Funding

Overhead rates and restrictions differ from state to state.

Industry Enhancements

Usually project sponsor-specific but may be charged the same overhead rates as industry memberships. Additional conditions may affect timelines, reversion of unspent funds, etc. This may require a separate account for each enhancement.

Contracts

Industrial and government contracts are usually negotiated on a case-by-case basis and may vary in terms of overhead, deliverables, timelines, etc. A separate account for each contract is typical.

charged, which budgeting and rebudgeting rules should be followed, how will special conditions be monitored) and will provide a heyday for an auditor. One useful strategy is establishing separate accounts for specific donors or sources of revenue. To the extent possible, each separate account is earmarked for a specific expense. (See section titled *The Accounting Function* in this chapter.) For instance, all the NSF or government agency money pays for administration, or XYZ Corporation money pays for lab equipment. Sub-accounts under a master account can fund each faculty project.

There is no simple fix for the revenue uncertainty which goes with running a center. As a consequence, control-wise directors prepare budgets which include a range of projected revenues, probability statements, and critical assumptions. (See Figure 8-4.)

Figure 8-4	Sample I/UCRC estimated revenue budget.

CENTER BALANCE SHEET BUDGET FY1997

SOURCES (in $k)	Low	Level	High
Memberships	240	300	360
Affiliate Memberships	0	30	30
NSF/Government Funding			
I/UCRC Program	25	25	25
TIE Grants	30	80	100
Other	50	50	150
Governmental Grants			
ARPA	50	80	100
NIH	30	50	80
Other	0	30	50
Governmental Contracts			
EPA	50	80	120
Other	40	60	50
State Funding			
DOT	35	40	60
State I/UCRC	50	50	80
Other	10	10	20
Special Projects			
XYZ Contract	40	40	75
ABC Grant	30	50	60
Other	20	25	50
Total Income	**700,000**	**1,000,000**	**1,385,000**

(Courtesy M. Griscavage, HSMRC, NJIT)

CENTER EXPENSES

Center expenses can be broken down into fixed (typically administration) and variable (research) expenses. Most centers can use expense categories used in federal awards: personnel, fringe benefits, tuition, travel, equipment, computer operations, contractual services, office supplies, research supplies and expenses, and overhead.

Fixed Expenses: Administration

Centers demand a great deal of time and effort for general administration, recruitment and retention activity, and technology transfer to operate efficiently and effectively. At a minimum, fixed administrative expenses will include salaries and fringe benefits for the director (usually via release time, summer salary), an administrative assistant or secretary, an evaluator and a bookkeeper/accountant; equipment needs; general office supplies and copying; and travel support for recruiting, retention, and technology transfer activities. Although most administrative expenses fit within standard budget categories, some do not, such as paying for meals at semi-annual meetings; handling such expenses may require consultation with your grants and contracts office.

Most I/UCRCs have lean administrative budgets, on average 18 percent of their total operating budget. Although there is no perfect formula for deciding upon the administrative budget, it's a mistake to shortchange this aspect of center operations. Centers need an adequate support team, travel, and marketing budgets. Generally speaking, under-budgeting administration costs (particularly recruiting and related expenses), represents a penny wise, pound foolish budgeting strategy.

Research Expenses

Most important is the research budget. Once the revenue budget and fixed expense budget are completed, calculating the aggregate research budget is pretty straightforward. Research budget = Revenues – Fixed Expenses. However, parts of the research budget are considerably more complicated.

Because principal investigators are responsible for achieving the goals spelled out in their proposal, it is important that each project be considered a separate expense center. The principal investigator is responsible for preparing, defending, managing, and controlling his or her own budget. The most appropriate time to secure the needed budget data is at the proposal stage before funding. Faculty researchers must submit a complete proposal, with a detailed budget so that the Center Director and IAB members can make an informed choice regarding the proposed research.

The project budget categories should be consistent with the center's and the university accounting guidelines. Although most centers allow faculty considerable discretion in framing their budgets, some centers require faculty to keep their budget requests within certain guidelines. For instance, 10 percent release time; one month summer salary; one graduate student; $2,000 travel; $500 supplies. Once approved, then the Center Director and budget administrator negotiate with the faculty researcher a final working budget. These details are posted to the center's master budget.

Ultimately, if you want PIs to operate like they are responsible for an expense center, center awards should look and feel like extramural awards. This goal can be achieved by having the university grants and contracts office establish subaccounts under one or more of the center's prime accounts. Some centers send researchers award letters from the university grants and contracts office or the center. While this can be time consuming, it provides for greater accountability, provides a mechanism for distributing overhead to participating departments, and ensures the principal investigator will get recognition along with the responsibility. Figure 8-5 shows a hypothetical hierarchy of funds for a typical I/UCRC.

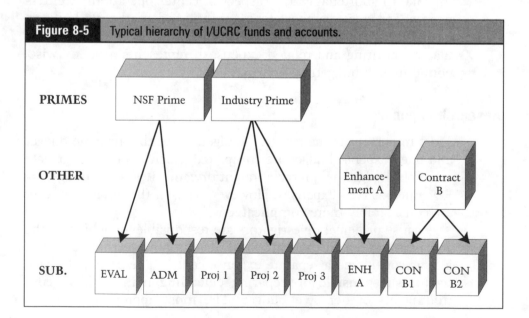

Figure 8-5   Typical hierarchy of I/UCRC funds and accounts.

To provide the PI adequate tools for budget decision making, it is recommended that, at the time of the budget assignment, any grant-specific controls and restraints be passed directly to the principal investigator(s) from the center administrator. Acknowledgment of any special requirements should be required from the PI for the record. Figure 8-6 shows an example of a memorandum of acknowledgment.

Figure 8-6 Sample memorandum of acknowledgment.

Your FY 1997 operating budget for this fiscal year is attached. There are three areas of concern which you need to be aware of and acknowledge to the Center Director.

- Only equipment specifically listed on your budget (if applicable) may be purchased. Equipment not listed will require prime grantor approval; allow time for written permission to be obtained. Equipment must be purchased no later than 60 days prior to the end date of your project.

- All budget transfers must have prior approval (e-mail, fax requests acceptable). For subcontractors, variances are permitted, as allowed for in the Prime Grant, without request.

- No budget extensions or carry-overs will be allowed.

Subcontract/budget documents are being completed and will be processed through your Office of Sponsored Programs, or equivalent authority. Please sign and return the annotated copy of this letter to the Director by fax or mail as acknowledgment of receipt of this letter. Thank you.

Acknowledged: _____

Project Number: _____

Date: _____

(Courtesy M. Griscavage, HSMRC, NJIT)

THE ACCOUNTING FUNCTION:
COLLECTING AND REPORTING PERFORMANCE DATA

A budget must be integrated into an accounting system. Since centers are constituent units within their respective universities, they are required to use and comply with the university's accounting system. While this relieves the center of a variety of burdens (e.g., writing payroll checks each month) it can also present a number of problems: specifically, a mismatch with a single PI-based system and timeliness of reports.

Most university grants and contracts accounting systems assume funding for an individual investigator. Such awards typically involve a fixed amount of money, from a single source, which arrives on campus once, with a set overhead rate, which can be spent by one or two PIs, within a fixed time period, and with little budgetary flexibility.

In contrast, the typical center award involves a variable amount of support, from multiple sources, often with different overhead rates, which arrive at different times during the year, which can be spent by a large number of PIs, over extended and multiple time periods, and with considerable budgetary flexibility. In short, center-related bookkeeping needs can present precedent-breaking challenges.

Fortunately, university financial staff are professionals who, if they understand your needs, will usually try to meet you half-way. Thus, many of these problems can be solved by sitting down with representatives of your grants and contracts office and negotiating an accounting system which is customized to your needs including different fund accounts, a system of prime and sub accounts, authorization to spend money on meetings and meals, billing system for members, etc. If, in spite of a good faith effort by both parties, you discover your financial needs cannot be met at the university level, it may be time to sit down with higher administrative officials.

Unfortunately, the second problem, getting timely feedback on expenses and revenues is a less tractable problem. If the experience of our I/UCRC colleagues is any indication, university-level accounting systems provide accurate but very late information for post-action auditing. It is not unusual for these systems to lack a procedure for recording encumbrances (e.g., already committed salary funds) and for postings to be three or more months behind. Center Directors who desire a modicum of financial control should develop a local accounting capacity.

Strategies for developing I/UCRC accounting capability vary. In some cases, a department or college-level accounting system may be more responsive and capable of providing timely and accurate information. When this is not a viable option, most centers develop and keep an unofficial set of books (e.g., set up in-house grant management software to record real-time expenses that could be reconciled with the university accounting system on a monthly basis). In some cases, centers have been designated university cost centers, with the authority to maintain their accounts. This has an extra advantage because it will allow the center, under certain constraints, to authorize expenditures before funds arrive. While the latter two strategies involve a significant investment of staff time, they result in a responsive financial control system and are well worth the investment.

COMPARING AND INTERPRETING FINANCIAL ACTIVITY

Comparing performance to an established standard involves comparing expenses against budgets. We will discuss two approaches, a balance sheet and a cost analysis. To be useful, both require timely feedback on financial activity.

A Balance Sheet Report

A balance sheet report represents the center's financial picture. It projects sources and uses of funds for a given time period. A bookkeeper's ledger, it has a summary of revenues broken down by funds and major expenses (see Figure 8-7). Since they highlight uncommitted funds, balance sheets are particularly useful when a center needs to determine how much funding is available to support new projects.

Since center memberships and projects typically include multiyear commitments, centers should also consider two- or three-year balance sheet budgets which take into account longer term commitments and forecasts. For instance, a center which has made a lot of multi-year commitments may not want to commit all its discretionary funds in a given year if it means it won't have the opportunity to start new projects the following year.

Cost Analysis Report

Another straightforward way of comparing financial activity is cost analysis whereby actual costs are compared with the original

Figure 8-7   Sample center-level balance sheet budget.

BALANCE SHEET BUDGET FY1997

Center Name:_____

Time Period: Fiscal Year 1997

Revenues	($k)	Expenses	
Memberships	300	**GENERAL ADMINISTRATION**	
Affiliate Memberships	30	Salaries and Fringe	117,800
NSF Funding		Office Supplies and Miscellaneous	7,000
I/UCRC Program	25	Travel	5,000
TIE Grants	80	Evaluation	8,000
Other	50		
Governmental Grants		**RESEARCH PROJECTS**	
ARPA	80	RESEARCH FOCUS I: Sci./Tech Base	
NIH	50	1. Project A-1, Prof. Smith (8/94–9/96)	85,000
Other	30	2. Project B-1, Prof. Jones (8/94–9/96)	75,000
		RESEARCH FOCUS II: Applications	
Governmental Contracts		1. Project C-1, Prof. White (6/95–1/96)	57,000
EPA	80	2. Project D-1, Prof. Black (7/95–4/96)	60,000
Other	60	RESEARCH FOCUS III: Technology	
State Funding		Project E-1	55,000
DOT	40	**ENHANCEMENT PROJECT**	
State I/UCRC	50	Project F-1, Prof. Blue (8/95-6/96)	65,000
Other	10	1:1 PROJECTS	
Special Projects		Discrete projects	340,000
XYZ Contract	40		
ABC Grant	50		
Other	25		
Total Income	**1,000,000**	**Total Expenses**	**(874,800)**
		Balance	**125,200**

(Courtesy M. Griscavage, HSMRC, NJIT)

budgets (see Figure 8-8). This kind of comparison would be particularly appropriate at the project or research theme level and would help PIs and managers monitor the spend rate of particular projects or accounts.

| Figure 8-8 | Sample project-level monthly cost analysis. |

Month/Year:__6/97__

ACCOUNT #: _____

| Project Number: | INCN-52 | Project Dates: | 5/25/96 - 5/31/98 |
| Project P.I.: | M. Evans | Institute of P.I.: | Another U. |

Description	Granting Agency	Match	Expended to Date	Variance
Faculty 1/8 AY: $6,500	6,500		3,250	3,250
Post Doc 18%: $4,395	4,395		1,753	2,642
Analytical technician: $4,375	4,375		2,917	1,458
Fringe benefits @ 28%	4,275		2,217	2,058
Research hourly (GA/RA)	4,770		2,000	2,770
Fringe benefits @ 9%	430		180	250
Supplies	5,000		2,100	2,900
Travel		1,000	200	800
Other operating expenses computer operations	1,200		600	600
Tuition remission, fees	7,200		3,600	3,600
subtotal:	38,145	1,000	18,817	20,328
Indirect cost 68% of salaries:	15,667		6,745	8,922
Equipment: Mixer $3,000	3,000		3,000	0
TOTAL:	**56,812**	**1,000**	**28,562**	**29,250**

(Courtesy M. Griscavage, HSMRC, NJIT)

CONTROL SYSTEMS AND DECISION MAKING

It is easy to get hung up in the minutiae of budgeting and accounting and "miss the forest for the trees." It is important to remember budgeting and accounting contribute to three control functions: go/no-go, steering, and post action.

Go/No-Go Control: Budgets as Planning Documents

Budgets should illustrate what you intend to do, when you intend to do it, and the amount of resources it will take to get it done. When a center submits a budget that commits a significant portion of its discretionary funds to purchase equipment, or to hire a technology transfer assistant, or to send a team to a meeting in Tahiti, those plans can be subjected to go/no-go control by the IAB.

The same is true for budgets submitted by PIs. However, one can tempt over-control by submitting overly detailed budgets. In general, IABs like itemized project-level and center-level budgets but do not care to know which meetings Dr. Levine plans to attend or precisely how the director will use the recruiting budget. In fact, some IABs have authorized directors to spend up to 10 percent of the research budget at their discretion on promising quick-breaking research opportunities. Thus, directors and PIs need to use their judgement and feedback from the IAB to determine how detailed a budget they should submit.

Steering Control

From a management standpoint, the most valuable aspect of budgeting is the ability to exercise steering control. When budgets are coupled with performance reports on spending rates and progress in achieving milestones, managers can interpret variances, decide if they are outside acceptable tolerances, and if needed, take mid-course corrections monthly or at least quarterly.

In order to exercise adequate control at the project-level, PIs need monthly or bi-monthly updates on their expenses to ensure that they are not underspending or overspending their awards (see Figure 8-8). Center Directors need the same information on all project awards, plus monthly or quarterly updates on achievement of project milestones. They may use this information to allocate additional resources in cases with impressive early research, or to close down projects which are floundering. Since there are often late or disputed payments, or unsigned contracts, etc., the Center Director must have information to monitor revenue flow and act when necessary.

Post-action Control

Once budget spending has been realized, I/UCRCs can measure how close research results match the plan. A final report and budget information provides the IAB with a lot of information on how much bang they got for their membership buck. This kind of control requires the center to produce performance reports which interpret revenues vs. expenditures; expenditures by program research areas; expenditures by budget categories; personnel costs broken down by budget category; and any of the preceding over time. This type of information can usually be communicated effectively via simple graphs like pie charts and bar charts.

Financial controls do not compensate for weak management. They are an effective, quantitative tool that can improve planning, help in asserting management control, and generally produce an organization that is effective, efficient, and on course.

APPLYING CONTROLS FOR OPERATIONAL ISSUES: USING INTERNAL ADMINISTRATIVE DATA

There are numerous areas besides finances within a center that the director may wish to control. This section discusses how to use administrative data, the kind of data contained in a Management Information System, for control of operational issues. Rather than discuss each area of control in only a general way, we present a specific case study that deals with the important concerns of all centers—member retention.

Selecting the Variable

Quite obviously, member retention is a key area that must be controlled. Simply looking at whether a firm is retained or not has little value. Like most post-action control information, feedback is usually too late to correct the problem. From another perspective retention equates with member satisfaction, one of few variables that the center can control.

Defining the Units of Measure

What are the appropriate units of measurement for satisfaction? Unfortunately, most directors don't have direct and accurate information on member satisfaction. A director would need to focus on process measures that appear to be related to member satisfaction. Feedback provided by IAB members and monitors during semi-annual meetings might prove useful, particularly if documented carefully. Complaints would be particularly valuable. A strictly objective measure would be how many complaints have been received. Satisfaction related to the frequency of personal and phone contact between a member and center personnel, and the number of projects a member rates "very interested" during the "LIFE" evaluation process are other measures. Members who check "Not Interested" in 40 percent or more of a center's individual projects on the LIFE form are candidates for withdrawal.

Establish Standards

A performance standard for variables might be 100 percent retention, even if some members leave for reasons beyond the center's control. Alternatively, very high satisfaction is a reasonable, realistic goal. However, interpreting very high satisfaction may be difficult. In terms of measures the standard might be something like these: no complaints logged during the past year, at least two personal visits to the members site each year, monthly phone contact reported, and at least three projects rated very interested.

Create and Implement Measurement Tools

Although the variables described above do not require a sophisticated measurement system, valuable information will be lost without some systematic record keeping system. One tool, for use by the director, might include a log or diary used to record conversations on types of changes made in projects. Another tool is a master log of member communications (see Figure 8-9).

This form would provide a vehicle for tracking frequency of contact with members. The complaint column is checked whenever the caller or visitor overtly voices a complaint (e.g., the level of research hasn't been up to your usual standards) or is perceived by the receiver to be making a covert complaint (e.g., I'd like to re-

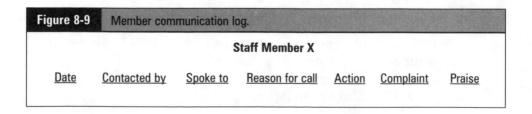

| Figure 8-9 | Member communication log. |

Staff Member X

| Date | Contacted by | Spoke to | Reason for call | Action | Complaint | Praise |

ceive the materials in a more timely fashion). Complaints must be handled right away.

Comparing and Interpreting

Comparing the actual performance to the standard is measured by the number of complaints or contacts that meet or don't meet the standards. To aid in interpretation, a contact log should describe the complaint (see Figure 8-9).

Actions

Actions are almost always remedial because the system is designed to inform the director how best to serve the members. When any shortcoming is detected, it is the shortcoming that should be fixed, rather than the system. If anything, the system may need to be more sensitive; for instance, something is amiss if a member leaves who appeared completely satisfied. The simplest kind of corrective actions may be based on the complaint log. All complaints should be discussed at the moment they arise, a decision made how to handle it, the action taken, and the member firm contacted with the proposed solution. Contacts can also be monitored periodically. One center reviews its contact log half way through the year and assigns faculty to visit members who haven't received at least one visit by that point. Another center asks PIs to report numbers of contacts in their progress reports and does not consider any new project without comment from at least two IAB members. Some centers schedule a meeting with members whose LIFE evaluation forms report less than three projects "interested." This is more likely to produce a positive outcome than a meeting scheduled after a member resigns.

This control system is designed to increase member satisfaction by paying attention to member concerns. In the long run we believe this will result in a more effective center with a larger membership.

A variety of other variables tap into satisfaction and retention. However, control systems based only on MIS data have drawbacks because such data is often poorly or inconsistently collected or highly subjective to personal biases. As a consequence, some centers strengthen their control systems with data provided by evaluation research.

CONTROL AND EVALUATION RESEARCH

According to Weiss (1972), the purpose of evaluation research is "to measure the effects of a program against the goals it sets out to accomplish as a means of contributing to subsequent decision making about the program and improving future programming" (p. 4). Substitute "center" for "program" and this definition reads like the concept of management control developed throughout this chapter. Both involve the collection of data to assess goal attainment and strive to help management and program sponsors to assess and improve organizational performance. Evaluation research even has an analog for the three forms of control we have described: planning evaluation corresponds to go/no-go control; formative or process evaluation corresponds to steering control; and summative evaluation corresponds to post-action control.

There are significant differences that have implications for your control system. Evaluation research usually involves collection of external not administrative data, particularly about outcomes and impacts. It uses sophisticated social science methods, research designs, questionnaires, interviews and statistical analyses to enhance reliability and validity and to strengthen inferences. Outside professionals also are required in evaluation research.

Although evaluations are usually mandated by an outside sponsor like the NSF, to serve their purposes, evaluation research, when it's done carefully and thoughtfully, can provide management with valuable feedback about program processes and outcomes.

Evaluation Research in an I/UCRC

For the past 15 years, the NSF I/UCRC program has mandated a standardized evaluation of all centers, executed by an external, independent evaluator. This was discussed earlier in this volume. The I/UCRC presents several challenges for an evaluator: I/UCRCs are composed of many constituencies—the university, NSF, faculty, students, the IAB, and the research field—and each of these may require different types of information. Further, evaluation of research is difficult due to the uncertain nature of the activity, the complexity of its processes, and the fuzziness and latency of its outputs. The I/UCRC evaluation system, which has evolved over the past 15 years, addresses these problems.

The I/UCRC Evaluator

NSF augments awards so that centers will have the resources to hire independent evaluators. The NSF standardized evaluation includes: (1) submitting a yearly Evaluator Report detailing the center's progress, (2) conducting exit interviews when members leave the center, and (3) administering and analyzing an annual process and outcome questionnaire to IAB members and associated faculty. The evaluator must attend the center's semi-annual research review meetings, other significant internal meetings, and semi-annual meetings of all I/UCRC evaluators. These duties are described in detail in the "I/UCRC Evaluators Handbook" (NSF, 1997).

As important as these formal requirements are for compliance and the information they may provide to the Center Director, I/UCRC evaluators may play a number of informal roles. They are skilled, objective observers. They may act as a communication channel between the center and the IAB. They may be asked to troubleshoot center problems or be roving ambassadors and information collectors at IAB meetings. They are the center's link to the network of 50 other center evaluators and a data bank of all center activities during the past two decades. In fact, the number of ways that a Center Director may use the services of the evaluator are constrained only by the Center Director's imagination.

It would be a mistake to only view these evaluation tasks as external mandates. Each of them has important utility within the center and each may be used to enhance the Center Director's control.

Evaluator's Report (ER)

For start-up centers, this report documents the ideas, plans, and efforts that led to the planning grant/meeting and formal proposal. For continuing centers, the ER documents critical incidents and provides important information about the evolution of the center. Internal uses for this information include monitoring progress, milestones and achievements, and describing problems and opportunities to be attacked in the coming year. Since center stakeholders sometimes feel more comfortable confiding anonymously to the center evaluator, this report can produce the kind of surprise that is the hallmark of a good control system. Some centers have found that giving new IAB members the most recent ERs is the best way to introduce them to the operations of the center (see Appendix 8-1).

Exit Interviews

This procedure involves an interview with all members who are about to or have already left the center. However, given all the effort required to recruit new members, it is obviously important to do everything possible to keep them within the center. One strategy employed by some centers is a "pre-exit" interview: At the first sign that a member firm is considering leaving, the evaluator phones them to ask why and if anything might be done to fix the problem. Some factors are beyond the center's control, such as a corporate decision to curtail external research affiliations. When this occurs, the evaluator documents the factors that went into their decision. This is an example of post-action control. The evaluator can also obtain information regarding the basis on which a member would rejoin the center.

Process and Outcome Questionnaire

The results of this data gathering activity form the center's best longitudinal data base. This feedback from member and faculty questionnaires can be incorporated readily into a steering control system. The process and outcome questionnaire forms the core of this activity. Most IAB representatives do not have the time to answer very long questionnaires so it is short enough so that individual centers can add a few site-specific questions. The process and outcome questionnaire was developed by a team of I/UCRC evaluators with input from IAB firms and NSF I/UCRC program officers and the questions have gone through extensive piloting and preliminary psychometric evaluation.

Using the Process and Outcome Questionnaire for Management Control

The I/UCRC Process and Outcome (PO) questionnaires, available from your evaluator, solicits industry and faculty feedback on program processes, various outcomes and center management's need for steering control. The questionnaire includes closed and open-ended questions. Outcome questions focus on the center's impact on R&D, commercialization and other benefits. Process questions focus on the research program, level of interest, satisfaction with quality of the researchers, administration, satisfaction with project selection process, general satisfaction and membership renewal intention.

The industry and faculty PO questionnaires are administered annually to all IAB members by the local center evaluator. Analyses are performed locally by the evaluator and nationally at North Carolina State University. This system facilitates quick local feedback and benchmarks local performance. We can illustrate how evaluation data can be used as part of a control system by using the same issue addressed in the previous section—member satisfaction.

Defining the Units of Measure

Member retention and satisfaction are measured by responses to rating scales. One item focuses on intention to renew membership (1 = definitely not renew to 5 = definitely will renew). Seven items focus on different aspects of satisfaction with the research program, and eight items focus on satisfaction with different aspects of satisfaction with center administration (1 = not satisfied to 5 = very satisfied). In addition, members report how to improve center performance in each of these areas.

Establish Standards

It can be very difficult to interpret the meaning of an average satisfaction score of 3.5 on a 5-point scale, but PO data are collected annually and program-wide and so meaningful standards for interpreting these data have been developed. One standard is to meet or exceed last year's rating on all items. Another standard is to score at, or above national norms for the I/UCRC program.

Comparing and Interpreting

Comparing and interpreting performance in this system is quite straightforward. Center mean scores for the current year can be compared to last year and to the "norm" for the entire I/UCRC program. If a center is performing on a par with the previous year and above national norms on all areas except two, these are the areas on which the Center Director should focus. See Figure 8-10.

Actions

What action should a Center Director take given this kind of feedback? To some extent the answer depends upon what the director already knew and various local circumstances. If the information constitutes a surprise for the Center Director, e.g., a member reports renewal is unlikely, at a minimum the director would want more information about the relative dissatisfaction with the research program's focus and relevance to short-term needs. The Center Director will want to find out which firms are uncertain about their renewal and try to change their minds. On the other hand, if the Center Director already knew about a problem, this may reinforce the course of action already planned. It's worth

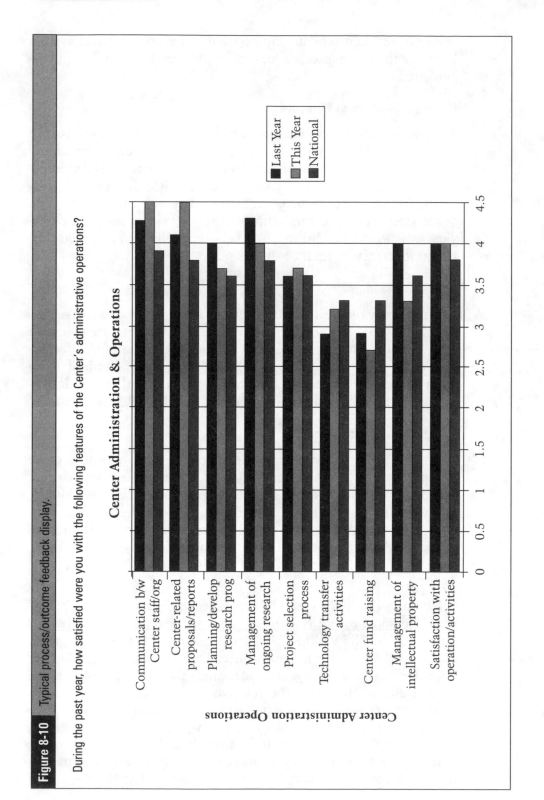

Figure 8-10   Typical process/outcome feedback display.

noting that standards, particularly outcome measures based on national norms, should be interpreted with caution. Firms look for different things from a center. Some outcomes reflect differences in values and expectations. For instance, investment in follow-on research is not an expectation of every IAB member, so it is not an accurate measure for every center. Like all control system data, PO feedback is only valuable if it is interpreted by a well-informed manager.

Summary

A Center Director should encourage the incorporation of evaluation into a broad and continuing system of management and control rather than isolated or occasional evaluations. The surest way to achieve this goal is for the Center Director to support and apply the work of the evaluator. Incorporating evaluation into a system of control is the same as adopting any new innovation and requires commitment education, and resources. The Center Director provides commitment and the National Science Foundation provides the education and resources in the person of an I/UCRC evaluator.

Evaluation is an important informational resource in the management and control of a center. The individual center evaluator, and his or her support infrastructure (NSF and the network of center evaluators), are resources that Center Directors need to draw on. As a minimum, it is the evaluator's job to keep the center in compliance with NSF guidelines. Many centers have found, however, that the independent evaluator serves an important role in the efficient operation of the center. As a Center Director, your job does not require you to perform evaluations; it does require you to attain the maximum benefit from the evaluation resources made available.

MANAGEMENT CONTROL CHECKLIST

Thinkers from Aristotle to Peter Drucker have written important books about how to maintain effective control. The following five rubrics encapsulize ways of maintaining effective control over an I/UCRC:

- Control begins with a clear sense of organizational purpose. When goals are set, strategies are developed to help meet them. All I/UCRCs began with a proposal of their purpose, goals and objectives which should be re-read from time to time to make certain that they are still appropriate. Everyone affiliated with the center needs to understand and appreciate them.

■ There is no one, best, control mechanism. Different areas and variables are amenable to control by a wide variety of tools that the director should use: university accounting procedures, questionnaire, center policies, voting protocol of the IAB, and personal judgment.

■ The concept of control should extend to all areas of the organization's operation. The director needs to control everything from financial and capital resources, project quality and timeliness, center personnel and graduate student production, to member satisfaction.

■ Decisive action is the hallmark of an effective control system. Deviation in time, cost, or performance warrants action to redirect the center's activity.

■ Effective control is a balance between over-control and lax control. Centers need to be especially aware of the university tendency for over-control of faculty. Directors must be specific and frugal in their requests for information from researchers and project leaders. It is possible to be in control without being controlling.

REFERENCES

Albanese, R. *Managing: Toward Accountability for Performance*. Homewood, IL: Richard Irwin, Inc., 1978.

Anderson, C.R. *Management: Skills, Functions and Organization Performance*. Dubuque, IA: Wm. C. Brown Publishers, 1984.

Brinckloe, W.D and Coughlin, M.T. *Managing Organizations*. Encino, CA: Glencoe Press, 1977.

Costinett, S. *The Language of Accounting in English*. NY, NY: Regents Publishing, Co., 1977.

National Science Foundation. *Evaluator's Handbook: NSF Industry-University Cooperative Research Centers Program*. Raleigh, NC: I/UCRC Evaluation Project, 1997.

Weiss, C.H. *Evaluation Research*. Englewood Cliffs, N.J, 1972.

APPENDIX 8-1

Evaluator's Report (Yearly) (ER)

General Instructions: Summarize the center's recent history (last 12 months or since the last history was prepared) by responding to the following questions.

1. **Goals and objectives**

Please describe the center's primary organizational and technical goals and objectives.

Instructions: This question can be answered by listing a center's official (written) and/or unofficial (but acknowledged) goals and objectives. Goals and objectives should be updated or elaborated upon (e.g., the basis for inferring informal goals) as needed. You should indicate if your answer reflects a change from previous years.

2. **Environmental/Institutional/Organization/ Research changes:**

Please describe any changes (positive or negative) which have occurred during the last year. Changes might occur in the following domains:

- *environment* (e.g., decline in industry's competitive position)
- *institution/university* (e.g., partnerships with other universities, shift in university priorities)
- *organization* (e.g., financial stability, structure, policy, planning, personnel)
- *research* (e.g., new or modified thrust areas).

Instructions: please address each domain. Emphasis should be on *significant* changes which might influence the center's ability to achieve its goals and objectives. Please attach an updated timeline which includes these changes.

3. **Center accomplishments**

Please describe any accomplishments or impact the center has had in the following areas:

- *knowledge/technical advances*
- *technology transfer*
- *educational impacts*.

In addition, comment on accomplishments which may reflect unique center objectives (e.g., forging international linkages, etc.)

Instructions: Evaluators are encouraged to obtain the information needed to answer this question from a variety of sources, including: program records (e.g., center's annual report), responses or comments provided in the P/O questionnaire, discussions with CD, IAB members and faculty.

4. **Analysis**

Based on the information provided above and other relevant information, comment on the health and vitality of the center. What are the implications of the various environmental, institutional, organizational and research changes? Is the center making adequate progress in achieving its objectives? What are the major obstacles and/or opportunities which may affect the center's ability to achieve its objectives during the next one to three years.

CHAPTER 9

KNOWLEDGE AND TECHNOLOGY TRANSFER IN COOPERATIVE RESEARCH SETTINGS

LOUIS TORNATZKY, *Southern Technology Council, Research Triangle Park, NC*

MITCHELL FLEISCHER, *Industrial Technology Institute, Ann Arbor, MI*

DENIS O. GRAY, *North Carolina State University, Raleigh*

KNOWLEDGE AND TECHNOLOGY TRANSFER

One of the primary reasons that companies join cooperative centers and programs is to be closer to the action in terms of linkage to new research and technology. Indeed, one of the primary reasons firms leave such centers is the failure of the center to transfer enough technology or useful research findings to industry. Despite the rapid growth of cooperative research centers, institutes, and programs in both academic settings and elsewhere over the past 15 years (Coursey and Bozeman, 1992; Etkowitz, 1991), these programs are always at risk unless there is a constant flow of technology to their sponsors. Unfortunately, IABs and directors of self-sustaining I/UCRCs graded their centers lowest on technology transfer among all operational areas (Gray, et al., 1991). Far too often the leadership of cooperative centers takes technology transfer for granted. As we shall see, member firms are often large, complex entities to which transfer will rarely take place without highly focused effort.

Changes in the Basis of Economic Competition

There are three fundamental reasons why knowledge and technology transfer are critical issues for cooperative research centers. The first concerns the impact the center has on its society, while the other two concern the very survival of the center itself.

Technology-based new products and processes are key components in how companies battle one another for markets and survival. The proportion of successful new products based on research-derived technologies is increasing (Mansfield, 1991; Nagle and Dove, 1991). The companies that are succeeding are those which have adopted a "first-to-market" business strategy (Sanderson, 1992; Gupta and Wileman, 1990; Reiner, 1989). Rapidly changing tastes and desires of customers are best addressed by being first with the most technologically feasible product. The implication for industrial participants in cooperative research programs is technological advantage must be extracted quickly, and the cooperative research program must facilitate it.

The Key to Member Retention

Not only are companies becoming more adept at competing with one another, they are also becoming more careful about their investment in R&D. While many companies have cut internal R&D and sought to leverage their R&D investments by engaging in cooperative relationships, they have also become much more attentive to monitoring its costs and benefits. Companies join a center for student recruitment, corporate statesmanship, and other reasons but the best predictor of whether a company will remain in a cooperative R&D relationship is whether they perceive benefits of *knowledge and technology transfer*. Everything else pales by comparison. Companies may believe that researcher X in university Y is doing some of the most advanced work in the world, but unless some of that new knowledge and technology translates into their industrial use, it is irrelevant.

Missing Skills, Missing People

Of the people who lead, manage, or do the technical and scientific work of cooperative R&D programs, only a small fraction have formal training or experience in knowledge utilization and technology transfer. They tend to be unfamiliar with—and too often hostile to—the behavioral, economic, business, and social science knowledge that is embedded in the practice of using research and technology for business advantage. Technology transfer tends to be neglected until the end of the year report of technology transfer results and impact. A senior technology transfer manager at Semitech compared "hunting-gathering" vs. "farming" (Smith, 1993). Hunting-gathering is the search for technology intermittently when confronted with a critical, emergent need. Farming is the investment in technology for the long-term, nurturing promising ideas, abandoning bad ones, systematically over an entire life cycle. When all works well, centers can help convert technology hunter-gatherers into technology farmers.

Is It Knowledge or Technology?

Without getting too deeply into the complex and somewhat confusing literature on technology transfer and related concepts (see Tornatzky and Fleischer, 1990, for an introduction), there are a few key concepts that are essential for the reader to understand, if only to enable us to all hold common definitions. Unfortunately, there is a fair amount of sloppy language and slippery definition in the field of technology transfer. In particular, there is much confusion about the difference among research results, knowledge, and technology. Typically, research results yield new knowledge. In contrast, technology involves a tool with which people can extend their living and working environments. The essence of a technology is its practical value; its doing something vs. its understanding. However, technology does not necessarily imply a physical artifact, machine, or device. Often, practical value or utility can be embodied in a formula, a piece of software, or set of procedures. The important point is that technology implies the application of knowledge having practical value and utility. Research results are not the same thing as a technology. Research results, whether empirical findings, statistical relationships, or new conceptual schema, are new knowledge. Knowledge is the bridge between research and technology, but different from practical or useful application, which is at the heart of technology.

Knowledge Use

Industrial participants *use new knowledge* from research results. For example, they use it for in-house proprietary development. The average I/UCRC firm reports they invest over $160,000 per year in follow-on funding (Gray & Meyer, 1993). They may use research results to suggest technological applications or to drive their own technology strategic planning. Knowledge use might be considered as the feedstock of subsequent technology development.

Technology Transfer

In contrast, the term technology transfer is much more immediately tied to business interests and objectives. It is embodied in tangible artifacts, devices, or tools. Technology implies practical value, and often that value is proprietary intellectual property protected by patents, trade secrets, copyrights, or licenses. Thus, technology transfer often involves legal and business transactions as much as knowledge. As far as the operation of cooperative research centers is concerned, the domains of knowledge transfer and technology transfer represent qualitatively different activities.

Technology transfer and knowledge are important to the participants in cooperative research centers but the way they are handled differs greatly. Because knowledge is not protected as is technology, publication is critical for the academic participants. In contrast, technology is almost always protected in some way, or its value is greatly diminished.

The Technology Life Cycle

Implied in this discussion is the notion that knowledge gets transformed or reconfigured as it evolves from research findings into a tool or product that can be used by a customer. These stages and phases are often described as the *technology life cycle*. This means that a given technology evolves or matures over time. For example, computer pointing device technology was basic research done at MIT and other universities which became applied research at Xerox PARC which developed the first mouse. A wide variety of product developments in mouse configuration, track balls, and light pens followed. The columns in Figure 9-1 show one version of a technology life-cycle from research to routinization.

The total life cycle involves a variety of different organizations and individuals more or less linked together. Not surprisingly, these individuals may have different views or perspectives about the nature of their work and its importance relative to other stages, phases, and participants. Of course, without all participants in the life cycle, there would be no practical application of technology. The rows in Figure 9-1 show the different types of individuals and organizations and when in the life-cycle they might be involved. Unfortunately, too often we see university professors disparaging the level of intellectual contribution required to turn their ideas into technology, and industry engineers disparaging professors for their lack of connection to the real world. A good "hand-off" between these groups is critical for the success of the life cycle.

A small but important microcosm of the total technology life cycle is played out in the context of cooperative research centers. Typical transactions and sub-stages that occur in the life of a

Figure 9-1   Technology life cycle.*

	Developing			Using		
	Research	**Development**	**Deployment**	**Adoption**	**Implementation**	**Routinization**
Environment	research labs	advanced manufacturing facilities	plants	plants	plants	plants
Organization	university, company R&D	technical centers	design centers, plants	companies	companies	companies
Work Group	I/UCRC+	company product development groups	manufacturing industrial engineering	manufacturing engineering	manufacturing engineering	manufacturing engineering
People	researchers	product, process design staff	production engineers	plant staff	plant staff	plant staff
Timeframe		Years to Decades			Weeks to Years	

*Adapted from Tornatzky and Fleischer, 1990.

center project include idea generation and project development, proposal review and project selection, project execution, review, and oversight, communication of findings, and post-project activities.

An Ongoing Process

Knowledge use and technology transfer are parts of an ongoing process which unfolds over time within the center and beyond. People and organizations play different roles in that process: *inventor, commercializer, technology champion,* and so on. The important point is that while these roles exist, they are not full-time jobs or responsibilities (or even legitimated) for those who occupy them, and that they all need to mesh with one another in order for the process of knowledge use and technology transfer to unfold over the whole life cycle. In order to get a sense of the potential complexities involved, the reader is referred to Chakrabarti and Hauschildt (1989), who describe the various roles that constitute the division of labor in innovation management.

PLANNING AN OPERATIONAL STRATEGY

The concepts just described may be expressed operationally in different ways, depending on the cooperative research setting. We will discuss operational options primarily in the context of our experience with the National Science Foundation's Industry-University Cooperative Research Centers (I/UCRC) Program. While we believe most of what we say will apply to most cooperative research settings, the reader should note any differences between this program and the one in which s/he operates, and act accordingly. This section will briefly summarize some operating principles, and then discuss their expression in terms of the project life cycle in centers.

Ensuring a Meaningful Voice for Industry

Almost everything a center does depends on a robust dialogue between industry and academia. The best way to ensure knowledge use and technology transfer is for this dialog to take place early and often in the project life cycle. The reader should refer to Chapters 5 and 6 for a fuller discussion of research planning and communication.

Benefits-Sharing vs. Proprietary Interests

The I/UCRC program is premised on several assumptions about corporate interests and behaviors, and the reasons that companies join centers. For one, it assumes that a consortium of companies can derive benefit from a process in which they guide the R&D agenda, and in which they share equally in the derived research. This typically results in procedures by which all member companies get early research results, and if a research-based technology is patented all get royalty-free licenses for internal use. Industry is at the same time trying to gain and maintain clear proprietary advantage over their competitors. One principle of center operations is to constantly maintain the balance between proprietary interests and collective benefits-sharing. If narrow proprietary interests prevail, leveraged research work won't take place; if benefits-sharing dominates, particularly in a way which erodes proprietary interests, companies may gradually loose business interest.

These processes tend to work well in most cases and centers, particularly when industrial members come from different industries or have different applications. The fact that most university research and proprietary technology is in such an early stage of the technology life cycle also keeps peace among the members. Consider the following real-life case from the I/UCRC for Dimensional Measurement and Control in Manufacturing at the University of Michigan.

> Members of the I/UCRC for Dimensional Measurement and Control in Manufacturing at the University of Michigan include all three of the major U.S. auto manufacturers, a machine tool manufacturer whose primary customers are the auto firms, and a vendor of non-contact gauging equipment whose primary customers are the auto firms. The center developed a new approach to optical measurement of sheet metal with the active participation of the gauging vendor and all three auto manufacturers. The gauging vendor has just begun the process of turning the technology into a product with all three automakers lined up to be its customers. The machine tool vendor is learning about the capability of the new gauging system so that the next generation of machine tool will meet the enhanced accuracy.

In this case a symbiotic relationship has developed among the university faculty, the gauge vendor, and the automakers, with the machine tool maker an avid onlooker who will benefit, but only in the long run.

When a technology has clear and important applications for commercialization but no center member company can move it to production, the scenario changes. Consider the following case from the Center for Aseptic Processing and Packaging at North Carolina State University.

> Members of the Center for Aseptic Processing and Packaging at North Carolina State University include some of the country's largest food processors and manufacturers and manufacturers of food processing and packaging equipment. The center developed and patented a thermal memory cell semiconductor device which measures the temperature of a food particle as it moves through the thermal system. Member firms were very excited about this technology because it might allow them to speed up processing times and win FDA approval for processing new food lines. Unfortunately, none of the firms was in the business of manufacturing semiconductors. In order to facilitate the commercialization of this invention, member firms waived their intellectual property rights. The center has spent a great deal of time developing a prototype and finding a commercializing partner. This process has taken more than two years and negotiations are still in process.

Successful transfer can occur, but it involves a great deal more effort and flexibility by both members and center. Later in this chapter we discuss alternatives to the typical non-exclusive intellectual property arrangement some centers may want to consider.

There are some rules of thumb for balancing shared benefits and proprietary interests. If a center goes along for several years and no company member or external partner generates process improvements or products from center research, then perhaps the agenda has shifted too far. On the other hand, if the fraction of one-on-one contract projects begins to exceed the core work, and there is limited enthusiasm for discussing early stage or basic projects, then the center may be turning into a university-based contract development organization. The solution in either case is to consciously and publicly shift the center's agenda.

The Role of Communication

One of the most common clichés in the technology transfer field is that it is a "body contact sport." Like most clichés this one has a large core of truth. The simple fact is that neither new knowledge nor technology is self-implementing. Moreover, one cannot assume that the potential users of knowledge or technology are waiting for it. In order for knowledge use and technology transfer to occur, it is important to communicate activities often, to as many constituencies as possible, in all media available to the I/UCRC. See Chapter 7.

Periodically members should receive some form of communication from the center or its faculty. This communication should be crafted to accommodate or overcome the communication system that exists within the member company. Center managers should not assume that the representative will pass on information to important others in his/her company. Often the representative is isolated by status or function. For example, a center representative from a company's R&D function may have little or no contact with people from the same firm's manufacturing function. The center must seek to develop multiple contacts within member companies so as to maximize the spread of information about the center and its activities. Some of the more explicit ways in which communication media can be deployed are as follows:

- **Academic Papers**. A key task in any university is to publish and disseminate scientific papers. Industrial participants can derive as much or more benefit from early or unpublished versions of the such papers. Make it a practice to provide drafts of papers and use industrial participants as early reviewers if they are so inclined. The Center for Advanced Computing and Communication at North Carolina State University and the Center for Dimensional Measurement and Control at the University of Michigan catalog all such papers in a technical reports series which is shown to prospective members and shared with new members. Publications are also made available on the Web. Other centers include research abstracts in their newsletters.

- **Personal Visits**. Although company representatives are supposed to disseminate center results within their organizations, some individuals do this job better than others. As a consequence, some centers require that all firms receive a certain number of visits each year and monitor this activity to ensure follow through.

- **Human Resources**. Graduate students trained under the auspices of a cooperative center and subsequently hired by industrial partners are a major technology transfer conduit. Some centers spotlight the work of students to get them working with company staff early in their training. Others have developed internship programs with member firms.

- **Doing Research**. In some centers, company personnel work side-by-side at a "bench level" with university faculty and students. In virtually all centers there is technical dialogue between company peers. Within the I/UCRC Program, NSF will cost-share "industrial sabbaticals" for faculty who spend at least a summer or semester working for a member firm. The firm must pay for part of the salary.

Transfer and Use Issues in Idea and Proposal Development

Project ideas come from many sources, not just from faculty. Successful cooperative centers have done a variety of things to ensure that a steady stream of project ideas emerge and reflect the effort of virtual teams.

- **White Papers**. One center asks industrial advisory board members to write short white papers on research issues that are then circulated among the IAB members and faculty.

- **Industry Presentations**. Another center has one industry representative each quarter make a formal presentation to the faculty and IAB members on the state of their field.

- **Brainstorming**. Other centers brainstorm separately from the normal center meeting. Brainstorming discussions are among faculty and industry members.

- **Request for Proposals**. Other centers use RFPs jointly crafted by center leadership, faculty and industry to generate proposal ideas.

- **Technology Transfer Plans**. At least one center asks for technology transfer plans in its project proposals. This forces faculty members to talk with industry about applications, concepts and practices.

The point of all of these techniques is to provide faculty and graduate students with some relatively clear boundaries and directions for useful proposals. Refer to Chapter 6 for a fuller discussion of additional issues and practices.

Transfer and Use Issues in Proposal Review and Project Selection

Perhaps the most highly leveraged technology transfer activity conducted by a center is project selection. Poor or undisciplined project selection will haunt the research agenda. The quality of the choices depends on the perspective of the stakeholder. Faculty and graduate students are inclined to pick projects with significant value to the scientific community and which will yield articles publishable in reputable academic journals. Although industry participants share those goals, they are more concerned about the problem-solving and business applications.

The cooperative center concept enables simultaneous accomplishment of these seemingly incompatible goals. However, in order for this to happen, it is important that the goals of the various stakeholders be discussed openly during project selection. Some portion of faculty project proposals should focus on expected industry relevance. Deliverables should be stated in industry terms. Development of this section should be based on prior interaction with industry participants.

Industrial participants need to play an active role in project selection, express their opinions, and be willing to work with faculty investigators to refine and re-craft a proposal. Industry participants should do more than vote up or down. See Chapter 6.

Transfer and Use Issues in Project Execution, Review, and Oversight

All should be attentive to transfer during project execution and should have a procedure for modifying or discontinuing projects.

During the semi-annual research reviews, there should be examination of any technical obstacles that will preclude practical or theoretical benefit from the project. If these obstacles cannot be overcome, the project should be discontinued. As the project progresses, do the originally-specified deliverables still make sense? Are there revisions needed? For example, if a research project begins to show promise of industrial applications, expected deliverables might be revised to a proof-of-concept prototype, sample material, or more tangible product. A review of budget will show if the project is over its expected spend rate, slow to start or needs new level of effort estimates.

Well-managed projects accomplish expected technical deliverables and facilitate the flow of knowledge use and technology transfer to industrial participants. Most centers should adopt fairly formal protocols, checklists, and benchmarks to assess the progress of projects.

Congruent with our previous discussion about shared benefits vs. proprietary interests, it is common that some companies will have a higher level of business interest in a particular project. Oversight and review will be enhanced if one or more industry "mentors" work closely with a project. This usually results in a better project as well as an acceleration of the technology transfer process.

Transfer Issues in Communication of Findings

In the university, publication of an article in a scientific journal, or presentation of a paper at a scientific meeting is the culmination of research but these modes of dissemination often do not reach the industrial audience. In order to increase the probability of knowledge use and technology transfer, the cooperative center must explicitly design and implement a dissemination strategy.

This implies several subtasks. One is to clearly identify the information users in member companies. That is, one should not assume that results will be transferred from the official IAB member to other users within his/her company. Some centers send their reports to the technical libraries in member firms. Others have their technical reports on-line so they can be accessed electronically.

Many industrial scientists and engineers lack the time or inclination to read full blown scientific reports. With little effort, it is possible to capture the essence in a much smaller document. Some cooperative centers have developed families of one page reports (often included in newsletters), executive summaries, or full-fledged academic versions. Other centers provide IAB firms with half-hour briefings on-site. Not only does more robust dissemination occur, but much good will is created as are ideas for follow-on projects.

Findings demonstrated in early-stage physical prototypes, software, or demonstrations are another means. Technology transfer is much easier when potential users touch and feel it. Centers with faculty who fail or refuse to take a research project from theory into practice lose an important opportunity to promote transfer.

Transfer Issues in Supplementals and Enhancements

Many centers become involved in *supplemental* or *enhancement* projects funded separately by IAB members and dedicated to more narrowly-defined research and deliverables (see Chapter 11). In some centers, these projects are *de facto* proprietary projects that do not share results with other members. Often, sponsoring companies have the right of first refusal to license inventions that result. In other cases, sponsoring companies are willing for the projects to be treated like any core project. In exchange, they get favored indirect cost and set the agenda for the project. Some centers double their research budget this way. Consider this example from the Center for Dimensional Measurement and Control in Manufacturing at the University of Michigan.

> One of the ongoing, shared projects in the Center for Dimensional Measurement and Control in Manufacturing at the University of Michigan is learning how to reduce variation in the production of large stamped body panels for automobiles. This involves a variety of smaller projects to understand how to measure and control such variation. One of the center's large auto makers funded an enhancement project to investigate specific processes for variation reduction. Results of the project are available to all center members including their competitors, who are also center members.

The project is conducted at one of their plants. One advantage to the auto maker is learning more than the others, since the project is in its plant. It also benefits from reduced variation on the specific process that is the focus of the project. This technology transfer is immediately tied to the business interests of the company. However, there is danger for dedicated, company-specific projects to dominate the overall center agenda and eliminate the incentive for other companies to participate.

Transfer and Use Issues in Center Evaluation

One means of retaining and accentuating that focus on technology transfer is to explicitly build it into periodic evaluation data-gathering. See Chapter 8. Besides a handful of questions that are asked in center evaluation surveys, centers should gather information from industrial participants on their knowledge use and technology transfer practices, industrial member roles, processes in the company setting, and additional IAB participants.

TACTICS AND IMPLEMENTATION

Given the preceding conceptual discussion, we can now move on to specific tactics and ways to implement them. In this section we will provide specific advice in five areas: (1) roles and responsibilities; (2) staff training and development; (3) procedures; (4) tools; and (5) intellectual property.

Center Roles and Responsibilities

The only way to ensure that knowledge use and technology transfer will happen is to assign the responsibility to someone. After the

Center Director's job, this is the second most important function in a center. If knowledge use and technology transfer don't happen, companies will leave the center. The technology transfer person should have a title equivalent to associate director and report to the Center Director. Ideally, the individual should have substantial industrial experience, knowledge and experience about the management and movement of intellectual property, and the ability to oversee the communication practices and programs of the center. Depending upon the size of the R&D program and the volume of results and technology suitable for transfer, this might be initially a part-time position. A retired industry executive or manager is often ideal. A senior faculty member with substantial industry exposure may also lead this effort.

If neither of these are available, other resources on campus may offer technology transfer help on a reduced cost basis. The university's office on patents and licenses may be able to dedicate some percentage of staff to the center. In some universities, this office may provide little or no useful advice. Student interns are a particularly rich source of help on some campuses. Several business schools have developed degree programs or specializations in technology management or its equivalent and are anxious to place promising interns.

Staff Training and Development

It is useful to assume that none of the faculty or students attached to the center know anything about the theory and practice of technology transfer or the promotion of knowledge use. All this suggests formal training of them can enhance the technology transfer process. Training ranges from a few-hours, to two to three days (Tornatzky, 1992). In most cases, anything beyond a half-day program will inhibit much-needed participation. Faculty members should be the prime audience. Avoid programs that concentrate on legal details of intellectual property. Try to find one geared to faculty interests.

It is also useful to involve or create separate programs for the industrial participants in a university-based center technology transfer training program. In fact, the blockages are often as much or more pronounced on the industrial side. The solution for center managers is to involve a wide range of company participants through joint training events involving both faculty and industrial partners.

Procedures

The desire to increase knowledge use and technology transfer will remain just that unless center procedures are instituted to make it a normal part of daily operations. Laboratory notebooks should be assigned to every faculty and student researcher with instructions for documenting technology development along with a center handbook, describing in 10 to 15 pages the technology transfer mission, goals, and procedures (see Figure 9-2). The handbook should be reviewed annually in an open center-wide staff meeting. The Center Director might also adapt the Association of University Technology Managers (AUTM) 1994 guidebook on technology transfer.

Figure 9-2	Technology transfer procedures manual.

■ **Invention disclosure and publication permission forms** should be readily available to all researchers attached to the center, along with instructions for their use.

■ **University policies** on technology transfer, intellectual property, royalties, licensing, and related issues should be distributed and discussed annually.

■ **Written guidelines** for communicating with industrial partners should be developed and circulated among research staff. These might include sample or form letters for routine correspondence.

■ **Market research templates** or approaches should be developed for exploring the market potential of a technology. These might include data collection and presentation. A template for a technology transfer prospectus should be developed.

Tools for Knowledge Use and Technology Transfer

In addition to the more mundane procedural aids described above, center managers should also think about the emerging set of tools which have recently been developed to assist the technology transfer function. A good metaphor for this development is that of *technologies of technology transfer*. Various computerized databases, expert systems and decision aids, paper and pencil checklists, and training games also promote knowledge use and technology transfer. For example, the Industrial Technology Institute has produced a live action simulation game called ADVANTIG to help people understand some of the problems of introducing company-wide technological change (Southern Technology Council, 1993). In addition, there are commercial databases of thousands of university-based researchers and their areas of expertise which identify research partners at other institutions. Databases of intellectual property are available for license in which centers may list their intellectual property. Databases organized by company technology enable technology transfer, and member and commercializing partner recruiting. A company called CORPTECH publishes national and regional directories of high technology companies and their products (Southern Technology Council, 1994). In fact, most universities' centers have access to such databases. The university's business school and marketing department may also help in marketing new technologies.

The Technology Transfer Society publishes a catalog which describes 58 tools and methods for assisting the technology transfer function (Nicol and Roeske, 1993). The Southern Technology Council (1994) also publishes a tools catalog. Center managers would be advised to become familiar with these tools.

Inventions and Intellectual Property

Intellectual property implies that an invention is or can be protected by law. Moreover, intellectual property often derives *value* from the fact that it can be protected. Many researchers fail to understand that an invention is different from a protected piece of intellectual property. They need to learn how to get to the latter, without impinging on their research creativity and productivity.

Invention Patents

According to U.S. patent law, an invention is patentable if it is:

- **Novel**. Not yet known or disseminated through any medium of communication;

- **Useful**. Has practical value so anyone skilled in the art can put it to use;

- **Non-obvious**. Non-obvious solution or application to someone skilled in the art.

The Invention Disclosure

In a university, when there is an invention from research work, an *invention disclosure* is filed with the institution's intellectual property or technology transfer office. This is evidence of the date of the invention, and identity of its inventors. U.S. patent law follows a principle of first to invent to define intellectual property ownership. The inventor may be asked to document work leading to the invention. All researchers should have an up-to-date laboratory notebook that can provide such information. In many nations, primacy is established by who *files* the formal patent application first. As this book goes to press, there is much debate about whether the U.S. should adopt this "first to file" approach to intellectual property.

Public Disclosure

Filing an invention disclosure does not secure patent protection so university researchers must be cautioned against openly discussing their research in public in formal speech, paper, published article, or informal conversation. Such public disclosure eliminates the possibility of protecting an invention by the trade secret approach or may preclude securing a patent outside the U.S. and thus eliminate effective entry into lucrative markets. It may preclude copyright protection, unless copyright has been claimed from the start. Finally, and perhaps most critically, it starts the clock on the U.S. patent process. At the point of public disclosure, the inventor will have one year to apply for a U.S. patent or lose all patent protection. Since the patent application process often can be lengthy, this is no trivial matter.

Obviously, the law concerning public disclosure has all the appearance of being contrary to the norms, practices, and habits of the practicing academic. How can one publish, interact with colleagues, and promote the free interchange of knowledge and still be involved in technology transfer? The solution lies in the *sequence* of how one does things. If the faculty researcher files an invention disclosure and files for a patent before publishing an article or presents a paper, the invention will be protected. Failure to do this is often the result of ignorance. More often, the faculty member is unaware of the importance of this sequence as a deadline for a favorite conference or journal approaches.

In the context of a cooperative center, if the faculty invention derives from center-funded research, the industrial participants will want to learn about the discovery. However, industrial participants and all visitors at center meetings should sign a non-disclosure agreement to promise to maintain the secrecy of the invention, but these agreements are inherently leaky and provide little more than a temporary protection against disclosure. Faculty and institution need to move smartly to secure more formal protection.

- **Patents**. This is the preferred protection for university-originated inventions to exclude others from making, using, or selling it. Once granted, the patent has a 17-year term. The details of the invention are published by the U.S. Patent Office. Most patent applications are turned down. It will take another couple of years of re-application and discussions before it is granted. Some organizations intentionally may drag out the process to secure a longer *de facto* protection period. Once granted, a patent can be licensed to one or more third parties.

- **Trade Secrets**. In some industries and technical areas, trade secrets are the preferred approach to securing intellectual property protection. A trade secret derives value from participants keeping quiet about the technical details of an invention. While some people argue this is impossible in academic settings, some inventions involve novel and useful technology that has little scientific value. The faculty inventor will have no interest in publishing such information. Other inventions constitute know-how or craft knowledge more easily protected through trade secrets. In one example, a master's thesis developed a sophisticated optical instrument that was ultimately licensed to a company as a trade secret. The scientific questions being addressed in the thesis were such a small part of the prototype instrument, the trade secret arrangement worked.

- **Copyright**. A copyright protects written expressions of ideas, rather than the idea itself. Besides seeking patent protection for the core invention, one might also seek copyright protection for relevant documentation, training tapes, records, or films. In addition, copyright protects software (although there are software patents as well). Copyrights are easy to obtain in a few months. The term of a copyright for an individual is life plus 50 years; for an organization, publication plus 75 years, or creation plus 100 years. Copyright notice should be on every technically relevant center publication or document. While protection is not complete until copyrighted material is registered, on a *de facto* basis protection is realized by that simple procedure.

- **Trademarks**. A trademark is a distinctive name or logo that is attached to goods or services. If there is some logical and catchy name that you have been using to describe the invention, go ahead and register it as a trademark. Eventually, if and when you get to the point of licensing the invention, the protected trademark adds more value. Trademarking is relatively easy to do, its term is as long as the trademark is being used, and it may have more value ultimately than the technology itself.

Toward a Center Strategy for Intellectual Property

Normal practice in NSF Cooperative Research Centers, when an invention has been developed, is to protect it through patenting or other means, and then make it available to all of the industrial participants on a royalty free, non-exclusive basis. In most cases member companies also share in the costs of patenting. This approach has worked well; however it may create some disincentives for full commercialization. This is particularly so when the costs of development are large and the time frame of getting to product is lengthy.

Each center-originated invention should be approached individually, with an eye toward maximizing the benefit to the center as a whole, and to the industrial members. Every invention has its own unique aspects, and center management should craft the response accordingly. As a consequence, some centers have adopted intellectual property by-laws in which non-exclusivity is the default but which involve a number of other options spelled out in a decision-tree. The decision tree might allow any one of the following: non-exclusive royalty-free for all members; limited but royalty-bearing license for member who shares in filing costs; exclusive license if only one member is interested; or exclusive license for a non-member if no members are interested. Mechanics of intellectual property agreements in the context of cooperative research (including sample contract language), can be found in a recent publication of the Government-University-Industry Research Roundtable (1993).

EMERGING ISSUES

Much of what has been described above derives from the accumulated experience of the NSF Industry-University Cooperative Research Centers program during the late 1970s to the mid-1990s timeframe. However, during this period developments have been occurring in other venues, which are, in effect, re-defining the terms of what cooperative research is, and how it is organized. Some of these developments are in an early stage, and many derive from consortia that are much larger or not university-based. Nonetheless, they may be instructive for center managers, researchers, and industrial participants. We will discuss four areas of new trends and developments: (1) next generation media and communications approaches; (2) new approaches to project selection and execution; (3) new structural models for cooperative research relationships; and (4) new trends in relevant public policy.

Next Generation Media and Communication

We are entering a new era with the use of electronic media in technology transfer (Anderson, 1993). One such new communication medium is the rapidly-growing system of digitized information networks by which text and soon video and audio can be sent to literally millions of users. The Internet provides electronic mail, news, and high speed file transfer services to millions of sites around the world. A number of centers already use Internet websites for sharing research results, center activities, student vita and other information. with their corporate participants. The I/UCRC at Purdue University, University of Florida, and Oregon University may be the most advanced in this area: (http://www.cs. purdue.edu/SERC).

A related communication medium of interest to center managers is the video conference. There is large literature which indicates that communication richness and the conveying of subtle meaning is enhanced by combining visual and auditory cues with words. Video conferencing exploits this to reduce the number and cost of actual face-to-face meetings, increase the number of virtual face-to-face meetings, and enable a great deal of delicate and critical business to be conducted. Center managers can start by contacting their regional telephone company. In most areas of the country it is necessary for each participant to be in a specially-arranged studio facility, few of which are in the public domain. This medium is most appropriate and effective for small meetings of 4-8 people, such as an executive committee or meeting with a group from a potential licensee company.

Another group of communication media comes under the label of computer-supported cooperative work (CSCW) or groupware. These are software systems by which a group of individuals sitting in front of a networked computer terminal work together. There are commercial versions. An example is Lotus Notes®. The most likely application for centers is participants planning a research agenda or exploring applications of a research finding (Olson and

Olson, 1991). The Center for Management of Information at the University of Arizona has developed such a tool, the Electronic Meeting System, to support I/UCRC research reviews. Virtual reality demonstration of technology in real time is possible for technology transfer applications, too.

New Approaches to Project Selection and Execution

Many of the newer approaches to project selection and execution are taking place in industrially operated consortia. Rather than selecting and funding a single research project in a problem area, waiting for results, and then deciding upon subsequent development or transfer plans, a bundle of related activities or projects is launched more or less at the same time. This might mean going to early technology prototype even while the research project is still being finished. The new model also implies mixing people from different stakeholder organizations at the bench level to engage in project work.

The New Public Policy Environment

Virtually every federally funded science or technology initiative has to be linked to technology transfer results, commercialization, and economic growth. There is a strong belief that cooperative relationships, joint ventures, and linkages are essential to realizing the economic growth potential of federal investments in technology. This is reflected in NIST Advanced Technology Program and Technology Reinvestment Programs. Major government efforts to address the education and training issues that are involved in moving to a high value-adding economy is an interesting opportunity for cooperative centers. Because they already involve industry and university in a consortial arrangement, a number of I/UCRCs have competed successfully for funding from these programs. Other centers should consider them. (See Chapter 11.)

New University Culture

Many university cultures conflict with these new technology transfer roles and behaviors. Few universities include helping industry or enhancing economic growth as part of their organizational mission. Faculty rarely get tenure or promotion for filing patents or securing licenses as they do for refereed publication. For university-based technology transfer to work, this must change.

This is not to imply that universities should abandon their traditional roles in both fundamental research and education. Rather, it implies the university should view itself from a larger perspective, one in which its traditional roles are a critical part of a much larger process. In fact, if we look back a century to the founding of land-grant and technical colleges in the United States, it becomes clear that the new culture we are advocating is not so very different from the very roots of the American university system as a practical place to improve society and its economic well-being.

SUMMARY

Knowledge use and technology transfer are critical outcomes from industrial member participation in cooperative research centers. Differences between industrial and university participants in a cooperative center can be overcome; indeed, that is the reason for establishing such a center in the first place. *However, building a center only increases the probability that technology transfer will happen*. Bridging this gap requires persistent effort by both sides. In particular both sides must:

- **Recognize the Need to be Proactive**. Both university and industry participants must recognize the need to establish procedures and take action regarding knowledge use and technology transfer. These things do not happen by themselves. Creating a staff position in the center with explicit responsibility for knowledge use and technology transfer will facilitate this.

- **Use multiple media for transfer**. This includes paper and presentations, one- on-one visits, meetings, websites, and oversight by industry.

- **Consider Use and Transfer in Project Selection and Review**.

- **Train Staff on Intellectual Property Issues**. Make sure all investigators and all industry participants understand the intellectual property issues involved in a center.

- **Establish Procedures to Protect Intellectual Property**. Have forms and procedures in place to make it easy for investigators to make disclosures, file patents, and protect trade secrets.

- **Keep Informed about Emerging Trends.**

REFERENCES

Anderson, H. *Virtual Proximity: The Promise and Reality of Electronic Media in Technology Transfer*. Paper presented at annual meeting of the Technology Transfer Society, Ann Arbor, Michigan, June 27-29, 1993.

Association of University Technology Managers. *AUTM Technology Transfer Practice Manual*. 71 East Ave, Norwalk, CT, 1994.

Chakrabarti, A. and Hauschildt, J. The Division of Labour in Innovation Management. *R&D Management*, 1989, Vol 19, No. 2, pp.161-171.

Coursey, D. and Bozeman, B. Technology Transfer in US Government and University Laboratories: Advantages and Disadvantages for Participating Laboratories. *IEEE Transactions on Engineering Management*, Vol. 39, No. 4, November, 1992, pp.347-351.

Etkowitz, H. and Peters, L.S. Profiting from Knowledge: Organizational Innovations and the Evolution of Academic Norms. *Minerva.*, Vol.29, No. 2, Summer, 1991, pp.133-166.

Government-University-Industry Research Roundtable. *Intellectual Property Rights in Industry-Sponsored University Research*. Washington, DC: National Academy Press, 1993.

Gray, D. Stewart, M., Gidley, T., and Blakely, C. *Self-Sustaining Industry-University Centers: Is there Life After NSF Funding*. Washington, DC: National Science Foundation,1991.

Gray, D. and Meyer, D. *Process-Outcome Survey Findings for the NSF I/UCRC Program: 1992-93*. Raleigh, NC: Psychology Department, North Carolina State University, 1993.

Gupta, A.K. and Wileman, D. Accelerating the Development of Technology-Based New Products, *California Management Review*, Vol. 32, No. 2, Winter, 1992, pp. 24- 44.

Nagle, R. and Dove, R. *21st Century Manufacturing Enterprise Strategy: An Industry- Led View*, Bethlehem, PA: Iacocca Institute, Lehigh University, 1991.

Mansfield, E. Academic Research and Industrial Innovation, *Research Policy*, Vol. 20, No. 1, February, 1991, pp. 1-12.

Reiner, G. Winning the Race for New Product Development. *Management Review*, Vol. 78, 1989, No. 8, pp. 52-53.

Nicol, M. and Roeske, J. A., eds. *Technology Transfer Toolkit*, Industrial Technology Institute and Technology Transfer Society, Ann Arbor, MI, 1993.

Olson, G. and Olson, J. User-Centered Design of Collaboration Technology. Journal of Organizational Computing, 1,1991, pp. 61-83.

Sanderson, S. Design for Manufacturing in an Environment of Continuous Change, *Integrating Design and Manufacturing for Competitive Advantage*. G. Susman (ed.). New York: Oxford University Press, 1992.

Smith, D. Relationships as Tools. Paper presented to Annual Meeting of the Technology Transfer Society, Ann Arbor, Michigan, June 27-29, 1993.

Southern Technology Council. Tools for Technology Change, *Regional Forum*, Winter, 1993.

Southern Technology Council Tools for Technology Change, *Regional Forum*, Summer, 1994.

Southern Technology Council, *A Catalog of Manufacturing Improvement Tools*. Research Triangle Park, NC: Southern Growth Policies Board, P.O. Box 12293, in press.

Tornatzky, L. G. Changing Academic Cultures: An Experimental Intervention. Paper presented at ORSA/TIMS Joint National Meeting, San Francisco, California, November 2-4, 1992.

Tornatzky, L.G. and Fleischer, M. The Processes of Technological Innovation. Lexington, MA: Lexington Books, 1990.

CENTER LEADERSHIP:

Putting It All Together

LOUIS TORNATZKY, *Southern Technology Council,*
Research Triangle Park, NC

KAY LOVELACE, *University of North Carolina, Greensboro*

DENIS O. GRAY, *North Carolina State University, Raleigh*

S. GEORGE WALTERS, *Professor Emeritus, Rutgers, University, NJ*

ELIEZER GEISLER, *University of Wisconsin, Whitewater*

INTRODUCTION

The role of leadership in starting and maintaining a NSF Industry-University Cooperative Research Center is central. Few NSF centers have succeeded without an effective leader. The center director (or founder) is essentially an intrapreneur who devotes an enormous amount of energy and expertise into developing and founding an enterprise. In the early stages of a center, the Center Director's gathering resources, obtaining commitment from industry, faculty, and university administrators are paramount. Later on, the Center Director's role is fine-tuning and routinizing operations and building leadership skills throughout the organization.

Growth and evolution of the I/UCRC are the result of the leader's abilities to develop a distinguished faculty research core, obtain industry support, and nurture leadership in other center members. This chapter focuses broadly on leadership in an I/UCRC and is less operational in its focus than other chapters in the text. We start with the notion of leadership and how it applies to the cooperative research center. We then address several key leadership issues in an I/UCRC including exercising intrapreneurship, spanning organizational boundaries, creating cooperative research teams, managing a changing center, and knowing oneself.

What Is Leadership in a Cooperative Research Center?

In our everyday lives, we often use the term "leadership" to characterize those we think of as born or natural leaders. Since few people feel that they measure up as natural leaders, they often feel uncomfortable when thrust into leadership jobs and assignments.

The result is that they choose to focus primarily only on tasks and activities in which they feel skilled, and neglect the other, less familiar activities of leadership. So it is with cooperative research centers.

Since the assigned I/UCRC leaders usually come from distinguished scientific and technical backgrounds, too often the tendency is to focus exclusively on tasks that are primarily technical in nature and to ignore the interpersonal and relational aspects of leading a center. The result is often failure. The intellectual power of a research agenda can carry a center for a while, but only leadership can enable it to blossom.

Most views of leadership are consistent in their assumption that leaders are people who can effectively influence others to carry out activities beyond those that they would normally carry out. Behavioral science researchers have investigated numerous leadership theories, including the commonly held belief that leadership is based overwhelmingly on personality traits or characteristics that some people are born with and others are not. Unfortunately, this "great man or woman" view of leadership leads many to conclude that they do not have the ability to carry out the tasks and roles involved. Contrary to this assumption, researchers have found there are few traits that consistently predict leader effectiveness. In contrast, researchers have found that many people can be effective leaders, given sufficient intelligence to conceptualize the demands of the job and sufficient motivation to carry out the tasks involved. *In fact, intelligence is one of the few measurable traits that consistently correlate with effective leadership.*

A second theory of leadership suggests that different organizations require different styles of leadership, e.g., military, universities, business and industry, non-profits, and government vary substantially (Lord and Mayer, 1990). What is expected of a leader in industry differs from what is expected in academic institutions. Since I/UCRC Center Director responsibility spans these two worlds, their leadership must accommodate both styles.

I/UCRC stakeholders are either affiliated with industry or the university. Industry stakeholders include IAB members, scientists in member firms, other firms in the industry associated with the

I/UCRC. University stakeholders include center faculty, students, and university administrators. The Center Director must influence stakeholders in two very different environments.

While the leader/director must be someone who can influence the center's stakeholders and constituents, what is it that leaders must do? One framework separates leadership responsibilities from management responsibilities. Bennis and Nanus (1985) characterized leaders as people who "do the right thing," i.e., they have a strategic overview of the purposes of the center and the work involved and this perspective guides their work. In contrast, managers are people who "do things right." Both are important in an I/UCRC, but they differ in terms of the required behavior and, sometimes, in terms of who can fill the role. An effective Center Director needs to adapt his/her behavior similarly. For example, a Center Director must assign space and facilities. In these situations Center Directors need not consult the membership and often they can be managed by a capable administrator allowing the Center Director to focus energy on "doing the right thing." (See Figure 10-1.)

Thus, leadership, rather than management, is called for when the situation is non-routine and ill-defined. Consistent with this view, Heifetz (1994) has asserted that leaders are people who motivate their constituents to meet challenges that require adaptation or learning. Heifetz explains that adaptive challenges consist

Figure 10-1	Situations calling for directive, administrative skills.

Situations

Simple	Assignment of space, facilities and other resources among projects and faculty.
Factual	Decisions on finances and budget. Decision agreements such as continuation of a research project approved by the IAB.
Predictable	Tasks for interactions with industry.
Repetitive	Preparations for IAB meeting.
Deadlines	Responding to requests from member companies to solve technical problems.
Mundane	Maintenance of lab equipment.

of gaps "between the shared values people hold and the reality of their lives, or of a conflict among people in a community over values or strategy" (p. 254). Adaptive problems require learning, both to define the problem and to develop and implement a solution. Heifetz argues that, because adaptive problems are complex and involve multiple sets of values, leaders must involve their followers in defining and solving them.

This perspective is particularly useful for looking at the work of an organization most centrally defined as a boundary-spanning unit. The hybrid structure of I/UCRCs involves multiple stakeholders/constituents with different values and priorities. For example, university researchers typically value freedom to choose their own research directions, creation of basic knowledge, and freedom to disseminate knowledge as dictated by the academy. Industry, on the other hand, values the potential competitive edge gained by entering an I/UCRC. Industry often hopes to actualize this by controlling research topics and the dissemination of results (Fairweather, 1991). These conflicting values are present within the context of the I/UCRC. Subtly, or not so subtly, Center Directors must exercise leadership if these contradictions are to be resolved to achieve a synthesis and direction.

Typically, such situations require input from individuals with diverse expertise and perspectives. Further, because individuals are more likely to implement plans in which they have had a voice, the leader can strengthen commitment to the center by involving other members in strategic decisions. In I/UCRCs, commitment to goals and the strategy of the center are essential because such commitment is more likely to engender a willingness on the part of other faculty to share the leadership responsibilities of the center. Figure 10-2 provides a list of some situations within an I/UCRC requiring participative, enabling leadership. Notice that these situations have far-reaching consequences often requiring consent and participation from center faculty and industrial members.

This does not mean that the Center Director is a facilitator but rather an advocate to constituents. The Center Director advocates development of a shared vision of the center's future. The I/UCRC director is often the first to articulate such a vision, but if it does not capture the imagination and support of members and constituents, the center is not likely to grow. Authority over I/UCRC constituents is limited so the Center Director must rely on interpersonal skills to accomplish this.

Figure 10-2	Participatory leadership situations.

Situations

Complex	Development of the research agenda.
Beneficial	Transfer of outcomes from the center's research program to industry.
Unpredictable	Termination of program or project due to unfavorable review by industry.
Unique	Discussion on foreign company becoming member.
Long-term	Cooperative agreements with another center.
Critical	Marketing the center to prospective members.

Summary

The previous perspectives on leadership inform our thinking about I/UCRC leadership because they suggest that: (1) understanding the need for intelligence, leaders are made, not born; (2) Center Directors must deal with internal and external constituents with whom they have differing degrees of influence; (3) Center Directors must distinguish situations in terms of their call for participative, enabling leadership behaviors vs. directive, administrative management type behaviors; and (4) Center Directors must use interpersonal influence to help their constituents meet adaptive challenges.

While these responsibilities are challenging, Heifetz (1994) provides a metaphor that is useful for thinking about some of the roles the leader must play. He suggests that the leader must be able to "get on the balcony," to alternate between participating and observing. Thus, to help the leader think about how to move the enterprise forward, he or she must step back to try to understand what it is that concerns constituents or causes them to be in conflict.

What aspects of managing a center are likely to represent adaptive challenges? While there are certainly many, we have identified six broad concerns that constitute adaptive challenges for a center: creating a new enterprise, technical vision, boundary spanning, team culture, developmental needs of a changing organization, and knowing oneself.

ACTING AS AN INTRAPRENEUR

The initiation of a cooperative research organization requires some of the more difficult aspects of leader behavior. The leader will undertake a bundle of actions which together constitute one of the hardest tasks imaginable—starting an enterprise from scratch. Such a task requires thinking and acting as both an entrepreneur and an intrapreneur. As defined by Webster, an entrepreneur is "a person who organizes and manages a business undertaking, assuming the risk for the sake of the profit." Although a cooperative research center is not strictly a business, the definition holds for what is expected of a center leader.

For one, clearly there is risk. There is a relatively high failure rate of organizations such as cooperative research centers. For every successful cooperative center launched, there is one center which failed in the stages of planning or early implementation. In addition to the large risk of organizational failure, there are many mini-risks along the way including lost opportunities, conflicts with administrators, collegial jealousies, and the cashing-in of valuable "IOUs" with industrial contacts. In order to build the center, the leader will need to be experimenting constantly in organizational relationships, personnel strategies, technical direction, and growth strategies. Most of these experiments will be initiated on the basis of minimal or zero information. There is much seat-of-the-pants risk taking involved in center leadership.

While university researchers seldom speak of "profit," the successful cooperative research center can yield much in the way of profit (defined as resource aggrandizement). Profit in a center includes the leveraging of the corporate members' research funds in the center, and the use of their own research funds. In the first instance, member companies profit by benefitting from research that is funded by their own contributions multiplied by the number of member companies. In the second instance, member companies profit by "outsourcing" their research activities to the cooperative center, while they receive high quality research at very little expense (relative to the cost of their in-house research). Faculty profit by increasing their research support and expanding their intellectual horizons. Further, there have been other individual rewards attached to success as the creator of a center. Faculty who take a turn at center leadership often end up becoming university deans. They also tend to function as a magnet for other funds and opportunities.

Yet a Center Director's situation is very different from the commercial entrepreneur. The Center Director confronts a more limited environment, with fewer options and more constraints (e.g., framed by a government sponsor, university, and industry rules and expectations). In fact, Center Directors' positions are similar to those of corporate intrapreneurs, or the entrepreneurs that operate within the constraints of a structured organization. Typically, intrapreneurship is "a process by which large organizations use their own members to originate and implement new ventures and products . . . to ensure institutional strength" (Perlman, et al., 1988). As an example of academic intrapreneurship, Perlman, et al. described an intrapreneurial process that was used to revitalize the University of Wisconsin at Oshkosh. In this process, a new Chancellor took bold action by proposing and championing radical scheduling and funding changes that better met the needs of the student body as well as those of the faculty. But, while he took decisive action, he involved faculty in developing support for the change that would fundamentally change their working lives. Much as proposed by Heifetz, he involved them in addressing the gap between reality and their values.

While corporate intrapreneurs often found their own company as they differentiate their activities, the leader-founder-intrapreneur in the university has the outlet of forming a separate institutional entity—the Center. Although the center has limited autonomy, it gives the university intrapreneur an outlet for some of the energy of creation that is characteristic of entrepreneurs.

While we have downplayed the idea of natural born leaders, there is a great deal of evidence that successful entrepreneurs tend to share a certain number of behavioral dispositions. Specifically, Perlman, et al. (1988) note that intrapreneurs are:

1. *Risk takers*: intrapreneurs seem more likely to take risks, albeit calculated and well-defined. They are "dreamers who do . . . [who] figure out how to turn an idea into a profitable reality (p.18)." Similarly, Bennis (1993) explained that leaders have the "ability to accept risk . . . . [they have the] capacity to make as many mistakes as . . . soon as possible and thus get them out of the way." Mistakes are seen as something to learn from and use; not as failure, but as the next step.

2. *Autonomous:* intrapreneurs often have personal needs such as autonomy, responsibility, and ownership which are met by developing a new innovation within an organization.

3. *Are focused on change and opportunity:* intrapreneurs ask questions such as "How can we capitalize on opportunity?" "What resources are needed for this effort?" "How is control gained over these resources?" rather than questions related to maintaining stability.

4. *Undertakers of difficult and complicated tasks.* As such, they are highly motivated people who have a specific goal that they pursue tenaciously.

Beyond any doubt, creating a new industry-university center is an intrapreneurial act that will require all of these traits. However, the need for intrapreneurial leadership doesn't stop once a center is created. Center Directors must be searching constantly for opportunities for a fit between center researchers and companies. This requires effectively spanning a number of boundaries. Here's a fictionalized example of a Center Director with this orientation:

> *Bob Rush is the director of a large I/UCRC. He was the catalyst for a newsletter which is distributed to several hundred individuals and firms which is considered the major forum for work in his center's area. He has also spent a great deal of time serving as an officer on various associations as well as networking with and getting known by all the movers and shakers in the industry his center serves. This has allowed him to be very effective in recruiting new members (most decisions coming from the top down, which is the opposite of most centers). It has led also to the creation of an international linkage with a foreign institute.*

DEVELOPING A TECHNICAL VISION

Developing or working with constituents to develop a vision is one of the key tasks of leadership (Bennis, 1993, Conger, 1991, Farris, 1988, Heifetz, 1994). Visions are statements of ideal future states based upon the most compelling ideas of what members want the organization to become. They are tools to "manage meaning" (Bennis, 1993). I/UCRCs that succeed are guided by a formal or informal vision. In some instances, the vision and the accompanying research plan result from a formal strategic planning process involving different center stakeholders. In other cases vision arises from one or two core leaders. They create a vision and an implicit mission for the emerging enterprise. This is a significant activity of early-stage I/UCRC leadership.

There can be organizational components of a vision: the center as an efficient entity in which the administration and the research functions are complementary and both work towards the goal of a prime research center; or how the center will work with the university, member companies, other universities, and international groups and institutions.

A compelling vision attracts companies, faculty, and other resources to any center. The language of the vision plays a critical role in its acceptance and accomplishment. Compelling visions are a result of the strategic expertise and knowledge of the leader(s). They are framed around appealing goals that have positive, culturally important meanings for the organization (Conger, 1991). Because centers span between institutions, their vision must incorporate both university and industry. See Chapter 5.

The technical vision of a center will need to be revisited continually and sometimes completely revamped as the center matures. For example, directors have exercised leadership by recognizing that a center's research vision was past its prime and acted as catalyst and facilitator of a process which provided a new and revitalized vision. Here's a fictionalized example.

> *Helen Scholar, director of an I/UCRC that performed work for the computer industry, spent her sabbatical at a major federal agency where she reviewed proposals and met with other scientists. She realized there that increasing computer speed and capacity would limit severely interest in the kinds of problems which currently defined her center but that this center had the capabilities to have a major impact on another industrial need. Upon her return, she articulated her new vision for the center. The center changed its focus and name and began addressing a broader class of design issues resulting in a resurgence in membership, revitalization and financial success.*

SPANNING MULTIPLE BOUNDARIES

The importance of effectively spanning boundaries while developing and managing a cooperative research center cannot be overstated. By boundary-spanning, we mean attention to groups outside the core in the center. In I/UCRCs, failure to attend diligently to a center's boundaries, particularly as defined by current and prospective members, can be catastrophic to health and longevity.

Research on boundary-spanning suggests that two types of activities are particularly crucial in developing innovative research groups or teams (Ancona and Caldwell, 1992). Ambassadorial activities are those designed to persuade others to support and provide resources for the team. Task coordination activities are those interactions with external groups to coordinate technical or design issues. It is important to clarify that it is not necessary for the center leader to perform both ambassadorial and task coordinator activities alone, but to ascertain that the activities are being accomplished by someone in the center. In fact, Ancona and Caldwell (1992) found it important for all members of the team to perform these activities.

Because the task of recruiting new companies to the center is ever present, it is important for the leader to get all participants to use every opportunity possible and every network available to serve as center ambassadors to potential new members. Individuals network differently. The more center members that participate in these activities, the more successful the center will be in identifying and recruiting new members.

In regard to member companies, PIs are probably in the best position to handle task coordination activities with bench-level scientists, but Center Directors are best to network center IAB members. IAB members are gates to a much more complex set of players and stakeholders back in the company. Effective center leaders will open these gates, and develop a much more useful — albeit complex—communication network in industry. They will spend much time reinforcing and developing this network of communication and, when possible, will influence the industrial members in various ways including their choice of appropriate IAB members. As well, the leader and key faculty may step into the company to become a "virtual" member of their internal teams.

Creating effective relationships with industrial constituents will not happen as a result of sending reports and memoranda to IAB members. The most effective center leaders allot time *every week* to visit the plants and labs of member companies. This never ends, and some centers have developed a shared leadership structure in which one of the co-leaders takes on this responsibility. In other centers, Center Directors develop incentives for faculty who recruit member companies.

Networking is also an excellent opportunity to model appropriate behavior to younger faculty and graduate students and thus increase their leadership competencies. Center leadership must adopt interaction which is open, responsive, and peer-to-peer. To increase boundary spanning capacity, center leaders should involve junior faculty and graduate students in these interactions.

In regard to the home university, a critical leadership and boundary management task is obtaining support and resources from other university administrators. The demands of this task depend upon the rank of the university administrator. For example, the Center Director must educate top university administration about the vision and purpose of the center and how it fits with the university's mission, the role and visibility of the center in the university's present and future, and the importance of university resources to the center. University administrators can also provide the center contacts with powerful others who might join or support the center by providing endowments and support for cross-disciplinary efforts.

The Center Director must also span boundaries between universities. As centers expand it is likely that all the technical expertise needed to meet the center's mission and the needs of the constituent companies will not reside in its university. Center Directors must identify and recruit faculty or create partnerships with other universities including multi-site centers (see Chapter 11). Here's a fictionalized description of a director whose actions embodied this principle.

> I/UCRC Center Director, Joseph Bridger, realized very early that his own university did not possess the breadth of technical expertise desired by his industrial members. This never threatened the success of his center in spite of strong opposition from local administrators who objected to sending support off-campus. Bridger was able to pinpoint unmet needs and subsequently identify and recruit talented faculty at other universities who could fill these gaps. Ultimately, one of these linkages resulted in a multi-university partnership which helped to strengthen the center technically and resulted in the addition of new members.

In summary, boundary-spanning activities are the lifeblood of a center. It is essential to recruitment and retention of members and to effective technology transfer. Center leadership must convey this in both word and deed throughout a center's whole life-cycle.

CREATING THE CENTER RESEARCH TEAM

Within the university, Center Directors have a unique role because they lead groups of their intellectual and organizational peers. Most frequently, they have no formal authority over these individuals and the persons they lead are often leading scientists and engineers who, in their own right, are typically characterized by their expertise, desire for autonomy, commitment to their work, and identification with their profession rather than their organization (Kerr, et al., 1977; McCall, 1981). These characteristics of scientists and engineers have implications for recruitment and for working with faculty colleagues in an I/UCRC.

Typically, a center's growth depends on a small number of core researchers whose competencies constitute the technical vision. Directors can enhance a center's success by developing a vision that appeals to two or three major stars whose competencies complement their own.

How a Center Director works with faculty peers is crucial. McCall (1981) found that more productive research groups had supervisors or leaders who, rather than exercising authority, fostered scientific productivity by recognizing good ideas, defining significant problems, influencing through expertise rather than authority, and providing technical stimulation. Similarly, Farris (1988) noted that the most effective R & D leaders were technical experts who provide effective critical evaluation of others' ideas. Experience suggests the Center Director can share the role with those unwilling to take on administrative roles, but willing to nurture other scientists. If the Center Director is not a technical expert, Farris's work suggests that the director should provide a climate of freedom for center members to develop and pursue their ideas.

McCall's (1981) and Farris's (1988) findings that successful influence is based on expertise rather than authority should comfort Center Directors who have expertise but, in most cases, have very little authority over their peers. Thus, Center Director-leaders must fine-tune their informal influence skills. In this vein, Cohen and Bradford (1991) argue that honesty and trust is imperative. Beyond being absolutely honest and straightforward so that trust is built and maintained, they suggest that effective informal influence is based on an exchange of needs and resources. Among the "currencies" that a Center Director-leader can offer center faculty are:

- vision (i.e., being involved in a task that has larger significance for the unit; organization, customers, or society)

- excellence (i.e., having a chance to do important things really well)

- new resources (i.e., obtaining money, budget increases, etc.)

- challenge/learning (i.e., doing projects that increase skills and abilities)

- recognition (i.e, acknowledgment of effort, accomplishment, or abilities)

- visibility (i.e., the chance to be known by significant others in the organization or profession)

- reputation (i.e, being seen as competent and committed)

- contacts (i.e., opportunities for linking with others) (Cohen and Bradford, p. 79).

In addition to being able to motivate others to accomplish the tasks of the organization, the group dynamics literature has argued that leaders need to address the social and emotional issues of the organization. In a cooperative research center, one of the most important social-emotional responsibilities of the leader is to create a team culture. But why should the Center Director want to create a team culture? Why not go along with the individualistic way that most university researchers operate?

There are several reasons why a team culture is important in an I/UCRC. For one, the very concept of a center implies a group process and product, not just an amalgamation of faculty. Moreover, the attractiveness of the product to companies derives from the assumption that complementary expertise is being pulled together. This, in turn, implies teams and teaming, at the level of both the project team and the overall center.

Teams need to be integrated into center operations along disciplines, research expertise and methodologies. Cooperative research in industrial settings is increasingly organized around multi-organizational teams representing different stakeholders during the technology life cycle. A project team may include people from different units or departments, different organizations, and different sectors. In terms of life cycle it might also include basic researchers, end-users, commercializers, and business-marketing interests. Center leaders need to assemble and hold together increasingly heterogeneous teams. This can be at odds with the prevailing norms and practices of the university.

Center projects should be examples for teams in action. A written center statement of the importance of teamwork can serve as a powerful reminder to center participants. The center must create powerful incentives for teams. If a center gives lip-service to the values of cooperation and then funds a series of egocentrically conceived and executed projects, teams are pointless.

Providing incentives for teams demands action by Center Directors. Insist faculty conduct peer review of research projects. Make teams and the use of co-principal investigators a project selection criterion. Share any praise with all members of the team. Hold monthly meetings of the center team. Develop follow-up action items for teams. Assign one researcher to train another. Host informal social events once or twice a semester. Some of the more productive and creative high technology companies have intentionally organized Friday afternoon social activities. However, all of these practices will be for naught if institutional policies discourage or fail to reward multi-investigator projects and joint publications and, by implication, teaming and collaboration. As a consequence, a leader must be prepared to point out these inconsistencies and, if necessary, challenge them.

LEADERSHIP AS THE I/UCRC DEVELOPS

Many things can be understood from a life cycle or developmental perspective. That is, we can conceptualize the birth, development, maturation, and decline of entities as diverse as flatworms and specific technologies (e.g., computer operating systems). In a cooperative research center, some things change and some don't. We have argued that the leader of a new center will need to:

- Develop a center vision
- Think as an intrapreneur who develops a new organizational entity within the university
- Span boundaries between the institutions involved in a center
- Develop and support multi disciplinary research teams.

While these tasks may not have the same urgency as the center matures, they will continue to be critical for the success of the center. One of the major leadership challenges is rejuvenating a stagnant or ossified R & D agenda by wiping the slate clean of the technical vision and strategic planning that was launched several years earlier. New industrial members may trigger a need to rethink the research agenda.

On the other hand, some of the Center Director's work does change over time. Three major tasks include routinization of procedures, developing leadership capabilities in others, and preparing for succession.

Routinization of Center Operations

Some of the center procedures and processes that can be routinized include:

- Staff meetings, distribution of minutes, and action items
- Process for reviewing and managing the research program, and for working with industrial clients
- Manuals describing procedures, forms, and other administrative tools.

These tools are described in various chapters throughout this volume and can, in many cases, be put in place by a center manager who is not the same person as the Center Director. Differentiating those responsibilities to be carried out by a manager and those to be addressed by the center director-leader is not a shortcoming of the director but rather an action that allows individuals to excel at what they do best. The point to be made here is that the leader must support the development and implementation of an appropriate set of stable bureaucratic procedures.

Shared Leadership

Throughout this chapter we have mentioned areas where leadership responsibilities are best shared, including recruiting industry firms, nurturing relationships with IAB members, and routinizing the structure of the center. Giving other faculty moderate administrative and leadership duties is one of the most effective ways to develop their managerial potential (Cordero and Farris, 1992). Leadership and managerial competencies within other center faculty will become increasingly important as the work of the center expands. Thus one of the most important jobs of the center director-leader is to nurture leadership competencies within other center constituents, including other faculty.

Succession

In the history of every cooperative center there comes a time for succession. A study of I/UCRCs showed that the Center directorships last, on average, only three years (Gray et al., 1991). The director leaves for a promotion or new position, returns to full-time laboratory research, or launches some new venture in another setting. Succession may signal a point of financial and intellectual stability that permits a different type of leadership. However, if the leader has not prepared the center for succession, it can mean a time of great turmoil and instability. In the study cited above, over half the firms interviewed said the turnover of directors had been very disruptive. The fictionalized description illustrates what can happen.

> Dr. Edward Mobile was considered one of the top scientists in automation. The I/UCRC he directed was one of the most successful in the country. He was solely responsible for every aspect of center administration. Over the years Mobile received and turned down a variety of lucrative offers to join industry. For a variety of personal and professional reasons he decided to accept an attractive offer. Mobile gave the university six months' notice and left succession to the university. The university did not mount a national search and appointed a relatively inexperienced colleague as director. In the opinion of most members, the center lost its technical vision and ability to communicate effectively with industry after this transition. Two years later, it lost almost two-thirds of its members and eventually terminated operations.

Center Directors may wish to groom a deputy director or an acting director in conjunction with a sabbatical, or reassigning the director's responsibilities to a deputy director. I/UCRC directors should detail viable plans for their succession. The plan should list I/UCRC activities and responsibilities and a commitment from the university's administration for an outside search. Center Directors must promise their successors a debriefing on the center's vision, problems, and a history of what did or didn't work, and any unique characteristics of the center. This can be in writing, audio or videotape recording. Finally, the Center Director should bring stakeholders into the succession process by eliciting their participation.

The process of succession must be managed by senior researchers, corporate members, or university administration. There is some evidence that an external candidate will be more likely to shake things up, and if that is what is desired in a transition, then an outside candidate should be sought. In a mature and stable center the best choice is a researcher already attached to the center who has shown some leadership inclination and talent.

THE IMPORTANCE OF SELF-KNOWLEDGE

It is clear that the Center Director role and tasks require more than many researchers feel capable of handling. But a director can share leadership with others in the center. This suggests the most important leadership quality is knowing oneself. Indeed, Bennis (1993) has argued that effective leaders know themselves and their skills and deploy them effectively. They also know their weaknesses.

For example, a Center Director might enjoy teaching and research but feel uncomfortable with an administrative role. S/he might feel quite comfortable working within the university but dislike making the necessary contacts with member companies. A director might be stimulated by and enjoy the headiness of a start-up period but be bored by developing the more routine aspects of a center's operation. An examination of one's preferences may reveal that it's time to move on.

For the center to be successful, it is also critical that the leader adapt to the challenges the center faces at any particular time. This may mean spending more time amplifying and fine-tuning the center's bureaucracy or, as we've discussed above, moving toward a shared or collective leadership approach. Exercising these options presumes the Center Director knows which challenges s/he is willing to tackle and which s/he is not.

Consistent with the notion of shared leadership is a rotation schedule in which successive researchers serve as Center Directors for three- to five-year periods each. This allows the senior research personnel in the center the opportunity to lead the center. The founder emeritus leader is still very important. If succession is graceful, the emeritus leader resumes a defined technical role in the center and eases transition of the incoming director. A bitter director emeritus hampers growth of the center. Handle this carefully; give credit and acknowledgment, and carefully move on. Rotating at the associate director level is another option. Compare this fictionalized example with the preceding.

> *Manny Lecture was the lead faculty member involved in the creation of a new I/UCRC. Shortly after the center was created, he announced that he had done some soul searching about his role. He had received too much satisfaction from teaching and doing his research and too little from administration to justify continuing in the role of Center Director. He gave the IAB and the university notice to find a new director but agreed to serve out the year. This allowed plenty of lead time for the transition and resulted in the hiring of a very effective director.*

On a more negative note, succession may be forced by "burnout" and declining performance by the founding director. This happens more often than academic administrators are willing to admit. Close attention should be paid to inattention to administrative detail, difficulty in relating to and retaining corporate members, and difficulty in forging and enlarging the technical vision of the center.

There are several ways to avoid burnout. First, the director may opt to reduce his range of responsibilities through delegation or the appointment of a deputy director. Second, the director may devote more time to research and teaching. Third, the director may take a sabbatical for one semester or longer. Once again, as this fictionalized description illustrates, knowing oneself can be the key to a positive outcome.

> In a center with close to 20 industrial members, nearing its sixth year of operation, the founder-director felt besieged by the demands of routine center tasks. After consultations with colleagues and the center evaluator, he decided to allocate a good portion of his routine responsibilities to a colleague, who assumed the position of an operations manager. This manager was responsible for the routine operation and the maintenance of the center, including resources allocation, conflict resolution and periodic control and review of activities. Complete responsibility for marketing and maintaining links with industry remained with the founding director. Thereafter, the center operations ran smoothly and membership increased.

SUMMARY

When leadership works, improvement is the effect (Bennis, 1992). Effective leaders make a difference in a variety of ways: people feel they make a difference to the success of the organization, that risk is part of life and mistakes are sources of feedback to tell us what to do next, feel part of a community, and feel work is exciting. The Center Director-leader is in a unique position to foster such empowerment, community, excitement, and connection within the university. The Center Director helps constituents learn and develop. The Center Director is rewarded by feelings of accomplishment in building an organization, success and growth, and knowing s/he brought together technical expertise to everyone's benefit.

ANNOTATED BIBLIOGRAPHY

Bennis, W. *An Invented Life: Reflections on Leadership and Change.* New York: Addison Wesley, 1993.

In this collection of essays, Warren Bennis, Distinguished Professor of Business Administration at the University of Southern California, reflects on three decades of experience as an university leader and leadership researcher. In this book, he emphasizes the importance of self-reflection, a tool which enabled him to conclude while president of the University of Cincinnati that leadership was about the relationship between the leader-as-individual and the organization. In addition, he reports on the findings of an extensive study of nearly 100 chief executives of corporations, heads of foundations, or heads of major government departments or agencies. In this study, Bennis and Nanus (1985) found that effective leaders are able to focus on a vision, communicate that vision to others, establish trust by being reliable and consistent, and have both a positive self-regard and a positive regard for others.

Cohen, A.R., and Bradford, D.L. *Influence Without Authority.* New York: John Wiley & Sons, Inc., 1991.

The central premise of this helpful book is that individuals in today's workplace are often not given the authority to accomplish the work they need to get done. As a result, they must fine-tune their influence skills. According to Cohen and Bradford, informal influence is built upon the principle of reciprocity. To exert informal influence, individuals must assume that the "other," or influence target, is an ally, clarify their own goals and priorities, diagnose the ally's world (goals, concerns, needs), assess their own resources relative to the ally's wants, diagnose their relationship with the ally, determine the exchange approach, and make exchanges.

Farris, G.F. Technical Leadership: Much Discussed But Little Understood. *Research-Technology Management,* 31, 1988, pp. 12-16.

In this article, George Farris, a leading researcher on R & D leadership summarizes what is known about technical leadership. He concludes that the effective technical leaders are strategic leaders, effective organizational players, technical experts, informal leaders, developers of personnel, creators of climates that stimulate technological thinking, and are responsive to their followers.

Heifetz, R.A. *Leadership Without Easy Answers.* Cambridge, MA: Harvard University Press, 1994.

Heifetz's definition of a leader is "someone who mobilizes constituents to learn to solve their adaptive problems." In example after example of

"messy problems," or those problems that are not amenable to technological quick fixes (e.g., Civil Rights in the South, the enforcement of environmental regulations when jobs are at stake), Heifetz carefully expli-
cates the process that leaders (e.g., Martin Luther King, Jr., Lyndon B.
Johnson, William Ruckelshaus) use to help their constituents develop
their own solutions to problems. This book is a refreshing antidote for
those leaders who, from their own experience, know that leadership is
more difficult than the experts say.

McCall, Jr., M.W. *Leadership and the Professional*. Technical report no.
17. Greensboro, NC: Center for Creative Leadership, 1981.

This report summarizes research on leadership and the professional by
addressing four topics, including (1) who is being led and how professionals are different from other "followers;" (2) what the leader can do to
enhance productivity among professional subordinates; (3) the impact of
the professional on the organization; and (4) the choice faced by a professional in becoming a "manager." In particular, this report is useful for
thinking about leading one's intellectual and technical peers, a task that
many Center Directors face when leading other faculty.

Perlman, B., Gueths, J, and Weber, D.A. *The Academic Intrapreneur:
Strategy, Innovation, and Management in Higher Education*. New York:
Praeger, 1988.

Perlman, Gueths, and Weber describe the intrapreneurship process that
was used to revitalize University of Wisconsin-Oshkosh. The book gives
a model of the intrapreneurship process, rich description of the journey
undertaken, and concluding thoughts on what did and did not work.

REFERENCES

Ancona, D.G., & Caldwell, D.F. Bridging the Boundary: External
Activity and Performance in Organizational Teams. *Administrative
Science Quarterly*, 37, 634-665, 1992.

Bennis, W. *An Invented Life: Reflections on Leadership and Change*.
New York: Addison Wesley, 1993.

Bennis, W. and Nanus, B. *Leaders*. New York: Harper and Row, 1985.

Cohen, A.R., and Bradford, D.L. *Influence without Authority*. New
York: John Wiley & Sons, Inc., 1991.

Conger, J.A. Inspiring others: The Language of Leadership, *The
Academy of Management Review*, 5, 1991, pp. 31-45.

Conger, J.A. and Kanungo, R. The Empowerment Process: Integrating
Theory and Practice. *Academy of Management Review*, 13, 1988,
pp. 471-482.

Cordero, R. and Farris, G.F. Administrative Activity and the Managerial Development of Technical Professionals. *IEEE Transactions on Engineering Management*, 39, 1992, pp. 270-276.

Fairweather, J.S. Managing industry-university relationships, *Journal for Higher Education Management*.

Farris, G.F. Technical Leadership: Much Discussed, But Little Understood. *Research-Technology Management*, 31, 1988, pp. 12-16.

Gray, D. O., Stewart, M., Gidley, T.R., and Blakley, C. Self-sustaining Industry-University Centers: Is There Life After NSF Funding? Washington, D.C.: National Science Foundation, 1991.

Heifetz, R.A. *Leadership Without Easy Answers*. Cambridge, MA: Harvard University Press, 1994.

Kerr, S., Von Glinow, M.A., and Schriesheim, J. Issues in the Study of "Professionals" in Organizations: The Case of Scientists and Engineers. *Organizational Behavior and Human Performance*, 18, 1977, pp. 329-345.

Lord, R.A. and Mayer, K. Perceptions of Leadership and Their Implications in Organizations. In J.S. Carroll (Ed.), *Applied Social Psychology and Organizational Settings*. Hillsdale, NJ: Lawrence Erlbaum Associates, Publishers, 1990.

McCall, Jr., M.W. Leadership and the Professional. *Technical Report no. 17*. Greensboro, NC: Center for Creative Leadership, 1991.

Perlman, B., Gueths, J. and Weber, D.A. *The Academic Intrapreneur: Strategy, Innovation, and Management in Higher Education*. New York: Praeger, 1988.

EXPANDING AND DIVERSIFYING THE CENTER RESOURCE BASE

DENIS O. GRAY, *North Carolina State University, Raleigh*

S. GEORGE WALTERS, *Professor Emeritus, Rutgers University, NJ*

INTRODUCTION

Centers are run as small entrepreneurial enterprises of the university. Like all small enterprises, a center's health and vitality depend on the availability of a variety of resources, particularly technical and financial. We have discussed the importance of developing your center's technical and human resources previously (see Chapters 5 and 6). In this chapter, we focus on the importance of financial resources and how to develop them.

There's a variety of reasons centers must focus a considerable amount of organizational time and energy on developing and implementing strategies for financial growth and diversification. First, most new centers start operations as relatively small research organizations. A first-year NSF I/UCRC typically begins operating with a budget of less than $500,000. This falls well below the level needed to sustain a cutting-edge, multi-disciplinary and team-based research organization, particularly one which aspires to national or international excellence. In addition, data indicate that the average 10-member center loses approximately one member each year. Centers also lose federal and state support. Unfortunately, this pattern holds true for even the best run centers! Thus, a strategy of growth and diversification is critical to both new centers which aspire to reach a financial and technical critical mass and mature centers which hope to forestall decline and organizational extinction.

The centrality of growth to organizational survival is not unique to centers. Virtually all organizations confront this issue, but fortunately there are a number of standard strategies for achieving a proper balance between growth and organizational health.

LIFE CYCLES, GROWTH AND COOPERATIVE RESEARCH

The need for organizational growth is widely recognized. Most organizations go through fairly predictable patterns called life-cycles which can be depicted by an S-shaped curve. While some organizations may be able to stay small and continue operating for an extended period, most organizational survivors generally follow a pattern characterized by period of introduction, followed by a period of growth, followed by a period of maturity, followed almost inevitably by a period of decline. Thus, organizations which want to survive long-term need to develop strategies to achieve growth and other strategies to sustain them as long as possible.

This is true for cooperative research centers. Centers are competing with other universities and research labs for a limited number of customers. A life cycle model shows how surviving centers grow over time. Figure 11-1 illustrates an NSF I/UCRC life-cycle.

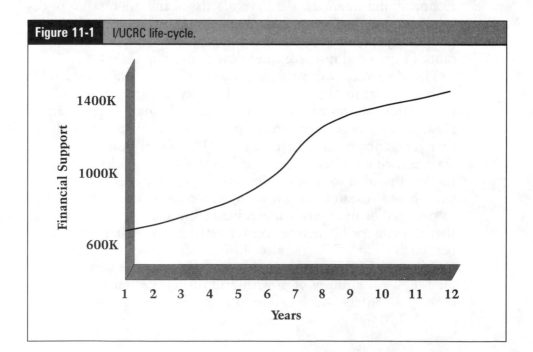

Figure 11-1   I/UCRC life-cycle.

Centers under two years of age have an average budget of $680,000. By the time a center is five to six years old, its average budget increases to $900,000. After eight years the average budget rises to almost $1.4 million.

Thus, long-term financial prospects for a new center with only $500,000 to start, are much brighter. Much brighter that is, if they can avoid complacency and develop a winning strategy for growth.

Strategies for Growth

According to Galbraith and Kazanjian (1986), there are four basic growth strategies: expansion of volume, geographic dispersion, vertical integration, and diversification.

Each of these strategies either expands the customer base directly or diversifies products or services to add new customers. Expansion by volume usually involves marketing or pricing efforts for your current product or services. Geographic dispersion involves attempts to add customers by locating a branch or franchise a distance away from your current market (for your current product or services). Vertical integration involves attempts to grow by offering new but highly related products or services. Diversification involves attempts to grow by offering products or services that are unrelated to what your currently offer.

While Galbraith and Kazanjian's framework is based on profit-making organizations, most of these strategies work for I/UCRC growth, with the exception of diversification to completely unrelated services. Centers grow by marketing or pricing strategies that expand the volume of customers for their current services (expansion by volume); or by developing a branch at another campus (geographic dispersion); or by offering new but highly-related services like applied research, development or even testing (vertical integration).

Selecting a Strategy

Choice of the correct growth strategy isn't always straightforward. It depends upon awareness of opportunities and needs which exist in your environment, like new sources of funding, technological developments, new markets, etc. Centers operating in industries which need precompetitive research or which face little competition from other research providers have a good opportunity for growth. Awareness of these needs and opportunities is important. In choosing a growth strategy it is crucial to obtain such information as which segments of the target industry are growing or declining, needs for R&D, willingness of firms to procure R&D outside organizational boundaries, university's expertise and industrial networks, and federal and state initiatives. We have discussed approaches to collecting this kind of information elsewhere, and encourage the reader to review this material (See Chapters 2 and 5).

Strategies need to be selected based on your ability and willingness to implement them. For instance, any growth strategy will require your organization to expend resources, in the form of time or money. If a center isn't willing to expend time or money in pursuit of growth, its strategy is doomed to fail. In addition, the more the strategy differs from current customers and services, the more difficult it will be to implement. Thus, if a center doesn't have the talent and skills needed to implement new services, it would be better advised to choose a simpler strategy.

Different growth strategies require different organizational structures. A center needs to be willing and able to change and adapt its organizational structure to conform with the needs of a given strategy. For instance, geographic dispersion and vertical integration will require more complex and managerially intense structures than is typical of a one-site or single service center. The greater the change, the more organizational redesign one may need to engage in. When selecting a strategy, anticipate structural changes, such as more division of labor or greater coordination, and assess your willingness and ability to execute them.

The imperative for growth is important but it entails risks too. Strategies that exceed organizational capabilities waste precious resources and risk chaos and decline. Galbraith and Kazanjian (1986) argue that the overriding principle for growth should be one of "controlled diversity." That is, expand and diversify the market and services in a way that strengthens and reinforces, rather than dilutes and weakens core competence.

This is particularly relevant to fragile boundary-spanning I/UCRCs. Growth should not be pursued as an end, but as a means of achieving the financial and technical critical mass necessary to make an impact in a focused area of research. Centers that understand and heed this dictum can capitalize on the opportunities which exist in their environment at various points in their life-cycle. Centers that don't, risk diluting or neutralizing the very qualities (e.g., a focused and cohesive research program, small personal and informal organizational structure) that have attracted and sustained current membership.

STRATEGIES AND TACTICS FOR
CENTER GROWTH AND DIVERSIFICATION

Once a center has built a solid foundation with a membership-based industrial consortium, a savvy administrator can choose a number of strategies to achieve growth. These strategies are organized into three main categories: expansion by volume, geographic dispersion, and vertical integration. Figure 11-2 lists the specific approaches within each strategy.

Figure 11-2	Strategies for growth and diversification.

Strategy	Approach
Expansion by Volume	Raising Membership Fees
	Developing Research Enhancements
	Adding Members and Grants
	Small Firms
	Federal Agencies
	Non-Profits and Associations
	Traditional Grants
Geographic Dispersion	Informal Time-Limited Partnerships
	Formal, Ongoing Partnerships
Vertical Integration	Providing Educational Services
	Providing Research-Related Services

Expansion of Volume

Expansion of volume involves attempts to increase a center's revenue without changing its precompetitive fundamental research. This does not mean that the center's research portfolio remains static. As discussed in Chapter 5, a center's research program must change and evolve.

Expansion by volume doesn't require significant resources, new services or major organizational changes. It is simple and straightforward. Growth is slow and incremental rather than fast and dramatic.

Typically, I/UCRCs expand the volume of work by increasing revenues from current members, and/or adding new members or sponsors. While some of the approaches we discuss here may have been used during your center's initial or ongoing recruitment effort, we think they warrant a brief review.

Increasing Work and Revenues from Current Members— Pricing Strategies

All NSF I/UCRC Centers set annual membership fees. One growth strategy is simply raising the fee. For instance, a Center with ten members at $30,000 per year would reap $50,000, a 17 percent increase, by raising its fee to $35,000. Strictly speaking, this is not an increase in volume, but it is a fairly common strategy for increasing revenues. By 1994, ten of the 18 oldest I/UCRCs (average age of nine years) raised their fees, seven maintained the same fee and one lowered its fee. The average fee increase was $7,500.

Relevant issues. This approach is fairly simple (at least on the surface). Negotiations are limited to the current membership, not an unlimited number of recruits, and results in a predictable increase in the center's revenues.

Unfortunately, unless your center enjoys a monopolistic position in its environment, this approach isn't as simple or as straight forward as it first seems. In order to increase its membership fee, a center must overcome a number of obstacles, not the least being that this strategy doesn't appeal to budget-conscious IAB members as much it does to overworked directors. The reality is IAB members often find it difficult to justify increased fees at a time when most budgets are getting slashed. Complicating this is the fact that a change in your membership rate often involves preparing a new membership agreement and bylaws and a new round of approval and signatures from upper level management and corporate lawyers. This prospect alone has been enough to terminate further discussion.

In addition, since an individual member may quit rather than pay an increased membership fee, a center needs near unanimous endorsement. A fee increase of 20 percent won't do much good if some members resign!

Because of all of these constraints, experience suggests all but the best-prepared proposals for a membership increase never get past the discussion stage and usually result in a recommendation for a renewed membership drive.

Recommended strategy. In spite of these cautions, some centers have succeeded in raising their membership fee. If this approach makes sense, here are a few suggestions on how to succeed.

1. *Do your homework:* Proposals accompanied by the following kind of facts and figures supporting an increase are more persuasive: number of years the center has operated with current fee; effect of inflation on the current fee; changes in technology, etc. that make operations more expensive; comparable costs including relevant overhead rates and related costs of salary, equipment, technicians for doing research within firms or charged by competitors; and level of time and effort for recruitment. Keep in mind most members will need to evaluate the cost/benefit of their past investments. Therefore, if possible, data about center-related benefits (see Chapter 8) should be presented to strengthen your proposal.

2. *Emphasize real consequences:* A most powerful argument for a fee increase is its effect on the matching dollars the center receives. Centers at risk for falling below minimum cost-sharing for a government sponsored program ($300,000 for NSF) have a good argument.

3. *Develop grassroots support:* Every director should have champions within the IAB to mobilize on behalf of a fee increase. A proposal for a membership fee increase presented by an IAB member is more persuasive than one by the director. Directors are also cautioned that even losing a single member who cannot convince his managers on the value of the increase can wipe out benefits from it.

4. *Time changes to coincide with other agreement changes:* Even if members support a fee increase, many will delay a change in fee rates until membership agreements are up for renewal or are being modified to limit attorney involvement. One center has solved this problem by institutionalizing fee increases into their membership agreement as a schedule of fee increases negotiated by upper management only once, at signing. Center membership agreements and bylaws can also be written to allow fee changes by a simple majority vote.

Research Enhancements

Some Center Directors are reluctant to approach current members about supplemental funding but should recognize that firms join an I/UCRC to buy rather than produce some of the research it needs. Once a good relationship develops and other research needs arise, IAB members are comfortable purchasing additional research. In fact, pursuing supplemental support from one's members is one of the most effective strategies for expanding your center's resource base. In 1993-1994, NSF I/UCRCs received $5.5 million (roughly 11 percent of their budget) in supplemental support. In fact, 75 percent of I/UCRCs get supplements and seven centers get more support from supplements than from membership fees! Support may be an enhancement project or a contract. Contracts usually are applied research for a single customer (see section titled Providing Research-Related Services in this chapter) and are managed outside the center.

Relevant issues. An enhancement is any project supported by supplemental funding consistent with the center's core research program, either fundamental or applied. Because the work is so similar to core research, centers can usually engage in enhancement research under the scope of center agreements and organizational structure.

Enhancement projects can come about in a number of ways. Examples include a project without support from the general membership but of high interest to one or more firms; accelerating or expanding an existing project; or a project idea put on a fast track. Enhancements involve much more intensive member-PI interaction. At one center with a great deal of enhancement activity, IAB members threaten to quit if worthwhile enhancements can't be developed.

Recommended strategy.

1. *Provide a routine and friendly administrative foundation:* Members don't want to waste their time waiting for paperwork to make its way through two bureaucracies before they can get an enhancement project started. Be sure your membership agreement and bylaws address enhancement and contract projects. To encourage enhancement support, most universities apply the center's reduced overhead rate as long as findings and intellectual property will be shared with all members.

2. *Encourage faculty to develop enhancement projects:* While some enhancements just happen, faculty need to be alerted to the potential for support and encouraged to develop new

projects which can be marketed as such. The best way is for faculty to talk to IAB members about their needs.

3. *Encourage IAB members to approach the I/UCRC:* At the same time, members need to be encouraged to come to the center and approach faculty with their research needs and ideas.

4. *Institutionalize enhancements into the research process:* If steps 2 and 3 succeed, enhancements will become an integral part of all your research planning, development, selection, and reporting activities. Enhancements should be specified in all calls for proposals, and research reviews. Core proposals that don't garner enough support, should be marketed routinely as enhancements.

Adding New Members and Grants

Recruitment of new members must be a central and ongoing part of any center's growth plan. In this section, we briefly highlight how to focus your recruiting efforts and discuss how some centers have increased their membership by targeting a number of non-traditional audiences including: small firms, government members and industrial associations.

Intensive Recruiting Campaigns

Successful directors recruit as an integral part of weekly duties, but there are also advantages to periodic intensive marketing or recruitment campaigns. It makes more efficient use of time, trips out of town, or trips to your labs, and such effort is a catalyst for reviewing and updating center marketing materials. Involvement of your center's faculty and board members can be refreshed during intense recruiting campaigns.

An intense marketing or recruitment campaign basically involves a smaller scale reprise of the efforts your center undertook when it recruited its first cohort of members: using one's network and other resources to identify prospects and contacts; revising and updating recruitment materials; qualifying and targeting prime prospects and organizing a group meeting. Since these steps were described in detail in Chapters 2 and 4, we will not repeat them here.

On the other hand, there are two important and related differences one should keep in mind when planning and implementing a recruiting campaign as an established center. First, you no longer need to sell your center based on its promise but, instead, should sell it based on its accomplishments. Therefore, devote time to systematically cataloging your center's scientific and technical accomplishments and recruitment advantages for members. This should be an important and early task. Remember that there is no better sales tool than a satisfied customer. Furthermore, it's absolutely imperative that you secure the help and involvement of your current members in selling the benefits of membership during your recruiting meeting. In some centers, industry members provide contacts and recruit specific members.

Small Firms and a Multiple-Level Fee Structure

Often membership prospects are interested in joining but just can't afford the established membership fee. More often than not, these firms meet the definition of a small business. In order to overcome the financial barriers to membership by this segment of your potential customer base some centers implement a lower secondary, tertiary, or sliding scale fee levels for associate membership. In 1994-1995, 16 of the 55 NSF I/UCRCs had a multiple fee structure to allow small firms to join at a reduced fee.

Relevant issues. Lowering the fee to accommodate smaller firms makes sense. First, small firms represent untapped and often technologically innovative markets. In addition, some larger firms value the opportunity to interact with smaller firms, particularly if they have a supplier-manufacturer relationship. Further, state governments often encourage and sometimes subsidize these arrangements making small business participation more valuable to the center.

On the other hand, multiple fee structures add complexity to recruiting, bookkeeping and management. Associate members' goals may differ from other members and can cause conflict within your consortium. Current members may resist subsidizing small members. This problem is probably the most serious. However, as we described in Chapter 3, most I/UCRCs deal with this obstacle by offering associate members abridged rights or benefits like limited voting rights, limited intellectual property rights, or limited access to some research results.

I/UCRC experience shows that reduced fees rarely increases membership significantly. In fact, many of the centers that offer this option have few or no associate members active! A number of factors may account for this. "Your fee is too high" may simply be a polite way of saying "I am not interested." Small firms may believe that their needs and goals will be overridden by full members, particularly given the restricted benefits that often accompany associate membership.

Recommended strategy. It's important to remember that small companies can be highly innovative and may contribute technologically to your center. If you think a multiple level fee structure may help you recruit some firms, here are a few suggestions on how to succeed.

1. *Clarify your goals:* Implementing a multiple level fee structure can take a significant amount of time. It's important to clarify the reasons for making this change. Do you anticipate a quantum leap in membership? Will this approach court favor (and perhaps revenues) with local or state technology officials? Do you anticipate associate members will add to the technological mix of your membership? If your goals aren't realistic and reachable, you would better be advised to invest your energies elsewhere.

2. *Test the waters with some key prospects:* Before you make a big investment of time, it's probably worth consulting with the firms you hope to recruit. Try to find out if they really believe membership would be possible under a reduced fee, what level of fee would be acceptable, and whether the typical trade-off of fewer benefits for a lower fee is acceptable. Remember you don't want people to tell you what you want to hear. Encourage candid assessments.

3. *Assess the impact of a reduced fee on current members:* Try to anticipate the impact of the new fee on your current membership. How many of them might qualify for and decide to switch to a lower membership fee?

4. *Develop grassroots support:* This change cannot be unilateral. If you are convinced that you have a good chance of achieving the goals you have in mind, it's time to solicit input and mobilize support for your plan among some key IAB members. Use their input to develop a proposal they feel they can get behind. In many cases, this proposal involves some abridgment of rights for associate members on issues like intellectual property, voting privileges, or both.

5. *Schedule changes to coincide with other agreement changes:* Changes to agreements and bylaws and another round of lawyers are necessary so it may make sense to delay until

membership agreements are up for renewal or are being modified.

Recruit, recruit, recruit. Need we say more.

Recruiting Federal and Military Agencies as Members

One of the primary reasons firms join centers is it is a cost-effective way to buy research. The same is true for federal agencies. Recent federal policies and programs encourage transfer of government research and development of dual-use (defense and commercial) technologies encourage centers to recruit actively government agencies as members[9]. Federal entities now account for roughly ten percent of the 700 NSF I/UCRC memberships (about half are military agencies or labs, another 20 percent are national laboratories). Some centers get over half their membership revenues from federal agencies. Sometimes, federal members support a center through multi-year institutional grant. (These are reviewed in section titled *Vertical Integration* in this chapter.)

Relevant issues. As the numbers suggest, the Department of Defense and other federal agencies are a good source of new center memberships[10]. Interestingly, representatives of most federal/military organizations find it difficult to sign a center membership agreement. However, this dilemma actually constitutes a competitive advantage for government sponsored I/UCRCs, since federal entities can join by transferring funds via the government sponsor. This is done by a Military Interdepartmental Procurement Request (MIPR) or its civilian equivalent. Many military organizations have significant needs for external research. This mechanism is used by them to transfer several million dollars in enhancement project support to NSF's I/UCRCs.

In addition to dollars, federal members may offer access to specialized equipment, talented personnel, and information on new and emerging technological advances. Further, regulatory agencies may pinpoint critical needs and comment on the value of proposed projects.

There are reasons for *not* recruiting federal agencies. Sometimes military needs (e.g., high performance, small production, high unit

---

[9]While some of the large-scale dual-use federal initiatives have been scaled back or eliminated by the recent Congress, some Department of Defense initiatives continue.

[10]State governments often fund I/UCRCs by becoming sponsors rather than members.

cost) and industrial needs (e.g., modest performance, high production, low unit cost) conflict. Research performed in federal agencies may compete with I/UCRC research for member research.

Recommended strategy. Recruiting a federal member isn't much different from recruiting an industrial member, so we encourage you to review the advice provided in Chapter 4. In addition, we advise you to do the following:

1. *Consult with industrial members:* If your center currently doesn't have any federal or military members, first consult your industrial members to clarify if their research goals are compatible. In one case, industrial members rejected military members. On the other hand, because of federal-industry procurement relationships, IAB members are likely to have good leads for recruiting federal or military members.

2. *Become familiar with MIPR procedures:* Experience indicates that the MIPR mechanism is a plus for federal agencies in joining a center. However, it seems to cause some universities a headache. In addition, MIPRs have been changing of late. Recent or contemplated MIPR changes include a 3 to 4 percent processing surcharge within NSF and additional signature requirements within the transferring organization. Check with NSF and your grants and contracts office on how you should handle MIPRs or interagency transfer of funds.

3. *Recruit, recruit, recruit.* Enough said.

Recruiting Non-Profits and Industrial Associations

Another way for expanding recruitment is targeting non-profit research organizations and industrial associations. Industrial associations include groups like the Electric Power Research Institute and the Gas Research Institute. Unfortunately, according to 1993-1994 data, only one non-profit and seven associations were I/UCRC members.

Relevant issues. There are a number of reasons why non-profits organizations haven't proven to be a significant source of memberships. Most non-profits are *research performers* not research consumers and often compete with I/UCRCs for industry's research support[11].

---

[11]Non-profits might be recruited by centers performing non-traditional research. For instance, Health Planning I/UCRC, University of Arizona, and Georgia Tech have non-profit hospitals among their members.

In contrast, many industrial associations sponsor research and do very little research internally. However, association membership raises questions. If an association joins a center, do all of its members get access and rights to center results? Should a firm join a center if they already pay dues to an association that is already an IAB member? Strategies for resolving these conflicts include: a membership which limits an association's ability to transfer and retain rights to center results, or to require a significantly larger membership fee. The latter strategy was employed by The Ohio State University (OSU) Center on Welding. It became a multi-million dollar arm of the International Welding Institute for a substantially greater IAB membership fee. However, it eventually severed its ties to OSU.

Recommended strategy. Here are a few additional suggestions.

1. *Choose this approach carefully:* Very few non-profit memberships have been recruited successfully. Be particularly wary of pursuing research non-profits that may view your members as potential customers for their own services.

2. *Consult with your members:* Several centers have succeeded in recruiting industrial associations as members, so they have been able to overcome the obstacles to membership we discussed above. Nonetheless, consult your industrial members on your plans to recruit an industrial association and any accommodation necessary for these organizations to join.

3. *Recruit, recruit, recruit.*

Competing for Traditional Research Grants

Most of the faculty involved in centers have a long track record of successful grantsmanship. Since only a few centers achieve the membership-based support required to fund all of their worthwhile research projects, there's no reason faculty should stop their proposal writing. Based on 1993-1994 data, roughly 20 percent or $3 million of the $15 million NSF I/UCRCs received from various federal agencies was generated by traditional single- and multiple-investigator research grants. The balance was generated by institutional awards discussed in section Providing Research-Related Services in this chapter.

Relevant issues. Why would a faculty member submit a grant application from a center and not from his/her academic department? If the department and center compete for overhead or prestige, the faculty member is caught in the middle. However, there are a number of good reasons for faculty to submit proposals from a center. Centers have specialized facilities and other technical resources; a reputation and track record that support proposals; grant applications often build on work done by the center team; centers ensure industry involvement and eventual transfer of results; and centers can offer leveraging opportunities.

Recommended strategy. A review of grant writing is beyond the scope of this chapter. Like all grant writing, what usually will succeed is quality, personnel, good ideas and a well written proposal. Here are a few helpful suggestions.

1. *Clarify turf issues:* Conflict between the center and department should be worked out before the proposal is written.

2. *Target promising funding opportunities:* Some agencies and programs will put a greater premium on center-related strengths (e.g., teamwork, multidisciplinary, industry relevance, etc.). You will probably have a competitive advantage when submitting your proposal to these programs.

3. *Facilitate team collaboration:* Center Directors may need to facilitate multi-investigator teams to collaborate on a strong proposal.

Geographic Dispersion—Multi-University Partnerships

Because of their relatively large size, U.S. universities have tended to operate independently when it comes to grant writing and center building. Not surprisingly, most I/UCRCs have involved a single university. However, funding for research is getting tighter. At the same time prospective center members complain about their inability to evaluate, let alone join, all of the university-based or government sponsored consortia. In this new environment, multi-institutional partners can reinforce or expand a center's resource base. Based on 1993-1994 data, 17 of NSF's 55 I/UCRCs involve multi-university partnerships, another 12 are exploring this option, and uncounted others have informal partnerships.

Relevant Issues

Partnerships diversify a center's technical capabilities and offer a broader, deeper, and diverse research program to market to new members. Firms prefer working with nearby universities or individuals with whom they've worked before. A partner university may already have relationships with organizations reluctant to be recruited otherwise.

Unfortunately, some directors and many university administrators believe partnerships result in cutting the financial pie into smaller pieces as support gets shipped off campus. This mentality is very shortsighted. Centers exist in a very competitive and dynamic environment: members join a center when they believe it provides access to valuable assets and leave a center when it does not. Partnerships, if developed properly, can result in a bigger pie or prevent it from shrinking, or disappearing altogether.

Partnerships are informal or formal. Formal arrangements are more likely to produce significant growth. They also require more effort.

Informal Time-Limited Partnerships

A large number of I/UCRCs expand their technical resource base by inviting faculty from other universities to submit proposals to their IAB, sometimes through RFPs, but more often Center Directors invite select faculty to submit a proposal. Awards are executed with a subcontract to the PI and his/her university. The subcontracting university and PI must agree to the terms of the center's membership agreement and bylaws. (See Appendix 11-1; Sample Agreement). Initially, this requires negotiation and paperwork but once established can be routinized. As Figure 11-3 describes, NSF programs can be used to subsidize some informal multi-university partnerships between NSF I/UCRCs.

Formal, Ongoing Partnerships

A large number of I/UCRC partnerships are formal and ongoing. Sometimes these partnerships are executed when a new center is

Figure 11-3	NSF-supported partnerships: TIE projects and other awards.

NSF is aware of the benefits of multi-university partnerships and can cost-share these arrangements via a number of I/UCRC and NSF programs. For instance, the I/UCRC program will, on a cost available basis, cost-share TIE Projects, projects between two or more I/UCRCs. A number of NSF programs which primarily target undergraduate institutions (RUI/PUI), historically black institutions; institutions in states with low R&D infrastructures (EPSCOR); and foreign institutions (USAID International Partnerships) have been used to subsidize partnerships. Because all I/UCRCs have similar bylaws, the administrative burden is less in TIE projects.

created. Mature centers are increasingly using partnerships as a growth strategy.

Relevant issues. A new center often arranges partnerships when a prospective government sponsor determines that a single university does not have the technical capabilities and/or industrial network necessary to flourish. Over the years, an increasing number of mature single-university centers have entered into partnerships. This phenomenon is generated by increasing competition for industrial support and a desire for growth.

Recognizing the value of these arrangements as well as the extra administrative overhead involved, NSF provides some financial support. As Figure 11-4 reveals, NSF supports these arrangements if each campus contributes both industrial members and technical capabilities. Similar arrangements may be available within other government programs. Although one university is the prime site, shared management is devised. The organizational arrangements needed to support this kind of operation is discussed in section titled *Strategies and Tactics for Center Growth and Diversification* in this chapter.

Figure 11-4	Guidelines for an NSF-supported partnership.

All Partnerships

1. Each partner university must recruit members;

   a. Full Partnership ($50,000 per year): requires at least $150,000 in membership support

   b. Associate Partnership ($25,000 per year); requires at least $75,000 in membership support

2. Universities operate under a single IAB

3. Universities operate under the same governance

4. Shared management

5. Each site supports the evaluation function.

Partnerships Involving a Previously Supported I/UCRC

1. NSF provides a new five-year award

2. Membership support added by the new partner is spent on that campus for at least two years

3. IAB supports projects without any constraints thereafter

4. Old site receives award plus a $10,000 supplement when the prime or managing site.

This strategy does not make sense for every center. University administrators are skeptical about the benefits of partnerships. Multi-university centers deal with multiple bureaucracies and require a high level of trust and coordination among their directors. They are also much more demanding administratively. Thus, some universities, particularly large, technically diverse universities, may not consider this alternative. For less well-endowed universities or ones trying to recruit within an industry that is being over-recruited by other universities, this approach represents a viable approach to survival, if not expansion.

Recommended strategy. If you believe your center would benefit from a formal multi-university arrangement, discuss it with your government sponsor. The sponsor's involvement invariably helps to enhance the center's vitality and does not result in a loss of members. Here are a few suggestions.

1. *Identify appropriate partners:* This is probably the most important step. Informal, time-limited partnerships only demand talented and reliable investigators of interest to you and complementary to your expertise. A formal ongoing partnership requires much more: an institution with a peer program with capabilities and assets complementary to your center's; a university administration which supports partnerships under government guidelines; and an entrepreneurial collaborator driven to create a viable center with a strong industrial network, and capable of sharing leadership. Compatibility, mutual respect and trust, and collaboration in planning and managing a multi-site center are prerequisites to success. Every transaction must leave a residue of trust on the part of both parties. Informal partnering can be an effective way of screening for these qualities. If you can't find all or at least most of these ingredients, you are probably going against the tide.

2. *Educate and assist prospective partners:* Potential partners need to understand the benefits of an I/UCRC, what it takes to put one together, how one operates, and the government guidelines. Sharing a copy of this handbook might be helpful. However, since you've already created a center you are undoubtedly your potential partner's greatest resource. You must be willing to invest a significant amount of time, spend scarce resources on travel, and engage in a great deal of handholding if the partnership is going to succeed.

3. *Gain a commitment:* Experience suggests many would-be partners drop by the wayside when they realize how much work it takes to recruit a half-dozen or so members. Well-intentioned collaborators can eat up a great deal of time before they figure out that they don't have the time or energy to create a center. Get an unequivocal commitment in writing for certain activities and milestones from a collaborator before you invest a significant amount of your time and resources in nurturing a merger. It might be wise to get the same from your collaborator's institution. Your government sponsor may provide a planning grant to help underwrite this effort.

4. *Create a sense of urgency:* It is easy to procrastinate without goals and deadlines. A merged center shouldn't involve an open-ended time line. As part of your agreement, agree upon deadlines for developing a prospectus, visiting top prospects, hosting a formal recruitment meeting, and submitting a proposal to NSF. Your semi-annual IAB meetings and your government sponsor's funding cycle help define your timeline.

5. *Start working early on administrative details:* Get started on preparing or revising your membership agreement and other legal documents early because it requires many meetings among university administrators. Appendix 11-2 provides a sample memorandum of understanding (MOU) for a joint center.

Vertical Integration

The third and final strategy for growth, vertical integration, involves offering new but related services to your current or prospective members, both educational and research. Diversification only makes sense for a mature and relatively stable center.

In order for this strategy to be successful, one must not only identify an unmet need in one's environment, but must also possess the skills needed to offer these services and be prepared to make the necessary organizational changes required. How similar or different the new services are to those already offered by your center will determine the level of effort necessary.

Providing Educational Services

Although research is emphasized, centers can also build on their educational capabilities, such as offering industry short-courses for a fee. At least one NSF Engineering Research Center has pursued this strategy and achieved considerable financial success. Several other I/UCRCs have received grants to provide educational services to different student populations for a small incremental increase to a center's resource base.

Relevant issues. Multidisciplinary I/UCRCs have a competitive advantage when competing for educational grants. Figure 11-5 lists a variety of programs within NSF which support educational initiatives. While such opportunities can expand your center's resource base and can be personally and institutionally rewarding, it's important to remember they can also strain your organization's capabilities and dilute a center's ability to achieve its central objectives. As a consequence, centers need to be very cautious in pursuing a growth strategy that involves assuming new and additional educational responsibilities.

A good rule of thumb for evaluating educational activities might be: the more they diverge from I/UCRC objectives and populations and the larger the scale, the more trouble and stress. Graduate education, faculty development, and transfer to industry initiatives that are small in scale and allow sufficient support to contract for needed services and resources are good options. For instance, you should be able to absorb small- and even large-scale educational initiatives for college undergraduates, but even a small scale pre-college program imposes a major administrative burden. Nonetheless, a number of Center Directors have found the personal satisfaction derived from these activities to more than justify the additional workload.

Figure 11-5	Educational and human resource funding in NSF.
Program/Mechanism	**Goals**
NSF I/UCRC	
Industrial Sabbaticals	Faculty Development
Research Opportunities for Undergraduates	Undergraduate Research Opportunities
NSF	
Pre-College Education	Enhance Pre-College
Combined Research & Curriculum Program	Integrate Research and Education
Minority Research Supplement	Encourage Minority Students

Recommended strategy.

1. *Clarify your goals:* Be clear on your purpose. If having an impact on education is important, pre-college educational initiatives can be very rewarding. If increasing your center's funding-base is, seek other initiatives.

2. *Target promising funding opportunities.* Agencies and programs that value center-related teamwork, multidisciplinarity, and industrial linkage will give a competitive advantage to your proposal.

3. *Consider collaborating with educational specialists.* University faculty in curriculum and instruction and related disciplines understand educational needs of non-college populations and are highly motivated to secure funding. It is useful to collaborate with them.

4. *Team up with center members.* Pre-college educational programs provide students and teachers with a broadened perspective on the world of work and the different roles scientists and engineers play in different settings. I/UCRCs have been very successful in funding these programs by gaining support and cooperation of IAB companies.

Providing Research-Related Services

Like educational services, research-related services can vary from relatively congruent to very different from current center services. Below we discuss two strategies for expanding your center's resource base. The strategies differ in terms of the novelty of skills and organizational accommodations they require.

- *Contract Research and Related Services.* Enhancements resemble a center's generic core research, but contract research and related activities (like testing and prototyping), involve applied research and explicit deliverables that are very different from core and enhancements.

   Most universities engage in a great deal of contract research and related services and need little advice on how to develop and manage this kind of activity. However, because contracts with center members usually require separate and complex legal agreements, they are administered separately from the center (although some centers will nominally count them in their budget). This works well when research is small in scope and infrequent. If a center wanted to grow by performing a significant amount of contract research, it would need to consider various structural adaptations (see section titled *Organizational Adaptations* in this chapter).

- *Competing for Multi-Year or Institutional Support.* I/UCRCs shouldn't be dissuaded from competing for large-scale, multi-year institutional awards. Just the opposite. NSF I/UCRCs received about $17 million from federal agencies and $6 million from state government, or one-third of their 1993-1994 in multi-year awards. Sponsors of these awards have included Department of Defense, Environmental Protection Agency, Defense Advanced Research Projects Agency, National Institute of Standards and Technology, and various state science and technology agencies. Obviously, I/UCRCs that are interested in expanding and diversifying should consider this funding.

Relevant issues. The reason I/UCRCs have been so successful in competing for large multi-year and institutional awards is that they already possess many of the assets which the sponsor is looking for or developing: specialized facilities and other technical resources (e.g., technicians); a strong technical reputation; an ability to work in multidisciplinary teams; formal involvement by industry; established mechanisms for transfer of results; a culture which accepts timelines and deliverables; and an administrative infrastructure to support large-scale projects. Add to this an established base of support which provides additional leveraging, and I/UCRCs have a real competitive advantage.

However, large multi-year institutional awards can constitute a major organizational challenge for an I/UCRC. The degree of organizational adaptation needed is influenced by how large is the award, how different are the mission and services it mandates, and how different is the mandated mode of operation. Relatively small awards, primarily focused on fundamental research and consistent with a consortial format, require only minor adjustments. Large awards involving job creation, economic development, or new extension services for a single sponsor require major adjustments and perhaps even dissolution of the center. See section titled *Organizational Adaptations* in this chapter.

Recommended strategies. Advice for traditional grants applies here too: target promising opportunities, practice good grantsmanship, facilitate collaboration and team formation. In addition, the following tips should prove helpful.

1. *Get the support of your IAB:* Not every funding opportunity synergizes your center's mission. Individual faculty must pursue any funding opportunity which interests them, but IAB may object to some large-scale projects as counter-productive or a dilution of effort. It would be wise to seek their advice and support. Initiatives like the Advanced Technology Program require industry involvement or leadership as a given.

2. *Consider partnering with other universities and non-profits:* Research sponsors expect a big, more technologically diverse bang for their buck. As a consequence, many require or expect proposals to include teams brought together from across several universities and/or not-for-profit research institutes.

3. *Seek advice and pay attention to review criteria:* Because these awards frequently have non-traditional grant objectives like job growth or economic development, many faculty will be out of their element in preparing a winning proposal. Close and frequent contact with the program manager and collaborators who have competed for these kinds of awards is highly recommended.

ORGANIZATIONAL ADAPTATIONS

As we have pointed out in Chapter 3, Organizational Structure, and at the beginning of this chapter, an organization's structure must be designed contingent on a number of contextual factors including: its size, the kind of work it performs, its environment, its strategy and goals, and its culture. Since growth has the potential to change most, if not all, of these factors, growth-oriented Center Directors must be prepared to re-engineer their center's structure in terms of its complexity, centrality or formality. In this section, we review the ways growth affects center structure. A review of the organizational structure can be found at the beginning of Chapter 3.

Increased Size

When a center grows it is supported by more members and is doing a larger volume of research. Size is the easiest growth-related change to accommodate organizationally. One can simply add more administrative and research capacity. For instance, centers have added a full-time director, another secretary, a full-time administrative assistant, or more researchers.[12]

Increased size may also dictate changes in the center's complexity. This is usually accomplished by deepening its hierarchy (vertical differentiation) and/or increasing the division of labor (horizontal differentiation). For instance, with respect to hierarchy, some larger centers create an IAB executive committee or add associate directors. With respect to division of labor, some larger centers have created a variety of associate director positions (e.g., technical, administrative, technology transfer), created or added to their program areas, and created new roles like computer technicians or research associates. As we will discuss in the next section, increased differentiation requires greater coordination.

Multi-University Partnerships

The degree of formality involved in a multi-university partnership influences how much and what kinds of organizational accommodations need to be made. Informal partnerships that involve subcontracting projects or a single joint project can usually be handled by a minor increase in organizational formality in the form of a contract or memorandum of agreement. Figure 11-6 presents a diagram of basic and informal partnerships.

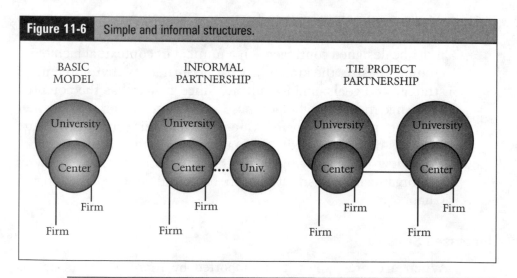

Figure 11-6   Simple and informal structures.

---

[12]If a center did not have the ability to add research capacity in-house, they might need to hire more faculty for in-house research or engage in the kind of multi-university partnership we discuss below.

Formal multi-institutional partnerships need to identify who is in charge, how decisions are made, how resources are divvied. Most structural changes are administrative. Figure 11-7 presents a diagram of simple and complex arrangements. For instance, multi-university centers usually become more complex in terms of hierarchy and division of labor. Almost inevitably, this means establishment of director, co-director, rotating, or site-director positions and a certain amount of decentralization of decision making.

To promote integration and synergy in the research program, NSF has discouraged completely decentralized units and prefers a single Center Director with site- or co-directors elsewhere. In order to accommodate the increased complexity and need for coordination, most centers adopt greater organizational formality through explicit job descriptions, written policies and procedures, and written agreements between institutions. Research continues to operate in a much less formal fashion.

The biggest challenge presented by a multi-university center's increased complexity and decentralization is how to achieve coordination without sacrificing flexibility and efficiency. In many instances, policies and procedures can be used to spell out areas where site directors have discretion and areas where directors must reach a consensus. For instance, should a site director be able to authorize participation of his/her site in a new proposal or must all new initiatives include both sites? At least one multi-university center found its sites competing with each other for an award for lack of a policy in this area. On the other hand, promulgating policies requiring shared decision-making on all issues

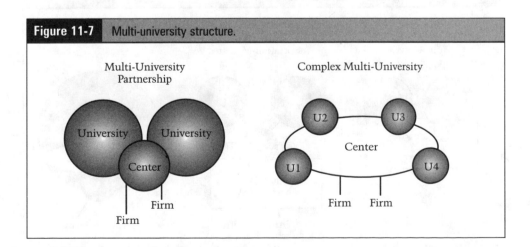

| Figure 11-7 | Multi-university structure. |

Multi-University
Partnership

University   University

Center

Firm

Firm

Complex Multi-University

U2   U3

Center

U1   U4

Firm   Firm

would be time-consuming and inefficient. In the final analysis, effective communication and a degree of trust between sites would probably be a good substitute for excessive reliance on policies and procedures.

Different Missions, Services, and Formats

An I/UCRC has three primary missions: fundamental research that has industrial relevance, enhance graduate education, and promote knowledge and technology transfer to industry. It attempts to achieve these goals by conducting and transferring industry-relevant fundamental research, much of it performed by graduate students, to a consortium of firms. However, multi-year institutional awards, particularly those sponsored by states and some newer federal initiatives, encourage or require recipients to pursue other missions, deliver very different services, and respond to the needs of a single sponsor. While these mandates are not inherently inconsistent with the goals of an I/UCRC, they may represent significant diversifications of a center's operations and create conflicts or overloads which require revising and perhaps reinventing a center's structure. Figure 11-8 presents a diagram of complex and hybrid structures.

When service, mission or format changes are minor, centers may implement many of the structural changes already discussed. For instance, create new roles or functions, centralize decision making more, or modify or add new policies or procedures.

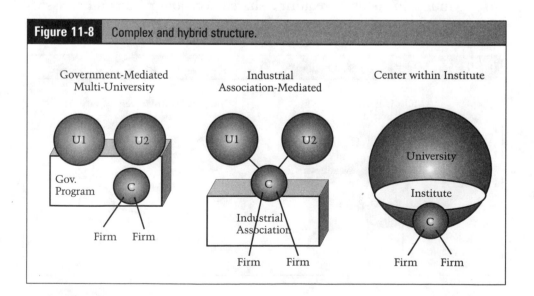

Figure 11-8   Complex and hybrid structure.

Government-Mediated Multi-University

Industrial Association-Mediated

Center within Institute

Dramatic changes in services, mission, or format requires more complex multidivisional organizations. For instance, most universities do not reward faculty for contract research or extension work. As a consequence, centers that perform a significant amount of contract research or extension might develop separate units or divisions staffed by full-time non-faculty researchers for this research (Figure 11-9). Similar strategies could be followed for grant-related educational services.

Centers can pursue a strategy of horizontal differentiation even further by creating separate, but loosely-coupled organizations. Perhaps the best example of this model is the collection of centers, institutes and labs which evolved from New Jersey Institute of Technology's (NJIT) Center for Hazardous and Toxic Waste Management, since renamed the Center for Environmental Engineering and Science.

The I/UCR Center for Hazardous and Toxic Waste Management (also known as the Hazardous Substance Management Research Center) headquartered at NJIT is the largest and one of the most successful of the NSF I/UCRCs (see Figure 11-10). Started in 1984 with a critical mass of $300,000 in IAB membership fees and ten members, it oversees five centers and programs within NJIT's Center for Environmental Engineering and Science with a total operating budget ranging from $6 to 10 million.

Figure 11-9	Surviving as a contract research center.

The Center for Electrochemical Systems and Hydrogen Research (CESHR) at Texas A&M University has been through major organizational changes over the course of its life. Initially funded in 1983 as a hydrogen research center, CESHR fell victim to the oil glut; there was little interest among energy companies in funding research in alternative energy sources. Membership peaked at nine companies, and had fallen to two by 1987.

At about this time, the university associate provost for research reviewed the center and research program. He decided that the quality of the research and of the faculty were such that it was worth investing. A new center director was hired, the university contributed $1 million, and the modus operandi was shifted from an NSF-type consortium to a contract research operation. CESHR retained two members who paid $20,000 per year for basic research. Federal grants, including a share of the $2.5 million line item for hydrogen research in the federal budget and contract research projects for industry are the primary funding. With an operating budget of close to $2 M in fiscal year 1989, CESHR was a highly successful contract research organization. Because results of individual research projects are owned by specific sponsors, CESHR ceased as an NSF I/UCRC.

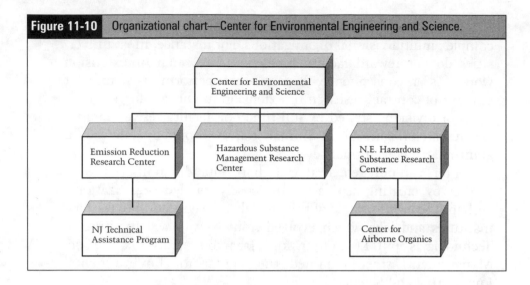

Figure 11-10   Organizational chart—Center for Environmental Engineering and Science.

The Hazardous Substance Management Research Center (HSMRC) has a threefold mission of research, service, and technology transfer. Through its industry-university collaborative research, HSMRC advances the state-of-the-art in engineering management of hazardous waste. The work of the Center expands present knowledge and application of effective, environmentally acceptable, and economically feasible hazardous waste treatment and remediation technologies. The Center currently has 15 industrial sponsors, six participating universities (New Jersey Institute of Technology, Rutgers University, Princeton University, Stevens Tech, Tufts University, and the University of Medicine and Dentistry of New Jersey), and an annual budget of almost $4.4 million. HSMRC also has two international research tie programs— the ReCoRD Center at the University of Lyon, France, and the QUESTOR Center at the Queen's University, Belfast, Northern Ireland.

The Emission Reduction Research Center (ERRC) is a National Science Foundation I/UCRC dedicated to research in pollution prevention in all environmental media, but with a particular concern to air emission reduction. ERRC, launched in 1994, is organized around clusters of companies in specific manufacturing areas. Industrial membership is currently seven members. The 1996-97 research budget is $415,000.

Northeast Hazardous Substance Research Center (NHSRC). Recognizing the fact that current scientific knowledge and existing science-based technologies are inadequate to fully address the identification, remediation, and management of hazardous substances, the federal Superfund Amendments and Reauthorization Act (SARA) authorized EPA to establish five university-based research centers. Two adjoining federal regions are served by each center. New Jersey Institute of Technology, in a consortium with Massachusetts Institute of Technology and Tufts University, was awarded the center to serve Federal Regions 1 and 2. This center was established in February 1989 to conduct research and training related to manufacture, use, transportation, disposal and management of hazardous substances. The center receives baseline funding of $1 million per year from EPA. Supplemental funding of approximately $1.5 million is provided from EPA, U.S. Department of Energy (DOE), and DOD in support of specific targeted research projects and four major new initiatives.

Center for Airborne Organics. The EPA has established a Center of Excellence for Exploratory Environmental Research in which the problem of deteriorating ambient air quality, particularly in our urban areas, is coming under significant research scrutiny in order to establish the scientific basis for corrective actions. NJIT has joined with Massachusetts Institute of Technology (MIT) and California Institute of Technology to form the Center, which became operational July 1992, and focuses its research on the transformation, transport, and control of airborne organic compounds. The Center operates on a budget of $ 1 million annually shared among the three consortium universities.

New Jersey Technical Assistance Program (NJTAP) for Industrial Pollution Prevention has gained visibility and credibility with industry as an extension service that provides environmental audits; functions as an information clearinghouse for literature and videotapes related to pollution prevention; delivers education and training; and adopts, develops, or aids in the development of novel pollution prevention technologies. The New Jersey Department of Environmental Protection (NJDEP) and EPA provide major funding for this program. Current funding levels are $400,000 per year; NJDEP support has just been renewed through 2001.

It would have been impossible for HSMRC to absorb all of these missions. Instead an umbrella institute was created and new centers added. The CEES Director, Dr. Richard Magee, reports to the office of the Provost and has a point person to manage each center. Here is a collection of centers with clear overarching goals. They adapt and respond to new events by practicing "planful opportunism." This collection of centers is subject to the same challenges of top-out that any I/UCRC faces. They may, however, be even more intense and complex.

However, it's worth remembering that while there are many organizational fixes for the challenges presented by center growth, some conflicts may be so great that they require choosing between one's center and an alternative opportunity. Every good strategy has a downside. Know what it is; moderate and monitor it. See Appendix 11-3.

SUMMARY

Many university-based centers, institutes, and labs provide services to industry underwritten by a single well-endowed federal or state sponsor for an extended or open-ended period of time. Such organizations typically do not need to develop a strategy for growth. They can achieve a critical mass overnight and devote themselves almost exclusively to performing research. Unfortunately, the long-term survival of these organizations often has more to do with satisfying their major governmental benefactor than their supposed customer base.

In contrast, cooperative research centers have much more in common with small entrepreneurial start-up companies. Survival, even over the short term, can never be taken for granted and must be the focus of considerable organizational energy. Ultimately, long-term survival depends upon the interplay of several factors: ability to develop and maintain a highly relevant and responsive research program, awareness of opportunities and needs they can meet in their environment, and selection and implementation of a winning growth strategy. While we have focused on growth here, the reader needs to remember any growth strategy is only as good as the research planning and environmental reconnaissance which supports it.

Various growth strategies appear to make sense for centers at different stages in their life-cycle. A strategy of expansion by volume appears to be the most straightforward and simple. It can be used throughout a center's life cycle. This strategy has the added benefit of building on a center's core competency and typically does not require substantial organizational redesign.

While geographic dispersion through partnership agreements can be used at start-up, this strategy has also become popular for mature centers, particularly those with static growth for core services. However, development of successful formal, ongoing partnerships take a great deal of time and attention to detail. Choosing the wrong institutional or administrative partner can divert energies and result in center failure. Long-term success requires a willingness to re-engineer the center structure and a commitment to open and active communication between participating institutions.

Finally, vertical integration, particularly the provision of new but related research services, offers the potential for significant growth but requires the greatest commitment and can unbalance or dilute a center's core competence. It probably only makes sense for mature and stable centers. Adding missions, services or using a format which is substantially different from the standard I/UCRC approach will almost inevitably require a center to re-engineer its organizational structure. A variety of structural accommodations which can compensate for the stress caused by these changes were discussed.

In the final analysis, Center Directors need to be wary of trying to enlarge their centers too fast or too far from their core competency, a goal Galbraith and Kazanjian (1986) refer to as "controlled diversity." Since centers succeed in getting other support in large part because of their membership base and their infrastructure, they are well advised to reinforce the core competencies that keep their consortium-based membership happy.

REFERENCES

Collins, J. and Porras, J. *"Built to Last,"* New York, Harper Business, 1994.

Galbraith, J.R., and Kazanjian, R.K. *"Strategy Implementation."* Structure, Systems and Process, St. Paul, MN, West Publishing, 1986.

Reagan, R. *"Facilitating Access to Science and Technology."* Executive Order 12591, 10 April, 1987, Section Four, International Science and Technology, The White House, Los Angeles, CA, Office of the Press Secretary.

Walters, S. G. *"A New International Industry/University/Government Cooperative Research Initiative, January 1988."* NSF Technical Report, ISTI/Directorate for Scientific Technological and International Affairs, Washington, DC, January 2, 1988.

Walters, S.G. *"Managing International Cooperative U.S., European Center Research Projects."* Proceedings, Congress Report, International Congress of Engineering Deans and Industry Leaders, Paris, France, UNESCO, October 7, 1993, pp. 137-143.

Walters, S.G. "*NSF-I/UCRC Annual Evaluator Reports for I/UCRCs,*" for Ceramics, Plastic Recycling, Wireless Information Networks, Center for Advanced Food Technology (NJCST) at Rutgers, and IUCRCs in Hazardous Substance Management Research, Emission Reduction Research at NJIT, and QUESTOR at Queen's University, Belfast, Northern Ireland. Newark, NJ, October 16, 1995.

APPENDIX 11-1
Subcontract Agreement

This agreement constitutes a Subcontract between the Center for X as an organized research unit of Y university , and Z <u>university,</u> hereinafter referred to as <u>Z</u>.

The purpose of this Subcontract is to carry out the tasks described in the proposal submitted to <u>X</u> by <u>Dr Smith,</u> the principal investigator(s), and entitled, <u>"Closure Integrity"</u> which is made a part of this Agreement as Appendix A. <u>Z</u> agrees to carry out the tasks listed and provide monthly updates on the progress of the work and quarterly reports giving a full account of the progress. At the termination of the grant <u>Z</u> will provide <u>X</u> with a report of the completed investigations (no later than 60 days following termination of the grant). <u>Z</u> agrees to adhere to the publication, software copyright, and patent policy as described in Appendix B. It is understood that if it is necessary for <u>X</u> to divulge certain confidential information, such as chemical structure of compounds or the nature of a process, to <u>Z</u> for the conduct of research for the public good, this information shall be treated in confidence until such time as disclosure is made by <u>X</u>.

Performance under this agreement shall begin <u>January 1, 1997,</u> and shall not extend beyond the completion date of <u>December 30, 1998</u>, unless the period is further extended through mutual agreement in writing.

<u>X</u> shall reimburse <u>Z</u> for all direct costs incurred in the performance of the research as set forth in the Budget contained in Appendix A. It is understood that <u>X</u> will not reimburse <u>Z</u> for any administrative or indirect costs associated with the research. Within the total estimated cost of <u>$62,585</u>, <u>Z</u> shall not shift more than ten percent of the funds from any category without written approval from <u>X</u>. <u>X</u> agrees to deposit by quarterly installments the total amount of the award with <u>Mr. Jones</u>, the financial official of <u>Z</u> during the designated period, with the initial payment made upon receipt of this signed Subcontract Agreement. Disbursement of said funds will be made by the financial official of <u>Y</u>. However, installments may be delayed by <u>X</u> due to lack of performance in accordance with this agreement and of the specified research schedule as noted in Appendix A.

<u>Z</u> agrees to retain and make available for possible <u>X</u> audit all books, records and other documents relative to this agreement for three years following completion or termination of the specific research programs or termination of this agreement, and to provide

X̲ a final expenditure report within 90 days of the contract period. Any funds unexpended by the end of the contract shall be returned to X̲ with the final expenditure report.

X̲, as an organized research unit of Y̲, shall not be liable for the actions of Z̲ nor shall Z̲ be liable for the actions of X̲. It is understood that Y̲, an agency of the State of _____, is limited in any claims that may be made against it for negligence up to $100,000 as provided by the State Tort Claims Act.

Z̲ agrees to comply with relevant federal and state executive orders, rules, regulations, and laws including OMB Circular A-21, and policies and bylaws of X̲ as noted in Appendix B.

Should unforeseen developments take place that necessitate an interruption of the said project, this agreement may be renegotiated upon thirty (30) days written notice by either party.

Z̲ shall not use the names or symbols of Y̲ and/or X̲ or of the investigators or any derivative thereof, in any advertising or promotional sales literature without the prior written consent of Y̲ and/or X̲ in each case.

Z̲ shall have complete direction of the approved project and other activities associated with the efficient conduct of the study. The proposed research shall be conducted under the direct supervision of the Principal Investigator who will be accountable to Z̲.

In order to effectively conduct the proposed project, Z̲ agrees to furnish such facilities and equipment as are required insofar as facilities of Z̲ will permit.

No waiver, alteration or modification of these provisions shall be binding unless in writing.

Neither this agreement nor any right, remedy, obligation or liability arising hereunder or by reason hereof shall be assignable by Z̲ without the prior written consent of X̲ and/or Y̲.

This agreement is binding upon and shall inure to the benefit of the parties hereto, their representatives, successors and assigns. No failure or successive failures on the part of X̲, its successors or assigns, to enforce any covenant or agreement, and no waiver or successive waivers on its or their part of any condition of this agreement shall operate as a discharge of such covenant, agreement, or condition, or render the same invalid, or impair the right of X̲, its successors or assigns, to enforce the same in the event of any subsequent breach or breaches by Z̲, its successors or assigns.

APPENDIX 11-2

Memorandum of Understanding Between
My University and Your University

This Memorandum of Understanding (MOU) is effective the ____ day of _____, by and among My University (hereinafter referred to as 'MY') and Your University (hereinafter referred to as 'YOUR'), to be known collectively hereinafter as 'INSTITUTIONS'.

WHEREAS, the parties to this Agreement intend to join together in a cooperative effort to support the Center for Partnership (hereinafter referred to as 'CAP') in its efforts to create concepts, methods, and tools for use in our area of science; to stimulate industrial innovation; and to provide INSTITUTIONS with strengthened educational and research capabilities in these fields.

WHEREAS, the activities of <u>CAP</u> are funded by (I) National Science Foundation (hereinafter referred to as 'NSF', (ii) Industrial Members (hereinafter referred to as 'MEMBERS', and (iii) other funds that may be received from time to time.

WHEREAS, INSTITUTIONS are desirous of formalizing certain agreements between them with respect to the subject matter contained herein.

NOW THEREFORE, for and in consideration of the mutual promises and covenants herein contained and intending to be legally bound, INSTITUTIONS hereto agree as follows:

1. <u>Center Funding</u>.

a. During the initial period of this joint center, each Institution will receive its own funds directly from NSF, will be responsible for recruiting its own MEMBERS, and will retain membership fees collected from its MEMBERS.

b. When NSF decides to make a single payment to one Institution for distribution between INSTITUTIONS, all membership fees will be deposited into a single account for distribution to INSTITUTIONS for core research selected by the Industrial Advisory Board (hereinafter referred to as IAB), as specified in the <u>CAP</u> Bylaws.

2. <u>Center Governance</u>.

a. By mutual agreement between parties, <u>CAP</u> will be governed by a common set of Bylaws (a copy of which is attached as Schedule A) and each party's Membership Agreement will have common terms and conditions. The <u>CAP</u> will have a common IAB, Academic Policy Committee, and Research Advisory Committee, with composition and duties as prescribed in the <u>CAP</u> Bylaws.

b. During the first five year funding period, and in accordance with the proposal submitted to NSF and the subsequent awards, the Center's Executive Director will be from <u>MY</u>. The Policy Advisory Board, with the concurrence of NSF, will determine whether, in the subsequent funding period, the Executive Directorship will remain at <u>MY</u> or rotate to <u>YOUR</u>. Site Directors are selected and appointed in accordance with the policies and procedures of each Institution, and as specified in the Bylaws.

3. <u>Cross-Funding of Research</u>. The transfer of funds between INSTITUTIONS for core projects selected by the IAB will be made without the assessment of the indirect costs normally associated with the issuance of a subcontract.

4. <u>Ownership and Administration of Intellectual Property</u>. Subject to the rights of MEMBERS contained in the Bylaws and Membership Agreement, all right, title, and interest in and to all Intellectual Property (hereinafter referred to as 'IP') shall be based on inventorship and shall be allocated as follows:

a. All IP invented by inventors solely at one Institution shall belong solely to that Institution.

b. All IP invented jointly by personnel of INSTITUTIONS will belong jointly to each Institution. In the event one Institution has a lead inventor or houses the laboratory of the Principal Investigator of a research project leading to the joint IP, that Institution shall administer the IP. In the event INSTITUTIONS have contributed equally to a joint IP, then the Site Directors and Deans shall determine who shall administer the IP. After identifying the Institution that will administer the joint IP, INSTITUTIONS shall negotiate in good faith an Inter-Institutional Intellectual Property Agreement, the form of which is attached as Schedule B, which agreement shall contain, *inter alia*, terms and conditions concerning the sharing of royalties and costs associated with the joint IP. The Institution administrating any IP shall keep the other Institution advised as to the activities in administering the IP including any progress on commercialization, patent prosecution, or copyright protection. AU such information received by either Institution shall be deemed confidential.

c.   Each INSTITUTION shall be responsible for the identification and evaluation of its sole IP and for informing MEMBERS regarding IP as outlined in the Bylaws and Membership Agreement. If MEMBERS and the inventing INSTITUTIONS agree that patent protection should be sought and if MEMBERS are interested in securing such protection, the process will follow the, outlined in the Membership Agreement. If MEMBERS are not interested in procuring protection for inventions, the inventing INSTITUTIONS may determine on their own whether protection will be sought, and that INSTITUTIONS may dispose of the IP as it sees fit.

d. INSTITUTIONS shall jointly review any joint IP, evaluate its commercial potential and inform MEMBERS regarding the joint IP as outlined in the Bylaws and Membership Agreement. If MEMBERS and INSTITUTIONS agree that patent protection should be sought and if MEMBERS are interested in securing such protection, the process will follow that outlined in the Membership Agreement. If MEMBERS are not interested in procuring protection for inventions, INSTITUTIONS will manage the joint IP according to the terms of the Inter-Institutional Agreement.

5. <u>License to Use Intellectual Property for Internal Use</u>. With respect to IP belonging solely to <u>YOUR</u> or <u>MY</u>, each party agrees to and does hereby grant to the other, subject to the terms of this agreement, a nonexclusive, nontransferable, irrevocable, royalty free license for educational and research purposes only (without the right to sublicense). This license shall include the right to utilize any information and materials published by <u>CAP</u>. Both <u>YOUR</u> and <u>MY</u> acknowledge that a separate license agreement may be required by the Licensor in order to convey the rights granted by this paragraph.

6. <u>Publication, Sale or Use of Research Results on Jointly Owned Intellectual Property</u>.

a.   Subject to <u>CAP</u> Membership Agreements, each Institution shall have the right to publish research results on jointly owned IP. It is provided, however, that the Institution desiring to publish such research results shall submit a draft of any such proposed publication to the other Institution at least twenty (20) days prior to the submission of the research results for publication. Either Institution shall have the right to delay any publication for a period of not more than sixty (60) days for the purposes of obtaining patent protection by giving the other Institution notice before the end of the twenty (20) day notice period provided hereinabove. For the purposes of this MOU, cataloging and placing reports of research results in the library of any Institution shall be deemed to be a "publication."

7. <u>Miscellaneous Provisions</u>.

a. This MOU may be revised by mutual agreement between INSTITUTIONS at any time.

b. In the event that any of the terms, provisions, or covenants contained in this MOU are held to be partially or wholly invalid or unenforceable for any reason whatsoever, such holding shall not affect, alter, modify, or impair in any manner whatsoever any of the other terms, provisions, or covenants not held to be partially or wholly invalid or unenforceable.

c. This Agreement shall be subject to the <u>CAP</u> Bylaws and Membership Agreement, and in any conflict, the Bylaws and Member Agreement shall have precedence.

10. <u>Period of Performance</u>. The period of performance of this Agreement will be concurrent with the <u>CAP</u> contract with NSF.

IN WITNESS WHEREOF, INSTITUTIONS hereto have caused this MOU to be duly executed by their duly authorized officers as of the day and year set forth next to each signature.

MY UNIVERSITY   YOUR UNIVERSITY

APPENDIX 11-3

Overview—Pros and Cons of Various Organizationally Compatible Strategies

Strategy	Pros	Cons
Increase Membership Fee	A simple strategy for increasing financial resources.	May be hard to sell when corporate budgets are tight.
	Doesn't require extensive investment of time on part of Center Director.	Requires near unanimous assent by center members to be profitable.
	May result in predictable percentage increase in annual revenues.	Getting approval of new agreement may be difficult.
		Requires a well-prepared proposal, lots of support, and good timing.
Research Enhancements	Proven strategy; constitutes 11 percent of I/UCRC budget.	Requires well-prepared proposal, lots of support, and good timing.
	Convenient for members; follow-on research done under center bylaws.	May pull center in a direction which is too applied.
Intensive Recruiting	An efficient use of recruiting time.	Must catalog and document center successes to use as part of sales presentation.
	Recharge faculty and member involvement	
	Familiar; same strategy as used when building center.	Major time commitment.

Strategy	Pros	Cons
Multiple-Level Fee Structure	Helps attract small businesses. May add to center's technological mix. Helps reinforce supplier-manufacturer ties. May coincide with state initiatives.	Adds complexity to recruiting, bookkeeping, etc. If goals differ, may cause conflict in consortia. May be difficult to reach a compromise on privileges offered to associate members. Rarely results in significant membership increase. Current members may opt for lower fee.
Federal and Military Members	Capitalizes on dual-use orientation. Proven strategy: ten percent of current members. Capitalize on MIPR mechanism of funding.	Federal or military goals and time-frames may conflict with industrial. Some agencies may want to recruit your members.
Non-Profits and Associations	May be prominent in the field.	Has not paid off for most centers. Rights accorded association members may be difficult to resolve. Some non-profits may want to recruit your members.

Strategy	Pros	Cons
Traditional Grants	Proven strategy: 20 percent of I/UCRC support.	May cause internal conflicts between department and center.
	Centers have competitive advantages.	Must be congruent with goals.
Multi-University Partnerships	Proven strategy; almost half of all I/UCRCs.	University administrators resist sharing resources.
	Partner university can diversify technology and industrial network.	Takes a lot of work and "hand-holding" to create new sites.
	Can add geographic balance.	Requires more administrative effort for coordination.
	NSF will assist.	
	Provides "one-stop shopping" for members.	
	Can use informal partnerships like TIEs to pilot.	
Educational Services	Broadens the center's mission.	Rarely pays large financial dividends.
	Adds "perk" some members may value.	May strain center's organizational ability.
	Can be personally rewarding.	Divergent populations (e.g., pre-college) increase strain.
	NSF may support.	

Strategy	Pros	Cons
Contract Research	Can add support for faculty.	May pull center in a direction which is too applied.
		Need to develop mechanism to keep separate from core.
		May weaken consortial ties that emphasize shared research.
Large Institutional Awards	Proven strategy; constitutes about 30 percent of I/UCRC budget.	Single dominant sponsor may divert center from industrial mission.
	Centers have competitive advantages.	May require major organizational restructuring.

ENVOI

S. GEORGE WALTERS, *Professor Emeritus, Rutgers University, NJ*

Vision, strategies, tactics, and operating details have been presented in abundance in these 11 chapters. Above all, remember these three points:

1. This is a premier model.

2. The variables critical to success are known.

3. The NSF three-stage screening process must be successfully completed before you are on your way to building and managing an NSF-I/UCRC.

THIS IS A PREMIER MODEL

The NSF/I/UCRC model works. These centers produce trained, educated student scientists and basic, precompetitive research. Center research has intrinsic merit evidenced by companies investing their money in new research activities for their own strategic and tactical needs. Each dollar of I/UCRC funds triggers $1.50 to $7 of company research activity. R&D dollar multipliers of 1.5, 1.7, and, at one center, 7.0 are common. This is a remarkable return on basic research investments.

Further, pooling of all monies and company and faculty collaboration to co-design, co-develop, and co-manage precompetitive research projects leverages IAB membership fees by 10, 15, 30, or more times.

VARIABLES CRITICAL TO SUCCESS ARE KNOWN

Precompetitive, interdisciplinary research of intrinsic merit is the kind of research universities perform. Industry competitors are more likely to share their expertise and pool their funding for these kinds of non-competitive projects.

A Center Director held in esteem by scientific colleagues who has entrepreneurial skill, is persistent, and is trusted, will excel.

I/UCRC structure, organization, and management stimulate interactive collaboration and initiation of center research and policies. Other knowns include composition, function, and fees of the IAB; minimum critical mass of $300,000; patents and procedures; awareness of public law 98-620 "march in rights;" university cost-sharing; publication delay; semi-annual IAB meetings; and evaluators and evaluation.

Recruiting and sustaining members are critical to the vitality of a center. Up to 70 percent of a Center Director's time is spent on marketing the I/UCRC to companies, faculty, students, administrators, federal and state legislators, and anyone else who can provide significant R&D dollar leveraging and high R&D dollar multipliers.

I/UCRC's organization structure, management protocols, policies, and reports stimulate knowledge exchange between faculty and companies and among companies. More importantly, knowledge and technology transfer between faculty and companies is accelerated.

One-on-one contacts, IAB meetings, poster sessions, evaluation surveys, LIFE forms, center coffee breaks, and social functions foster feedback and exchange of ideas with researchers and the center leadership.

Knowledge transfer begins when an IAB member collaborates with faculty. IAB representatives contact individual researchers, track research progress, use LIFE forms, offer suggestions, material, equipment and special instrumentation. They also take advantage of on-site visits, and one-on-one discussions during the two day IAB meetings. Center members get early diffusion of new precompetitive research knowledge, technology, and artifacts long before they appear in journal articles or published proceedings.

Making certain that the value of the research knowledge reaches those who can authorize the steps necessary to transform center precompetitive knowledge into a form which can then be made to fit a company's particular strategic and tactical needs is the ultimate challenge of knowledge transfer.

The director must manage the entire I/UCRC organization so that the promise of its prospectus is fulfilled. New formal and informal information systems covering all center activities must be tailor-made to fit the I/UCRC non-hierarchical, boundary-less organization and then be dovetailed into the university, member companies, and NSF information systems.

The center and the university information system should be sensitive and responsive to rates of change. The center must generate periodic comparative analyses of activities. Operating, accounting, budget and progress reports which are 60, 90, 120 days after the fact are not much help in taking on-line corrective action.

I/UCRC evaluator reports and variance analyses provide a broad scan of all center activities. Variance signals situations which must be examined further. Causes, consequences, and the effect of various alternative solutions must be gauged before appropriate action.

Control by fear alienates. Incentives are better but lean in a university setting. The best control is to have people in I/UCRCs who understand center values, share them, and commit to them emotionally to do the right thing in an ethical, timely, cost-effective way.

A Center Director has two primary responsibilities: to improve constantly the asset base and research productivity of the center, and to put in place plans and programs of industrial relevance which provide quantum jumps in the asset base, and in research output of intrinsic merit.

Said the Red Queen to Alice, "You have to run faster and faster just to stay in the same place," which is very relevant for I/UCRCs. For instance, student researchers will graduate. New outstanding students must be recruited. Outstanding faculty retire or may be hired away. They must be replaced. Companies withdraw from the center. New members must be recruited.

Intensive recruiting, integration of research and diversification of research are some strategies. Tying research programs with other centers, other agencies, i.e., national laboratories, ARPA, and building multi-site I/UCRCs, are others. Let there be enough ambiguity in structure, protocols, and strategic planning to stimulate persistent, dynamic growth.

THE NSF I/UCRC SCREENING PROCESS

The ideas presented in this handbook really do work. I/UCRCs can be adapted to fit other models and the local situation and terrain. I/UCRCs work in the U.S. and overseas. In February 1997, QUESTOR Centre at Queens University, Belfast, Northern

Ireland, was awarded the Queen's Anniversary Medal for Achievement. This center was formed in the I/UCRC image. It has a tie program with a U.S. NSF I/UCRC at New Jersey Institute of Technology, and an NSF I/UCRC evaluator.

As you have read, there is more to setting up and managing an I/UCRC than a proposal of scientific merit. The NSF/I/UCRC is the foremost piece of social technology for managing cooperative research. Besides good science, you have to build and effectively manage an organization. Successfully completing the NSF three-stage screening process proves that you can.

ACRONYMS AND ABBREVIATIONS

AAC	Academic Advisory Committee
ARPA	Advanced Research Project Agency
ATP	Advanced Technology Program
AUTM	Association of University Technology Managers
Adm.	Administration
C	Center
CD	Center Director
CEO	Chief Executive Officer
CFO	Chief Financial Officer
COP	Center Operations Proposal
CP	Concept Paper
CV	Curriculum Vita
DARPA	Defense Advanced Research Project Agency
DOD	Department of Defense
DOE	Department of Energy
DOT	Department of Transportation
ERC	Engineering Research Center
EPA	Environmental Protection Agency
EPSCOR	Experimental Programs to Stimulate Competitive Research
ERDIP	Experimental R&D Incentives Program
Eval.	Evaluator
FY	Fiscal Year
Fac.	Faculty
IAB	Industrial Advisory Board
I/U	Industry/University

I/UCRC	Industry/University Cooperative Research Center
Indus.	Industry
LIFE	Level of Interest and Feedback Evaluation
MIPR	Military Interdepartmental Procurement Request
MIS	Management of Information Systems
MIT	Massachusetts Institute of Technology
Mem.	Member
NASA	National Aeronautics and Space Agency
NIH	National Institutes of Health
NIST	National Institute of Standards and Technology
NJDEP	New Jersey Department of Environmental Protection
NJIT	New Jersey Institute of Technology
NSF	National Science Foundation
OEM	Original Equipment Manufacturer
OMB	Office of Management and Budget
ORU	Organized Research Units
OSU	The Ohio State University
PI	Principal Investigator
PO	Process/Outcome (Questionnaire)
PP	Planning Proposal
PUI	Primarily Undergraduate Institutions
RFP	Request For Proposal
RUI	Research at Undergraduate Institutions
S&T	Science and Technology
SARA	Superfund Amendments and Reauthorization Act
SB	Small Business
SBA	Small Business Administration
SHP	Structured Historical Profile
SIC	Standard Industrial Classification
U	University
USAID	United States Agency for International Development

INDEX